THE
FATE
OF THE
WEST

THE
FATE
OF THE
WEST

The Battle to Save the World's Most Successful Political Idea

BILL EMMOTT

The Economist Books

Published under exclusive licence from The Economist by
Profile Books Ltd
3 Holford Yard
Bevin Way
London WC1X 9HD
www.profilebooks.com

The greatest care has been taken in compiling this book. However, no responsibility can be accepted by the publishers or compilers for the accuracy of the information presented.

Where opinion is expressed it is that of the author and does not necessarily coincide with the editorial views of The Economist Newspaper.

While every effort has been made to contact copyright-holders of material produced or cited in this book, in the case of those it has not been possible to contact successfully, the author and publishers will be glad to make amendments in further editions.

Typeset in Milo by MacGuru Ltd

Printed and bound in Great Britain by Clays, St Ives plc

A CIP catalogue record for this book is available from the British Library

ISBN 978 1 78125 734 0
eISBN 978 1 78283 299 7

FSC
www.fsc.org
MIX
Paper from
responsible sources
FSC® C018072

For Carol

Contents

Figures

Introduction: The idea of the West

FOR AS LONG AS ANY OF US CAN REMEMBER, to be modern has meant to be Western, and to be Western has meant being at the forefront of pretty much everything – of science, of social change, of culture, of affluence, of influence, of power in all its forms. Not everyone has liked this state of affairs, even inside Western countries themselves, but regardless of sour grapes or ideological discontent this Western dominance of modernity has become such an established fact that we have lost sight of quite why it is so. We have also lost sight of quite who we mean by "Westerners", albeit for the benign reason that neither modernity nor the features that bring it are any longer exclusively associated with geography, any longer exclusively the possession of western Europe, North America and those countries elsewhere that shared European origins through colonial histories. Japan, Taiwan, Slovenia and South Korea are now as intrinsically modern and Western as are Sweden, France and Canada. For what they share is not geography, not history, but an idea.

It is a powerful idea, one that matters. It matters, most obviously, because it has brought levels of prosperity, well-being, security, stability, peace and scientific progress that in previous eras would have felt simply inconceivable. It matters, right now, because it is under threat and under attack, not principally from outside the West but from within. It is under attack for the good reason that it has recently failed to deliver enough of what citizens have come to expect of it, notably fairness, prosperity and security, but with the bad consequence that people and forces that stand for distinctly unWestern ideas, chief among them Donald Trump, have risen to prominence and power. Those ideas could, if allowed to prevail and become entrenched, destroy the West and much of what it has achieved.

Such a defeat would be a tragedy, of historic dimensions. For the idea of the West has provided more freedom and opportunities to more people in every country that has adopted it, than any other way of organising a society has ever achieved before. It truly has been the world's most successful political idea, by far. One reason why so many have liked it, and why others have been converging on it, is that when nurtured it brings a virtuous circle, by which freedom and the widespread chance to create new things and lead relatively unconstrained lives bring prosperity, stability and security, which in turn provides the social trust and economic resources that make further progress possible.

We often call this idea "liberalism", or "liberal democracy", but neither term quite commands either the heart or the brain. The heart demurs because the words sound too technical, philosophical or academic to stir the passions. They can anyway confuse, as to some Americans the term "liberal" has become an insult connoting what they see as the excessive use of taxpayers' money to cosset undeserving citizens and distort markets, while to others, especially in Europe, by adding the prefix "neo" the same word can insult by connoting an advocate of brutal market forces. The brain rebels at this confusion but also demurs on grounds that "liberal democracy" is a tautology – how could there be an "illiberal democracy", since democracy is supposed to give power to the *demos*, the people? – or that in modern use the word democracy must carry little meaning beyond describing a mechanical process than can be used or abused at will.

Behind those phrases, however, lie two other crucial words – one could call them ideals or even lodestars. The first is openness, for the Latin *liber* or freedom expressed through liberalism is both a desired outcome for the individual and a statement of the condition of any society in which such a collection of free individuals resides. Such a society is one that is thereby open to new ideas, new elites, new circumstances and new opportunities whether of trade in goods and services or of culture and science. It is thus a society not directed by a central intelligence but formed by the collective desires and actions of its members. Which leads to the second ideal or lodestar: equality.

Openness has required a steadily advancing notion of equality in order to make its bracing winds work and be accepted by society at large over the long term. Otherwise, conflicts inevitably arise between free individuals, with no means available to temper or resolve them, as some come to feel neglected, disadvantaged, powerless or left behind. This is exactly what has happened recently in the United States and in many countries of western Europe. The feeling of equality has been lost, neglected or simply eroded.

This conflict-resolving, socially soothing "equality" is not principally one of income or wealth – though widening gaps between rich and poor can affect equality's practical meaning, for good or ill – but rather of voice, rights and treatment, of having an equal say and participation in the openness that is being established. It is what in ancient Greek democracy was called *isonomia*, equality of political rights, which also crucially encompasses equality before the law. Thus in shorthand we can call it citizenship.

In ancient Greece *isonomia* had, and has since had, various extensions such as the equal right to speak in a parliament, but such things represent particular choices made by particular political systems. It is the principle of equality of rights and of voice for all adult citizens that connects together all countries that operate according to the rule of law, that protect freedom of speech and information, and that choose to provide political accountability through regular free elections based on a universal adult franchise.

The sense of shared interest that such equality represents has further encouraged societies to choose to make collective provision, through laws or the use of tax revenues, for some "public goods" that are deemed to be of general societal benefit, such as access to mandatory and state-financed education, to forms of social welfare in case of hardship, to broadly available and affordable health care, and to security provided by armed forces and police. That *isonomia* is the sort of equality that has been enjoyed by Japanese and Americans, French and Swedes, Australians and British alike, even if its precise form differs greatly from place to place, from culture to culture.

We are, and always will be, unequal in all sorts of ways – income, wealth, talent, profession, personality, social status – but in principle in a Western society we are, or should be, equal in our basic civic rights and in the political voice that this gives us. This equality of rights serves to flip the emphasis in society away from central, dictatorial direction and towards a more organic, bottom-up character. It provides the protection of property, ideas and actions that allows or encourages us to take risks, create new things, make investments of time and money. It represents, too, a fundamental humility, in contrast to the utopian arrogance of communism and fascism or of any dictator claiming to be omniscient and omnipotent. It is what provides the social trust, the legitimacy, that allows a society to absorb and adapt to the shocks and transformations that openness has brought, and will always bring.

This Western idea has been enormously successful. Now, however, the idea is in trouble, deep trouble. A feeling of decline has set in in the Western heartlands of the United States of America, Europe and – a true Western heartland from at least the 1970s onwards – Japan. The decline begins with economic failure and disappointment, and moves on to ageing, less vigorous demographics and then to a new sense of impotence in influencing world affairs. This feeling, and the ailments that lie behind it, are producing new divisions between countries and within them, creating cracks in the structures of international collaboration that Western countries built during the decades after 1945 and which helped to add to our collective strength and resilience. These are pessimistic times, times of disintegration and of the rekindling of old nationalisms. Our knowledge of where such forces led us during the first half of the 20th century rightly adds to our pessimism and foreboding. Even many of those who voted for Trump or Brexit in 2016 must now share that foreboding. Their votes were cries of anger at the establishment and the system they see as having failed them, not necessarily endorsements of the ideas that he represents or that Brexit will bring.

Trump's 2016 campaign, like the campaigns of other anti-establishment political movements on both sides of the Atlantic, was right in many ways about the problems faced by, and felt by, citizens of Western countries. But to be right about the problems does not make you right about the solutions. The three main solutions that America's president stands for are all deeply threatening to the future of the West: he has said he will withdraw from free-trade agreements and use protectionist measures to benefit American companies and punish foreigners, an approach not used systematically by any US administration since the 1930s; he has indicated that he does not consider the security alliances the US has struck since 1945 as any longer part of America's essential national interest, casting doubt even on whether under his presidency the US would stick by the mutual defence obligation in what has been the country's most important and strongest postwar alliance, NATO; and he has set about seeking not only to tighten up American control of immigration (as many countries wish to do) but also to discriminate in immigration procedures according to country of origin and by implication religion, which would take US immigration policy back, too, to the 1930s.

Such solutions threaten the West, first because they would replace openness on trade, an openness governed by agreed international rules, with a reversion not only to closure but to a system of commerce based on threats and brute power. In such a system, the chosen measure of success is not the amount of trade nor its benefit to consumers, as has prevailed since 1945, but the size of trade surpluses and deficits, a view of trade more common in authoritarian times. Secondly, it would threaten because it would increase divisions among currently liberal, open, friendly nations, reducing the flow of ideas between them as well, crucially, as trust. Thirdly, it would threaten because by casting serious doubt on long-standing alliance structures and commitments it would inevitably lead countries to hedge their bets and form new relationships with non-western nations, breaking a basic assumption that liberal nations are more dependable and trustworthy for each other than are other countries.

Peter Thiel, a Silicon Valley billionaire who supported Trump, has fostered the notion that while the new president's voters took him seriously but not literally, his critics made the mistake of taking him literally but not seriously. Yet whether or not his policy ideas should be taken literally, what is serious is that they suggest he does not understand the problems he – or any western government – needs to solve.

Our current ailments can, and should, be blamed on the long aftermath of what in 2008 was the greatest financial calamity that Western countries had seen since the 1930s, a calamity that had as its cause a devastating blend of complacency, negligence and corruption in preceding years. That calamity had inequality of political voice and power high among its origins, and the failure to deal properly and fairly with its consequences is also a symptom of inequality. A system in which the banks that created the calamity have been supported, and in which their present and past executives have stayed rich, but in which 15 million homeowners in the US saw their mortgages foreclosed upon in 2008–12, is not a system likely to feel fair.

A rapid recovery in jobs and incomes from the 2008 calamity might have quelled the anger, whether in the US, the UK, France, Italy or elsewhere. But it didn't happen. Nearly a decade later too many citizens feel trapped in dud jobs, dud circumstances, dud education. More deep-seated forces, including technological change, the impact of ageing populations and growing income inequality had already been causing strains before 2008, strains which could and should have been dealt with by governments had they been more attuned to the equality of citizenship and better at preparing their societies for the longer term. But they had not been and were not, and the vastness of the financial calamity then swamped everything.

The result is that many of our societies have lost confidence in the combination they have enjoyed of openness and equality, as they have lost the prosperity, security, stability and well-being that this blend had brought. Instead of supporting each other, acting together as our lodestars, the principles of openness and equality find themselves in conflict with one another, in more and more of our societies, making various forms of closedness increasingly popular as potential solutions and increasingly demanded by those who see themselves as having been left behind as unequal citizens.

To understand this malaise and to overcome it we need to recognise that, powerful and successful though it is, the Western idea comes with at least one important weakness, one that needs to be overcome at regular intervals. This is that the way in which a Western society works is so free, so decentralised, so lacking in any blueprint or fixed manner of doing things that its essential virtues are easy to take for granted and even easier to neglect or distort. Which means, in turn, that it is easy for that essence to be undermined and subverted, not just by ill-wishers outside but by inadvertent, self-interested and sometimes malign insiders. Openness, equality and their expression through democracy can, over time, serve to weaken, undermine and potentially destroy their own foundations.

That, as this book will seek to show, is what has happened in the US and the UK, in France and Italy, in Japan and Germany, most dramatically in the run-up to 2008. For that reason, the idea of the West and our understanding of what it means need periodically to be refreshed and reinvigorated so that this weakness can be overcome. To stay modern, Western countries need to jolt themselves out of their innate complacency, to revisit the essential values that have made them so successful, and to revive and if necessary reinvent them. Yet to be able to achieve such jolting, revival and reinvention the West needs at the same time to win the battle of ideas against those now arguing for solutions of closure, of isolationism, of exclusionary nationalism. President Trump is nothing if not a jolt, but he is likely to be a jolt in the wrong direction. And his disregard for facts and the truth, shown repeatedly during the campaign and since, threatens to keep citizens in ignorance or misled denial rather than waking them up to reality .

There is also, however, a fundamental motive for optimism and for a greater confidence in ourselves, one that is based on the most fundamental strength of the Western idea. The very reason Western societies have survived and thrived is that with openness and equality has come a vital characteristic: the ability to evolve, in the face of new threats and conditions, internally and externally. The Western idea, if it is protected, preserved and when necessary revived, contains within it a power of evolution that has proved superior to that of any other form of social organisation.

Recent history gives us a simple but compelling example. In 1956 Nikita Khrushchev proclaimed to a group of Western ambassadors: "Whether you like it or not, history is on our side. We will bury you." As we now know he was proved wrong. The reason is that the Western system proved far more flexible, more evolutionary, than was the Soviet system over which Khrushchev presided as premier.

It was not a matter of having history on your side. It was a matter of having the ability to adapt and learn new steps while history was leading everyone on its merry dances. The Soviet Union's problem was that it proved rigid and closed, unable to evolve as a system or as a society, so in the end it toppled over. Meanwhile, the countries we know of as the West adapted and changed, in their different ways. Like their communist rivals they faced crises and social disorder of various forms during the period of the Cold War: the 1968 youth movements in Europe, civil rights and anti-war protests in the US, terrorism in Italy and Germany, strikes and separatist violence in the UK, protests and environmental troubles in Japan. They often mused during those troubles that the good days might be over. They were often divided against each other. But they found ways to adjust and to deal with these sorts of problems through evolution rather than revolution.

The source of the West's evolutionary power has been its openness, its equality of rights, and so its social trust. Levels and forms of these ingredients have varied between countries and continents, as well as over time. There is ample room for debate about how open, equal and trusting societies can or should be, on many dimensions. But all have shown – so far – the ability to roll with history's punches, to adapt, evolve and find new ways of doing things and new things to do. Our concern now must be whether that ability remains intact enough to be repaired, or whether it might now be or soon become fatally weakened.

Such a concern is not new. When Oswald Spengler, a German historian, published his epic two-volume book *Decline of the West* at the end of the first world war, he had in mind a Western civilisation which he considered to be European-American, and he had a concept of it that was less about ideas than about cultures.[1] It is not surprising that, at the end of such a devastating and ultimately pointless war, Spengler saw the European-American civilisation as being in its twilight or sunset period. Plenty of others felt similarly gloomy. His argument went further, however: he posited that history had consisted of a series of civilisations, of high cultures, each of which passed through cycles of rise, maturity and decline. It was now the turn of the Western, that is the European-American world, to slip into decline and, ultimately, to be replaced.

Since Spengler gave his civilisational cycles roughly 1,000 years each, we should perhaps not be too quick to consider him wrong less than 100 years later. The second world war, culminating in the dropping of two atom bombs on Japanese cities, was a pretty apocalyptic event, one which could have led to even worse destruction had either Germany or Japan succeeded in developing nuclear weapons to compete with those of the US. Between the two world wars Mahatma Gandhi is said (possibly apocryphally – no firm citation has been found) to have been asked what he thought of Western civilisation and to have responded drily: "It would be a good idea." Had the second world war turned more widely atomic, it could have been a dead idea.

It did not and we have flourished, instead, for more than 70 years, adding more and more countries to the list of flourishing Westerners as more nations converged on the ideas that bring modernity. The question that stands before us now, wagging its fingers and shaking its head at us in a somewhat Spenglerian manner, is whether or not this period of flourishing has come to an end, or at least is coming to an end. The West may no longer be definable in the civilisational terms that Spengler deployed 100 years ago, nor is it simply European-American. But plenty of people think that it is in decline.

We are living in a time when openness is under challenge, when equality of rights and treatment is under greater doubt than for many decades, and when social trust is looking frayed. We seem to be losing faith in the idea that we ourselves created, through a long process of trial and error, of how best to arrange our societies. This loss of faith is putting in danger the very thing that made us not just survive but also thrive: the ability to evolve, to adapt to changing circumstances, to overcome threats and predators.

The fate of the West now, and in the decades to come, is in the hands of that evolutionary ability, and thus of our ability, as citizens of Western countries, first to resist attempts to close doors, borders and minds, and then to identify, agree upon and remove the major obstacles that have built up and are blocking such evolutionary change. There is ample cause for optimism. Our record, as Western countries, of confounding our own doubters and of dealing with our own demons, should give us confidence that once again this fight can be won. But nothing, of course, is inevitable. The fight is on.

If the idea of the West is to prevail, we will have to follow again our lodestars and keep this firmly in mind: without openness, the West cannot thrive; but without equality, the West cannot last.

1

Let battle commence

A liberal is a man too broadminded to take his own side in a quarrel.

Robert Frost, 1874–1963

So much of liberalism in its classical sense is taken for granted in the West today and even disrespected. We take freedom for granted, and because of this we don't understand how incredibly vulnerable it is.

Niall Ferguson, *The Observer*, 2011

This civilisation has not yet fully recovered from the shock of its birth – the transition from the tribal or "closed society" to the "open society" that sets free the critical powers of man ... the shock of this transition is one of the factors that has made possible the rise of those reactionary movements which have tried, and still try, to overthrow civilisation and return to tribalism.

Karl Popper, *The Open Society and its Enemies*, 1945

THE REACTIONARY MOVEMENTS are trying again. They may not believe they wish to overthrow civilisation but are nevertheless leading us back towards a form of tribalism, one which will put civilisation at risk along with all the freedoms that we take for granted. The claim by Marine Le Pen, leader of France's Front National, that today's true political contest is one between globalism and patriotism is a firmly tribal one, even if the French tribe is large. So is the "America First" slogan of Donald Trump, the US president, which echoes earlier nativist calls in his country during the 1920s, 1890s, 1850s and 1840s that doors should be closed in order to favour some established citizens against newcomers or immigrants. Theresa May, the UK's post-Brexit prime minister, showed that a battle was raging in her own mind over openness and the politics of national identity when in a speech in October 2016 she stated: "If you believe you are a citizen of the world, you're a citizen of nowhere." It is not just that she won't take her own side in the quarrel. She seems unsure which side she is on.

This battle, this clash between tribalism and openness, reflects feelings not only of fear but also of doubt. Doubt about our ability in the open societies to cope with the many threats we see to our civilisation, threats to the way of conducting domestic and international affairs that our advanced, wealthy societies stand by and try to live by. Doubt, even, about the rightness and the sustainability of the open society itself in the face of all the threats outside our doors and of the financial catastrophe that the US and western Europe brought upon all of us from 2008 onwards. Such worries are not unreasonable. After all, we have made quite a mess of things of late.

The external threats are real, for the instincts of tribalism remain strong and always will. Closed societies of the sort advocated and dreamt of by leaders of the Islamic State,[1] or by the violent jihadists of Osama bin Laden's al-Qaeda who preceded them in instilling horror and fear in Western hearts by killing 2,996 people in the US on September 11th 2001, or by the likes of Boko Haram in Nigeria and equivalent organisations elsewhere in Africa and Asia, will always have an emotional and spiritual appeal. This is why some tens of thousands of people have run from inside open societies towards Islamic State's supposed "caliphate" in Syria and Iraq, looking for a sense of belonging, identity and personal or religious purpose, even as many millions more have run away from it, looking for safety and freedom. Such traitors to openness have brought death and destruction to the very cities in which they grew up and lived, from Brussels to Paris, from San Bernardino to Nice and Berlin. This tribalism is no transitional phenomenon, even if you measure transitional in terms of millennia.

The world still, moreover, has a large supply of dictators, eager to bully their peoples, their neighbours and often us. For it remains abundantly clear that closing societies, imprisoning thereby the critical powers of man, is powerfully attractive for any dictatorial ruler or ruling regime that wants to reinforce or entrench their authority and thinks they can get away with it. The idea that authoritarians can no longer do so, promoted in 1993 by that great capitalist autocrat Rupert Murdoch, who said then in a speech that satellite television and other telecommunications technology posed "an unambiguous threat to totalitarian regimes everywhere",[2] and further fostered by such commentators as the *New York Times*'s Thomas Friedman in his 1999 paean to globalisation, *The Lexus and the Olive Tree*, has since been disproved comprehensively.

They can still get away with it and often do. Those who run closed versions of modern nation-states, including Russia, which purports to be a democracy, and China, which doesn't, still relish the decision-making freedom and control that closedness gives them and have plenty of tools with which to constrain the flow of information and ideas into and within their territories. Seeing their success in asserting such control, some other countries that had become open and fairly Western in their ideas, such as Turkey and Hungary, have recently been tempted to slide backwards and close some doors. The greater shock is seeing that temptation take hold in well-established Western societies too.

Dictators' treatment of their own people is a tragedy but only rarely a threat to others. However, they become a wider threat when they try to undermine the rules and conventions by which Western societies have sought since 1945 to keep the world peaceful – or, at least, more peaceful than it would otherwise be. In the past decade the leaders of Russia and China have both decided to set their own rules internationally, to lay their own facts on the ground, most recently through the annexation or seizure of territory in Ukraine and the South China Sea respectively, where their actions have challenged accepted precepts about international borders, the rule of law and the United Nations Charter, to which both countries were founding signatories in 1945 while under previous authoritarian regimes. Power politics still trumps international law.

The histories of the Soviet Union and of communist China show that such authoritarian regimes can last for many decades and generations, and today's Russia shows that even when they seem to have died they can resurrect themselves in a new form. The recent uprisings in the Arab world show that the demise of one authoritarian regime can readily lead to another, often after an all-too-short intermission of openness. We should not be surprised by this – after all, in 1917 the overthrow of Russia's tsarist regime was followed by two revolutions inside a year, the second of which introduced totalitarianism – but we often are. The age of authoritarianism is far from over.

Such are the constant realities of domestic and international affairs. To say so is not to diminish such potent threats and sources of dismay but rather to put them into historical perspective. The much more important question is what those fortunate enough to live in open societies should think, and do, about these threats. Does today's reappearance of those realities make openness unwise and unsustainable? To protect ourselves, do we need to let the authorities tap our phones and e-mails, treat citizens unequally just in case they might be dangerous, build fences along our borders as Donald Trump has advocated, or bring in emergency powers as France has done? Should we withdraw from international institutions of shared sovereignty and collaboration such as the European Union, to "take back control" as the UK voted in 2016 to do? Are we now so powerless to influence world affairs for the better that we had better abandon trying to do so, hiding in our domestic fortresses instead?

Currently, nerves are fraying and confidence is low. Just as happened in the 1920s and 1930s, siren calls are being heard about the inherent weakness of democracies, about how openness makes you vulnerable, about how true patriotism is at odds with the greatest current expression of openness: globalisation. Many anti-immigrant, pro-closure politicians, from France's Le Pen to the UK's Nigel Farage, from Hungary's Viktor Orban to the US's Trump, have been heard to comment admiringly about how decisive and effective is Russia's leader, Vladimir Putin, in contrast to the constrained ditherers of the West. The implication that proved so deadly during the interwar years in Europe, that democracy might be for wimps or for losers, is creeping back.

Yet in response to this we need to reflect harder on what are the true origins of our current malaise. The temptation to look outside, to blame foreigners and dark external forces, is always strong, but that does not make it right. What is it that has made us less prosperous and feel less secure? What is it that is making sizeable parts of our societies feel that they have been left behind with such unequal rights and insecurity that they are willing to support radical forces that would throw away openness purportedly to restore their sense of equality or shore up their sense of identity?

The answer to both of those questions lies chiefly at home. It is our own failures, within our societies, that have created these problems and feelings, and which pose a bigger, more lasting danger to us than do Islamic State, President Putin, or China, whether politically or economically. These failures emanate not from any civilisational destiny but rather from errors, pressures and especially interest groups inside our societies and political systems. They come from our own forms of tribalism and from those tribes' eternal desire to recreate divisions and destroy social unity. The right slogan is not "America First", nor is the right approach a stop-the-world-I-want-to-get-off economic nationalism. Instead we need to clean up and repair our democratic and economic systems. We need to understand, and then defeat, the enemies that lie within. We really do need, as Trump has said, to "drain the swamp". If, however, we just close the doors, raising barriers to trade and competition, we will merely increase the damage being done by monopolists, cartels and those with excessive political power. Selfishness, and the ability to pursue it, will become greater, not less.

Ironically, those selfish groups and pressures that have become the enemies of democracy and economic freedom are often the beneficiaries and consequences of openness. They are often apparent friends of the open society that have, sometimes unknowingly, become its enemy by steadily eroding its basic foundations and undermining it, most often by taking Western values for granted or by pursuing their own interests and exploiting the complacency that long periods of stability naturally engender. These "frenemies" and their effect on the political and economic behaviour of open societies are the principal subjects of this book, because they are the most important foes to defeat. They are the true sources of the sense of inequality that is currently threatening the openness that has enabled us in the West to flourish. They are the explanation for Trump, for Brexit, for Le Pen. A strong West has always been able to cope with a turbulent and troubling world. It is thanks to our frenemies that what we currently have is a weak West.

*

In the affluent, developed countries of North America, Europe, Japan and other parts of the West, it is easy to forget how new are the genuinely open, liberal societies that we enjoy today. It is easy to take those societies, and the freedoms and living standards they have brought, for granted. Margaret Thatcher was fond of saying that "when people are free to choose, they choose freedom".[3] Were she alive today she might add "and when they have had freedom for a long time, they often forget how lucky they are". She would have been aghast at the thought of an economic nationalist, an America Firster, in the White House.

When Karl Popper, an Austrian-born philosopher, was drafting his book *The Open Society and its Enemies* in the late 1930s and early 1940s, truly open societies were new, few and in grave danger of becoming even fewer. In 1943 Japan, Germany, Italy, Spain, Portugal, Brazil and Argentina, among others, were governed by dictatorships which limited freedoms of many kinds. To that list of then closed and suppressed societies can be added all the countries that were under the grip of European and Japanese colonial empires, of German wartime occupation and of Russia's communist empire of the Soviet Union.

In many of those countries, young democracies had been swiftly snuffed out in previous decades, rather as they have recently been in many of the countries of the post-2011 Arab uprising. The first world war, the collapse of the Ottoman and some European empires, the burdens of post-war debt and then financial collapse in the 1930s produced such severe economic weakness and such a chronic sense of political despair that a search began for alternative formulas, chiefly of closure and of collectivism. That is why the main targets of Popper's philosophical attack at that time were Plato, Hegel and Marx, for in his view the arguments for collectivism that these long-dead philosophers' ideas fostered and legitimised lay behind the then fashion for totalitarian solutions, and took the world to war for a second time within a generation.

One of the earliest books by Peter Drucker, another Austrian, who later became famous as a management guru, was entitled *The End of Economic Man*.[4] Published in 1939, it explained the rise of totalitarianism in Europe by placing it firmly in the context of the social upheavals caused by the first world war and the collapse of empires, and of subsequent economic failure. All of this produced a severe loss of trust in political elites, which resulted in mass support for leaders whose chief appeal was spiritual, magical or even primeval rather than rational or intellectual. Today's populist political leaders, from Le Pen to Trump, are seeking to make a similar appeal, albeit in less catastrophic times. They are in effect seeking to change the political subject, away from practical policy solutions they say have failed and towards a more emotional, nationalistic approach.

Let us, however, fight them by changing the subject back again. The seven decades since the second world war have seen an extraordinary flowering of democracy, transforming the open society from being the world's exception to being almost, though not quite, the rule. This flowering has brought with it an extraordinary period of prosperity. The openness that the Western powers created, in culture, trade and technology, has brought that prosperity under the protection of an international order, the policing of which has been led by a United States that has seen global prosperity and peace as being part and parcel of its national interest. What is in question now under President Trump is whether the US is going to renounce that international order and global role, deciding instead to adopt the far narrower definition of its national interest that prevailed in its previous period of isolationism and protectionism from 1920 until 1941.

To do so would be to put at risk a remarkable run of progress, the benefit of which the US has shared. In 2015, on the measure approximating to political openness and liberty that is used by a respected Washington, DC-based think-tank, Freedom House, 88 of the world's 195 countries were rated as "free", or 45% of the total, representing 40% of the world's population. Meanwhile 48 countries, or 25% of the total, representing 35% of world population, were rated as "not free": their number includes Russia, China and most of the countries of the Middle East and Africa in which Islamic State and other violent groups are operating. The remaining 30% of countries, 59 in all with 25% of world population, are "partly free" and thus could be described as being up for grabs between the open world and the closed.

During the 1990s, the Western assumption was that the number of the "partly free" would slowly decline as more and more people gained the choice, as Thatcher put it, and so would choose to join the free and open world. That did happen during the 1990s, most notably in central and eastern Europe, and freedom and democracy became solidly entrenched in both Taiwan and South Korea. But the movement since then has not all been one way. In the first two decades of the 21st century the number counted as only "partly free" has grown and a few countries have relapsed into the non-free category, most notably Russia. Freedom and openness have receded, a little.

This is a setback, but not one that justifies the pessimism or self-flagellation that often greets it. Looked at over the longer term since 1945 and especially since the end of the cold war in 1989–91, the trend has been much more towards the flowering of openness and equality than their fading.

Today's affluent, mature democracies vary a great deal in their social and political institutions and cultures. No one could honestly say that Japan and the US, Australia and France, Ireland and Denmark, the UK and Italy, to pick but four pairs among the advanced open societies, are politically, socially, economically and culturally identical or even in close resemblance to one another. They are points on a long spectrum, of capitalism, of democracy, even in some ways of openness itself. After all, the open society is an invitation to celebrate and encourage variety and diversity.

Nevertheless, these pluralistic societies of the West share some important characteristics, both positive and negative. For the current purpose, eight such shared characteristics can be identified, ones which help clarify our basic values as well as showing how it is that those values have come under such pressure and challenge.

1 Success

The first shared characteristic is simply that all have seen success, of a sustained nature, across the board, from economics to culture to science, even to sport, a success that is related to their openness, because the new ideas and competition that openness has brought have themselves brought prosperity and achievement. A few countries have been successful in that way for centuries; the rest now for decades and generations, especially for the more than 70 years that have passed since the end of the second world war. Openness in some cases preceded full democracy: the philosophical and scientific "Enlightenment" that occurred in Europe, principally in the UK, France, Germany and the Netherlands, in the 18th century was the product of a spirit of liberty, tolerance and the welcoming of new ideas and elites that blossomed even under still-powerful monarchies, and then gained new, especially economic, force with the industrial revolution that was led by the relatively democratic UK in the late 18th and early 19th centuries.

Openness can be relative, and moves in steps, not all of them forwards. Still, the open societies, at all their stages of opening, have consistently been the world's leaders in every major field of development for at least the past 300 years.[5] Many historians attribute China's loss of its pre-eminence 300–500 years ago to its imperial dynasties' decision to close the country's borders to most trade, and to restrict scientific and commercial enquiry.[6] Today, there is no country that has stayed for a sustained period among the world's top 25 in terms of overall living standards, as measured by the UN Human Development Index, that has not been open and thus Western, except for Hong Kong, which as a former, rather open, British colony is a special case. Countries specialising in oil production pop in and out of the top 50 as the oil price rises and falls, but among them only open Norway manages to stay in the top ranks for long.

2 Failure

Yet a second feature, shared by almost all the advanced open societies, is that they have recently seen failure, on a grand scale. The main expression of that failure has been massive financial crashes, as in Japan and Sweden in the early 1990s, but above all in the US and the western part of the EU in 2008, a crash which had global consequences. Such failures have hurt living standards, pushed governments into huge debts, destroyed feelings of hope and opportunity for entire generations, and led to today's challenges to the open society.

The financial calamities of Japan and Sweden in 1990–92 and of the US and western Europe after 2008 should not be seen as if they were external surprises somehow akin to asteroids, coming to Earth from outer space and causing huge damage. Nor, however, should they be seen as somehow inherent and unavoidable "crises of capitalism" that arise, as Karl Marx claimed, from ineluctable historical processes. They occurred thanks to some very terrestrial but powerful forces and policy mistakes.

The forces responsible include the rise of formidable financial interest groups among banks and big companies. Let us not mince our words about what took place. Those forces distorted or disarmed public policy as a result of the interplay between those interests and politicians and policymakers, sometimes through corruption, sometimes through persuasion and delusion. A long period of success, known to economists as "the great moderation", generated the complacency that left Western political systems open to such delusion and subversion. A similar complacency and a similar diversion of political and public attention by interest groups took hold in Japan during the 1980s in the run-up to that country's crash.

All these Western sufferers are struggling to recover, struggling to learn the right lessons from their failures. A common but damaging mistake has been to conclude that these failures were somehow technical matters, the result simply of faulty policies rather as the wrong settings on a computer might make it crash or the wrong tuning of a racing-car engine could make it stall, so that once the settings have been corrected better performance will follow, given time. Instead, they reflected a bigger phenomenon: the way in which democracy's own weaknesses can lead to disaster, as interest groups win the democratic game, as the rules of the game are subverted and as the game's elected custodians – that is, governments – have their eyes diverted away from what is happening by the desire for instant political gratification.

3 The rule of law and constitutional legalism

Such failures have occurred before. When they have done so, another vital shared characteristic of open societies has softened the impact and lessened the degree to which the failures have divided countries and destroyed institutions. This feature is the separation of powers among political institutions, with checks and balances between them, all within a system of the rule of law. Open societies are not made open and successful simply by virtue of holding elections. They have succeeded and survived through what has been called their "constitutional legalism".[7]

Put simply, this means that open societies use laws to provide all their citizens with equal rights, and then surround the processes of making and enforcing these laws with structures set in constitutions so as to protect them from subversion or manipulation. Constitutions define the powers of political institutions and dictate the agreed means by which those powers can be changed in the future. Those who make the laws are accountable by democratic means but also to the law.

In this regard the contrast is stark between the open societies and countries such as Russia or Venezuela where elections are winner-takes-all affairs in which laws are arbitrary tools of power and constitutions can be changed at will or ignored. When in 2001 President Hugo Chavez of Venezuela was asked during a visit to *The Economist* about recent constitutional changes in his country, he responded brazenly: "We have an excellent constitution. I wrote it myself." Reaching into his jacket pocket he pulled out a little blue book, signed it and handed his constitution over as a gift. He was not, safe to say, presiding over an open society.

The faith, or at least belief, in constitutionalism and equality before the law can be dated back centuries, to the Magna Carta (in Britain in 1215) or to Roman law and the principles of *civis romanus sum* ("I am a Roman citizen", a millennium or more earlier), or even as far as the Babylonian Code of Hammurabi from Mesopotamia in around 1750BC, all well before elections on universal franchises were being held. Such documents were, however, widely disregarded in the years that followed. Power often trumped the law, but battle between the two had at least been set forth.

The provisions of the Magna Carta for the rule of law and equality before it were not widely honoured in Britain for a further 500 years, at best. Neither in Britain nor in the newly born United States of America did these principles become firmly established until the 19th century, which was the period during which both countries made dramatic economic and social progress, progress which brought with it a widening of the democratic franchise. Yet the US still denied equal civil rights to many African-Americans until the 1960s and denied women equal voting rights until 1920. The UK denied women equal voting rights until 1928, and maintained until the 1960s a colonial empire in which equality before the law was largely denied. Equal marriage rights for same-sex couples is the latest extension of this principle of equality before the law, an extension that remains in dispute in many countries and cultures.[8]

The fundamentals of open societies remain works in progress. This is what makes them impressive – they evolve and improve – but also vulnerable.

4 Social trust

One fundamental feature of the open societies has been thrown into particular doubt by financial calamities and the ageing of populations. As already noted, success has arisen from being open to trade, to ideas, to the entry of new generations of political, intellectual, cultural and commercial leaders – and, crucially, to being able to accept and absorb change, sometimes quite disruptive change, without suffering major political or social disorder. This acceptance and absorption has been achieved thanks to high levels of social trust, established through equality before the law, through the universal franchise for elections, but also through the provision of publicly funded welfare safety nets and old-age pensions along with more long-standing public goods such as education.

The way this has been achieved has varied from country to country, with extensive welfare provision more important in Europe and Scandinavia, high degrees of job security more important in Japan and Italy, geographical and social mobility more important in the United States. Social trust was built up slowly during the post-war decades, sometimes as the outcome of political or social conflict amid rapid economic and technological change.

For example, there was mass migration from rural areas into cities in Japan, Italy and elsewhere during the 1950s and 1960s, and painful deindustrialisation during the 1970s and 1980s of regions that had traditionally specialised in coal, steel, shipbuilding or other rustbelt sectors, in the US Midwest, Germany's Ruhr, France's Alsace-Lorraine, Belgium's Wallonia, or the UK's midlands, north-east, lowland Scotland and south Wales. Such change brought considerable trouble and strife, but nowhere did that strife lead to a revolution. Where particularly nasty conflict occurred, as in Italy during the 1970s "years of lead",[9] or the US with its many violent protests in the 1960s about race, civil rights and the wars in Indochina, or France with its "*événements*" of 1968, or Japan with its student protests of the 1960s, such turmoil was in the end contained and mitigated without threatening the country's political system as a whole. At times, though, conflict was ended by handing out welfare entitlements and special legal rights, the price for which in public finances and economic rigidity is only now being paid.

Public finances have been severely hurt by the 2008 financial crisis, and ageing populations are putting further strains on public-pension and health spending, as Chapter 9 will explore. This is casting doubt on the future affordability of welfare states and thus of the social trust that they buy or reinforce. One of the main problems is that yesterday's payments to buy social trust do not necessarily deal with today's or tomorrow's problems, but there is fierce resistance to any cutting of what groups consider to be entitlements. The farmers who were bought off with subsidies during rapid rural–urban migration in the 1950s and 1960s now block the streets with manure if their flow of public cash is threatened. Coalminers and steelworkers did similar things in the 1970s and 1980s. Some progress has been made in Europe, the US and Japan in reducing such entitlements, though not enough. Today's far more costly equivalent to the farmers and miners are pensioners, not because they receive public pensions that are generous in size but because they receive them for far too many years, as retirement ages have fallen and life expectancy has risen.

The single largest contributor to public debts, beyond recession, is public-pension costs, and the single most important solution to those debts, beyond economic growth, will need to be a radical change in the way in which people think about their working lives. With life expectancies rising to 80–100 years, it makes no sense for people to think of their working and thus main taxpaying lives as making up less than half of that period. To do so violates the basic equality of citizenship and participation that has made Western societies work so well. Economists' term of art – "dependency ratio" – to indicate the balance between those who pay taxes by working and those who receive them in public pensions gives the game away. An open and equal society cannot survive high "dependency ratios", for that would institutionalise inequality and produce conflict between payers and receivers. There will have to be some trade-offs if such conflict is to be avoided: working for more years will have to become easier than it is today, incentives for workers to retire and for companies to prefer younger employees will need to be altered, and public education will have to be redirected to facilitate retraining.

Welfare states are not ends in themselves. Their purpose is one of enabling change to take place without destroying security and a sense of belonging, of achieving a sufficient sense of trust, fairness and social justice to enable the country as a whole to continue to make progress, balance its books and provide whatever other public and private goods are desired. Whenever the welfare state becomes unfit for that purpose, it needs to be rethought and reinvented – but not abandoned, except in the unlikely event that the purpose itself has become obsolete.

5 Rising inequality

We live, by common consent, in an age of rising inequality. Technology, changing mores, weaker trade unions and less regulated economies since Margaret Thatcher and Ronald Reagan removed barriers to market forces in the 1980s have reversed the trend towards greater equality of incomes and wealth in most Western countries that had been seen during the previous post-war decades, and much attention has been given to this trend. Governments today place less emphasis on using taxation and welfare spending to redistribute, and so equalise, incomes than they did in the 1960s and 1970s, although tax and spending are still generally quite redistributive. Nevertheless, income inequality is not the biggest problem in Western societies.

The most problematic sort of inequality now is the sort that generates or is associated with unequal legal and political rights for different groups of citizens, because such inequality is causing divisions and conflicts that risk undermining faith in social and political systems themselves. This sort of inequality makes people feel powerless and breeds a sense of injustice. Pension entitlements are one example, though the division they cause between the young and the old, the taxpayer and the recipient, has not yet become a noisy or hostile one. More painful is the inequality of legal rights that has spread in many countries – notably Japan, France and Italy – among employees who hold differing forms of contract, some permanent and secure, others temporary and insecure, which is reflected also in the low wages and weak bargaining power of temporary workers. This in turn is making demand in those economies weaker and so harming their ability to create new, more secure jobs.

Most problematic of all is the inequality of political voice and rights that has come most spectacularly and clearly from rises in the wealth of the richest fractions of society and of big corporations. This is the biggest reason why income inequality matters. If such wealth becomes so entrenched that political influence is grossly distorted and all hope of social mobility and advancement through education becomes blocked, societies will have ceased to be truly open. If democracy simply means the best politics and policy that a billionaire, a banker or a technology monopolist can buy, democracy will soon die or be overthrown.

6 Immigration

There is a further question about equality, one that has become especially salient over the past decade: equality for whom? Or, put another way, are the rights of existing citizens diluted or otherwise materially affected when new citizens are added through immigration, and if so should that dilution give citizens a right of veto over further immigration? It is an eternal question, one that provokes more xenophobic answers whenever two conditions apply: when unemployment is high and/or incomes are depressed; and when war and other disorder in nearby countries increases the flow of would-be immigrants from a trickle to a flood or otherwise augments feelings of insecurity.

It is not hard to grasp why immigration causes controversy. To stop their populations from declining and to bring in youthful energy, all Western countries need immigration. But voters tend to disagree, since immigrants are foreigners, speak different languages, come from different cultures and might – especially in weak economic times – compete for jobs. Refugees can also seem dangerous, since they are fleeing violence at home and can be readily suspected of bringing that violence along with them.

According to the UN Population Division's *International Migration*

Report 2015, refugees form a small if headline-grabbing part of the overall phenomenon: of the 244 million people worldwide who were living in a country other than the one they were born in (the UN's definition of migrants), only 8%, or 19.5 million, were counted as refugees. The total stock of migrants has risen from 173 million in 2000 to its current 244 million, a 69 million-strong people movement in the past 15 years, which is equivalent to the combined states of California and Texas, or the whole population of the UK, upping sticks and moving home. Migration is not a new phenomenon, and the rising absolute numbers also reflect the world's growing population. But the 2010–15 growth rate of migration of about 1.9% a year (down from 3% in 2005–10 and 2% in 2000–05) has outpaced global population growth of 1.2% a year. Advanced, wealthy countries play host to more migrants (71%) than do developing countries: nearly a fifth of the world's total number of migrants, or 47 million people, reside in the United States alone, which took in about 1 million migrants per year, on average, between 1990 and 2015.

Migration poses a genuine challenge to the idea of openness and to its bedfellow, equality. For it raises the difficult question of how much is too much. Is it when the proportion of foreign-born in a population reaches 24%, as it had in 2014 when the Swiss voted in a referendum to abandon their treaty with the EU allowing free movement into Switzerland of EU citizens? Or the much lower level of 13.9% that it had reached in the UK in 2016 when the British voted to leave the EU, partly on similar grounds? Is national identity threatened by immigration, or is Britishness enriched by the fact that the mayor of London, Sadiq Khan, is the son of a Pakistani immigrant?

At its peak in the 1890s, the share of foreign-born in the US reached 14.8%, not far above contemporary levels of around 13%, but in the post-war era it fell to a low of 4.7% in 1970. On paper, the argument for immigration is uncontestable, especially when you can point to incredibly successful immigrants such as Sergey Brin of Google, Andy Grove of Intel or Stelios Haji-Ioannou of easyJet. But in practice, the argument is hard to win, for long. Tribalism runs deep.

7 Rising expectations

Some things, however, do change. A seventh common feature is that the citizenry's expectations about democracy, the rule of law, living standards, political ethics, rights of all kinds and even social mobility have risen steadily during the post-war decades. These higher expectations are partly the result of cultural change but also of the broadening of public education and of rapid and continuing improvements in information and communications technology. Openness has played a big part too: the cost of travel has slumped relative to average incomes and the flow of ideas around the world has become easier. Westerners are far more cosmopolitan in their habits and interests than at any time in the past, even those who profess to have a grudge against globalisation. Moreover, we can vote in snake-oil salesmen so we sometimes do – helped by complacency about our civil and political liberties, amid the belief that we will always be able to reverse our decisions next time we vote.

There was no golden age in the workings of Western societies, or in their economic performance. Democracies develop, but so do expectations of them, of what they can and should deliver, of how they can and should work. Measures of alienation or disillusionment, such as electoral turnout or polls showing mistrust in government or politicians, are often interpreted as indicating a new dysfunctionality in democracy. Although, as Chapter 3 argues, there is indeed evidence of some forms of dysfunctionality, such trends also need to be seen in the context of higher expectations and greater transparency. And, one might add, the steady increase in the number of channels for our grumbles. Twitter and Facebook have a lot to answer for.

8 International collaboration

Lastly, as different as they may be, open societies commonly believe in working together internationally in their shared interests. They have many more, and more extensive, alliances with each other than do closed societies, as Chapter 10 will show. All the advanced open societies have believed, even if to varying degrees and with differing opinions, in collaboration to solve common problems, set common rules and fight common enemies.

This belief is seen in the many collaborative military and political arrangements set up since 1945, including NATO, the European Union and the US-Japan Security Treaty, and the multilateral institutions and treaties the West has initiated and developed, including the United Nations and its sister organisations the International Monetary Fund, the World Bank, the International Maritime Organisation and the World Trade Organisation. We can even include here global sports associations such as FIFA for football and the International Olympic Committee. Many non-open societies also belong to such organisations, but their genesis lies in the open societies' belief in collaboration with one another, as well as in the desirability of extending the domestic virtues of the rule of law into international affairs.

This belief and practice is the main explanation for why the UK's vote in 2016 to leave the EU came as such a blow internationally: it represented a kick in the teeth to some of the country's closest allies and a renunciation of one of the deepest forms of international collaboration yet attempted. It is probably also why Trump liked the idea of Brexit, given that he too is a professed sceptic about international collaboration. Since 1945 alliances have proved long-lasting, but that does not make them permanent.

*

These eight shared characteristics represent a way of doing things, of organising national and indeed international affairs, that is resilient but under strain. Failures have led many to doubt whether past success can be repeated. Social trust has been lost thanks to inequality in political voice and rights, and to the fraying of welfare states. International collaboration has come to be seen as onerous, costly and even coercive. No wonder that the West, along with the liberal order it set up, is in crisis.

Open societies often think they are in crisis, shortly before finding their escape route from it. Sometimes the perceived crises have concerned a particular set of the advanced countries, sometimes they have encompassed all of them. Often, like now, the pessimism has coincided with, or emanated from, an economic setback. For example, in 1975 the Trilateral Commission,[10] a high-level think-tank-cum-conference-unit that had been set up two years earlier on the initiative of philanthropist David Rockefeller with the aim of bringing together the democracies of Japan, North America and western Europe, published a book called, guess what, *The Crisis of Democracy*.

That particular episode featured a nasty recession and high inflation following the trebling in oil prices enforced by Arab producers in 1973, widespread industrial and social protests in many countries, American failure in the Vietnam war, and a prevailing pessimism about East–West relations, that is, the cold war between the West and the Soviet Union. The Trilateral Commission's book quoted Willy Brandt, chancellor of West Germany from 1969 to 1974, as having said just before leaving office:

Western Europe has only 20 or 30 more years of democracy left in it; after that it will slide, engineless and rudderless, under the surrounding sea of dictatorship, and whether the dictation comes from a politburo or junta will not make that much difference.

Brandt might have felt gloomy about democracy for reasons close to home: his resignation was forced by the discovery that an east German spy had been working in his private office. Yet as we now know he underestimated two things: first, the possibility that the surrounding sea would soon turn substantially democratic, with Portugal, Spain and Greece all losing their dictators during the mid-1970s and with the eventual collapse of the Soviet empire in central and eastern Europe; and second, the adaptability of democracies, their ability to learn from crises and other travails and either to muddle their way out of them or in some cases, such as the UK under Thatcher in the 1980s and Sweden in the 1990s, to engage in quite fundamental reforms.

David Runciman, a professor of politics at Cambridge University, described in his book *The Confidence Trap* his view of how democracies have dealt with crises during the past century:

Democracies are adaptable. Because they are adaptable, they build up long-term problems, comforted by the knowledge that they will adapt to meet them. Debt accumulates; retrenchment is deferred ... Democracy becomes a game of chicken. When things get really bad, we will adapt. Until they get really bad, we need not adapt, because democracies are ultimately adaptable. Both sides play this game. Games of chicken are harmless until they go wrong, at which point they become lethal.

There's the rub, in Runciman's view. The genius of democracy is its ability to evolve, to adapt. The stupidity of democracy is its frequent preference for taking the easy life by deferring that adaptation, beyond the next election, the next economic cycle, even the next generation. One day that stupidity might, he implies, prove democracy's downfall.

Although the advanced democracies do exhibit both overconfidence and complacency, they do not thereby have a controlling brain that is truly capable of such psychological traits. Open societies are the product of millions of opinions and decisions by citizens, politicians, civil servants, companies, media, schoolteachers, academics and more, often wearing more than one of those hats, generally not feeling directly responsible for the outcome of whatever they do. Such decentralised systems exhibit negligence more than overconfidence, carelessness more than complacency.

Moreover, Western democracies do not err simply by deferring hard decisions. They also, through their own processes, make such hard decisions harder to take. It is the very process of democratic competition for power that produces the rigidities and distortions that hamper adaptation. It is not just that politicians seek power through short-term promises or measures, and avoid thinking beyond the electoral cycle. Much greater harm is done by the natural, but selfish, behaviour of myriad private actors in seeking advantage in the democratic contest, and then succeeding in holding onto it. Success in a democracy is about becoming winners, and accruing power, privileges, resources and rights as a result. Yet it is the winners that make democracy risk failure when they win too well. That may sound rather un-American, but the US is one of the biggest victims of such victors' manipulation.

Classic political analysis of democracy has for centuries focused on one, albeit vital, aspect of this excess of success: how to deal with the danger of a tyranny of the majority. This problem continues today every time victorious governing parties conclude that they thereby have a mandate to do whatever they like and even to try to ensure that today's majority becomes permanent, as has happened in Hungary since 2010 and in Poland since 2015. But the problem is much wider and more insidious than this. The rigidities and distortions that build up in democracies, through actions fair and square as well as unfair, are more frequently tyrannies by minorities, by groups that share an interest: by bankers and lawyers, by farmers and trade unionists, by doctors and pensioners, by oil companies, pharmaceutical companies, carmakers, and many more.

George Soros, a billionaire investor and philanthropist, who set up his Open Society Foundations to campaign for and support the establishment and extension of liberal democracy all over the world, most notably in his native Hungary and neighbouring central Europe, argued in his book *Open Society* that the enemy was what he called "market fundamentalism". Although a blind, often naive faith in markets did lie behind the huge policy mistakes by central bankers such as Alan Greenspan (chairman of the US Federal Reserve Board from 1987 to 2006) that led to the 2008 crash, Soros's argument underplays the key weakness, the most deadly trait of democracy: the ability of powerful special interests, some of them commercial and even "market fundamentalist" but many not, to capture and turn to their own advantage laws, regulations and public resources. It is the interplay of private actors and public powers that most harms – and in the end threatens the survival of – the open society.

That these selfish interests are all minority groups ultimately makes it possible, in principle, to form a majority consensus to deal with them, or at least some of them. There is nothing new about special interests, nothing new about declaring them the political enemy. In the US the cry against special interests has become habitual, even traditional, especially when tied to a claim to represent "the people" against "Washington".[11] When Trump promised in 2016 to "drain the swamp", he was following that tradition. Nor is there anything new about the fact that success in defeating special interests is always partial at best. What happens, though, is that the rigidities and distortions accrete gradually, rather like barnacles on a ship's hull. At first their accretion doesn't seem to make much difference. If allowed to persist and to accumulate, however, it makes a huge difference.

The power of evolution which open societies possess so magnificently is engaged in an eternal struggle with the barnacles that build up on their hulls so as to slow that evolution down. If those barnacles could only be regularly scrubbed off, democracy would be in a much healthier state. That they are not routinely scrubbed off is in part because of a basic trait of humanity: that we take things for granted, especially the good and even fundamental values that have been handed down to us by previous generations.

Freedoms of speech and of information, the rule of law, equality before the law, civil liberties of all kinds, clean, uncorrupted government, even the proper workings of electoral democracy: these come to seem not just as gifts to us by earlier generations that had fought or worked hard for them but as facts of life, as part of the social and political landscape, to be ignored, neglected or at times of stress traded away.

We are surrounded by seductive temptations to trade off freedoms and principles for more pragmatic goals. We are tempted to give up privacy and liberty to permit police and security services to survey all that we do in the hope of catching criminals or terrorists. We are tempted to encourage public servants to get into closer contact with business, even to work for private firms for long periods, so as to make them more commercially savvy, regardless of the resulting likelihood of favouritism and outright corruption. We are tempted to subsidise one industry or protect a big firm against foreign competition in order to preserve a particular set of jobs today, regardless of the consequences tomorrow. We are tempted to put constraints on the media and freedom of information, ignoring the benefits such constraints provide to those in political or corporate power. We are tempted to allow our security authorities to lock up or constrain people they may be suspicious of, dispensing with the normal requirements of due process of law and fair trials, or order to make ourselves feel safer, ignoring the possibility that such powers might end up being used against innocent people, people like us.

Openness, in societies, is not a once-and-for-always condition. It requires work, persuasion and vigilance if it is to be maintained and, crucially, if it is to continue to be supported by the population at large. It requires effort to explain, justify and defend the basic liberties and values that we trade away in such a cavalier or negligent fashion. And it requires an understanding of what are the self-harming tendencies of our democracies. President Barack Obama put it in typically inspirational words in his speech to the Democratic Party Convention in support of Hillary Clinton in July 2016:

> Democracy works, America, but we gotta want it, not just during an election year, but all the days in between.

We've also got to fight, at regular intervals, to deal with democracy's own frailties and to protect thereby the values and rights that make it work. Adam Smith wrote in his 1776 book *The Wealth of Nations* of how in economics a seemingly "invisible hand" of self-interest produces outcomes that are generally of public benefit – but not always. In democracies, self-interest also works as if by an invisible hand, in open competition. But the outcome, again, is not always to the public benefit. The public needs to realise this. It needs to be taught to watch out for it. Most important, it needs to teach itself such vigilance. The price of liberty, runs a famous American quotation sometimes attributed to Thomas Jefferson, is eternal vigilance. It is a vigilance that is required against internal threats as well as against external ones. Currently, the biggest single source of such threats is inequality. Which makes it ironic that the latest supposed battler for equality in the US is a self-proclaimed billionaire with a taste for glitzy buildings carrying his own name in large letters.

2

Inequality and fairness

Money can't buy you friends,
but it does get you
a better class of enemy.

Spike Milligan

We have lived a painful history,
we know the shameful past,
but I keep on marching forward,
and you keep on coming last.
Equality, and I will be free.
Equality, and I will be free.

Maya Angelou, "Equality"

"THE SYSTEM IS RIGGED." That claim was more or less a mantra during the 2016 electoral cycle in the United States, being chanted most notably by Donald Trump and by Hillary Clinton's rival for the Democratic nomination, Senator Bernie Sanders. Moreover, in the UK's referendum on membership of the European Union in the same year, the official campaign to leave the EU framed the contest as "the people versus the elites". Similar claims are made by populist and other insurgent parties in other European countries. But what do such slogans really mean?

In a partial or pretend democracy such as Russia or Zimbabwe we would know that "rigged" meant that ballot boxes were being stuffed, the media manipulated or the opposition intimidated. Although Trump occasionally veered towards that sort of allegation, this was not his main thrust, which was to portray Clinton as being part of a wealthy, selfish political and economic establishment whose interests were now at odds with those of ordinary voters. Yet this idea of "elites" and "the establishment" is itself not very enlightening. What is an "establishment" in democracies that change leaders every few years, many of which have made a fetish of choosing young prime ministers and presidents to symbolise change? The rise of Trump's predecessor, Barack Obama, like that of Bill Clinton a quarter of a century earlier, had demonstrated the openness of the US political elite, not its closedness.

The grievance that is being summed up by words such as rigged or by opposition to elites and the establishment is in truth closer to the idea contained in Maya Angelou's poem "Equality" than to old notions of class conflict or of socialist demands for income equalisation. It is a grievance about being left behind, which is the same as saying you are being left out. It is thus a grievance about being an unequal citizen, a citizen with fewer rights than others, with less of a political voice than would or should be expected in a democracy. That grievance may well arise from an unfavourable outcome, such as being unemployed or poor, as grievances usually do. But to go beyond jealousy or resentment and provide fuel for nationwide political movements, the grievance needs also to be directed at the perceived causes – just as the civil-rights and gender-equality movements that Angelou's poem related to were claims about causes, not demands for redistribution of income.

The principal cause of today's grievances is easy to find: the financial collapse of 2008 and the long-lasting economic pain that has followed it, along with the sense of betrayal and systemic failure that it has engendered. That collapse and that pain has been piled on top of the less widespread, but still real, suspicion of "globalisation", by which is principally meant cheap competition in manufactures from China and other emerging economies, and the job losses such competition has caused in towns that specialised in manufacturing. The two are linked, because it was free global movements of capital that made the 2008 crash the true calamity that it was. The crash also destroyed – or deferred, for at least a decade – the hope that the losses from globalisation were just a transitional matter, to which economies and societies would sooner or later adjust. In the face of all this, elites are being targeted not because they are elites but because they have failed to live up to their responsibilities. They have failed to deliver either stability or recovery. And yet they – the rich, the powerful, the well connected – are perceived to have done well themselves even while others have suffered from their failures.

If income inequality as such were the issue, it would have come to the forefront much sooner. Such inequality has risen virtually throughout the West, from the US to Japan, from Germany to the UK, during recent decades. But it did so without earth-shattering political consequences, because the inequality came without an abiding or at least sufficiently strong sense of unfairness. What connects the various political movements worldwide that are now seizing on this issue is the greater sense of injustice that has come from the 2008 crash, and above all the feeling of political and civic inequality that the crash, its causes and its remedies have engendered.

Money, whether as income or wealth, matters chiefly as a warning signal that inequality is becoming entrenched, not just socially but also politically, so much so that the chance of anything being improved from the point of view of those who see themselves as powerless victims feels low or even non-existent. This is what is meant by accusations that the system is rigged. It amounts, in the end, to a belief that in the West equality of political rights, the *isonomia* of the ancient Greeks, has at best been damaged, at worst become a fiction. The idea of the West, with all the dynamism it has brought, does not depend upon incomes or wealth being equal or even close to it. But it does depend upon political rights being equal. It does depend on people mostly considering their societies to be fair.

*

Open societies, the advanced democracies, have never been fully fair in any meaningful sense of the word. But they have made progress and muddled through in political terms because enough people have believed that within those societies they could make their way passably well, with a reasonable set of opportunities open to them and without grossly unjust obstacles in their way. Not all the people, of course. But enough to keep things moving, in proportion to changing expectations and perceptions of what is fair and unfair.

Such a belief can be made grandiose through constructs such as "the American dream", the notion that upward social mobility is available to all. Ironically, just at the time in 2008 when in a once-unbelievable sense that dream came true and an African-American of fairly modest origins, Barack Obama, was elected to the nation's highest office, disillusionment set in and became widespread, and not just in the US. In its eight years in office, the Obama administration achieved many things, most notably its signature extension of health care to more than 20 million previously uninsured Americans through the Affordable Care Act. What it did not manage to change was the sense that money talks and that it buys not just economic advantages but political ones too, advantages that endure through generations. Even in the US inequality is not just, or even mainly, a matter of cash. It is a matter of opportunities, education, marriage, political voice, the way economic inequality begets a new, more deep-seated and potentially pernicious form of inequality.

Economists can dispute most things, especially those involving statistics. But however you look at it or measure it, inequality of both wealth and income has plainly increased in recent decades in the advanced open societies of the world, which account for almost all of the 35 member countries of the Organisation for Economic Co-operation and Development (OECD), the official think-tank which is one of the most assiduous collectors of transnational data on economic issues.

In late 2015 the OECD released a new study, *Income Inequality: The Gap between Rich and Poor*, which showed that during the 1980s the richest 10% of the population in OECD member countries earned seven times more than the poorest 10%. Now, the richest 10% in those 34 countries earn nearly ten times more than the poorest 10%. The share going to the top 1% of the population in one of the most unequal countries, the United States, doubled during that same period, to more than 20% of total pre-tax income. Between 1985 and 2013 the level of income inequality rose in all OECD countries except Belgium, the Netherlands, France and Greece, in each of which it was little changed, and Turkey, in which it declined. There were especially sharp rises in inequality in some countries that had previously been associated with relative equity, including Finland, Sweden, New Zealand, Japan and Germany.

Looking at the difference in attitudes to the gap between rich and poor in, say, the US, France and Sweden, it is clear that culture and history play a big role in determining whether great wealth is seen principally with admiration, envy or active hostility. Few are the countries in which anyone cares much about the extraordinary incomes earned by sports stars, for their wealth can be considered a kind of lucky break (which could have happened to anyone) compounded by dedication and hard work (which makes them deserve it). Entrepreneurs such as Bill Gates of Microsoft, Sir Richard Branson of Virgin, Masayoshi Son of Softbank and Daniel Ek of Spotify also get something of a free pass in public opinion, receiving more admiration than envy. The same tolerance or lack of concern is not, however, generally applied to the vast sums earned by chief executives of big companies or leading investment bankers, for while it might grudgingly be accepted that such people do work hard, many assume, rightly or wrongly, that the means by which they have obtained such good fortune contain at least some elements of the rigging of markets.

Chief executive pay is a notorious example that has proved impervious to reform. Corporate boards call in remuneration consultants to certify how their CEO's total pay compares with those of competitors, a process which looks to have the merit of independence and objectivity. But the same consultants work for many companies competing with each other in the same sector. Boards declare that their CEO's pay ought to be positioned in "the top quartile". Who wants to position their CEO in a low quartile? But since everyone wants to be in that quartile, all their salaries are bid up. Bankers' bonuses are another vexed issue. This time, the notoriety occurs not because the pay market itself is rigged – top banks compete fiercely for staff – but because the competitive process leads to the granting of bonuses on the basis of activities that are in a market benefiting from a public subsidy, in the form of a willingness to rescue banks and their depositors in the event of crisis, and the true profitability of which will not be certain for several years to come.

The corporate management question is eternal: does it inspire ordinary and junior workers to see in the annual accounts that their chief executive earns hundreds of times more than them, or does it make them less loyal and more resentful? Whatever the answer, which no doubt depends on other corporate policies alongside those of pay, the disparities vary greatly from country to country. British readers may be surprised to see their country ranked so low on this measure in Figure 2.1, the figures for which come from the chief US trade union confederation, the AFL-CIO, but this is probably because the companies that hit the headlines with high CEO pay are an elite of international firms whose bosses swim in the same pool as their American counterparts, while the bosses of more middling, domestic companies do not.

Like other economic processes, inequality is an outcome of many factors, most driven by markets, some driven by or affected by government. As such, it cannot be described as entirely "natural", since it is plainly influenced by taxes of all kinds, redistributive transfer payments from the public purse, access to education and much else besides. Some studies show that rising inequality

FIG 2.1 **Ratio of CEO pay to average worker's pay at listed companies, 2011–12**

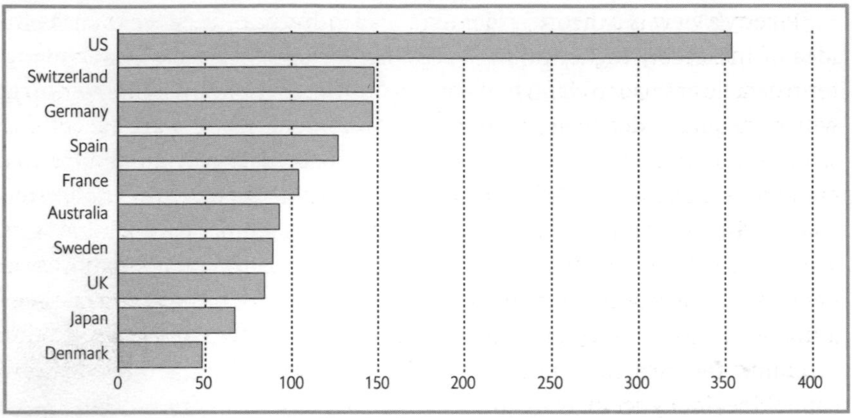

Country	Ratio
US	~355
Switzerland	~148
Germany	~147
Spain	~127
France	~104
Australia	~93
Sweden	~89
UK	~84
Japan	~67
Denmark	~48

(Horizontal axis: 0, 50, 100, 150, 200, 250, 300, 350, 400)

Sources: AFL-CIO; *The Economist*

harms economic growth, while others see correlation rather than causation. The economic performance of the US, over the long term, should alone be enough to convince that inequality per se does not inevitably act as an economic drag. This does not mean that, to match its wealth and productiveness, all other open societies should aim to match its levels of inequality; too many other factors are at play, including cultural ones. Nor does it mean that the US will always be able to look benignly upon further increases in inequality: there could be a point, even there, where inequality starts to be economically counterproductive. But it means that the connection between inequality and economic progress is complicated.

The now famous bestseller about inequality, *Capital in the Twenty-First Century*, by Thomas Piketty, a French economist, avoids many of these debates. Instead it opts for a deterministic warning, which Karl Popper would have termed "historicist" and modern critics think of as Marxist, arguing that in the absence of government intervention the gap between rich and poor will rise inevitably and inexorably, because Piketty believes that the income generated by capital will turn out to be higher, over the long term, than the rate of economic growth and thus higher than the growth in income from productive employment. This constant widening of inequality and this constant advantage of capital over labour will, he says, cause social and economic instability if left unchecked. He argues that it is an intrinsic feature of capitalism.

Piketty's view is a theory rather than a scientific finding, since to make the idea of inexorably higher returns to capital fit his unavoidably patchy long-term data he has had to claim that some long periods (basically 1914–75) during which inequality declined and this relationship did not hold are exceptions, while the current period (which for his purpose began in most advanced countries in about 1975) of rising inequality counts as a return to the rule. Two world wars and a great depression form his argument for why 1914–75 was an exception, though it is unclear how he can believe that major wars or depressions have been permanently abolished, especially as we have just seen a financial crash of 1929 proportions. His theory also contradicts some other economic theories, most notably one that posits that diminishing returns to capital inevitably set in, at a certain point.

Nevertheless, whether or not his theory is correct, one of its most important characteristics is that it treats government intervention as being, in effect, an independent variable. In other words, while political choices about taxation, spending and education may affect inequality, and he says did do so particularly strongly in 1945–75, inequality does not itself in the theory affect the way in which those political choices are made. But, as Piketty observes elsewhere in the book, in practice it does. And this is an intrinsic feature of democracy.

The degree to which it does differs from country to country, with the US, as is often the case, at one extreme and getting more extreme all the time. The ability of Michael Bloomberg, a billionaire media owner, to finance his electoral campaigns to be mayor of New York, or of Donald Trump to use his real estate and casino wealth to finance his presidential campaign, are only the most evident symptoms.[1] Such symptoms would not have been seen in that form 30 or 40 years ago. At that time individual wealth was not at such extremely high levels – though there were plenty of exceptions – but also political campaigning was not as costly and there were tighter rules governing donations.

Trying to control political donations had long been a losing battle as new ways were constantly being found around the restrictions. But in recent years the war has been lost, at least for a while. The US Supreme Court ruled in 2010 (for corporations) and 2014 (for individuals) that money must be permitted a more or less unfettered role in election campaigns on the grounds that to restrict it would be tantamount to restricting free speech and so would be unconstitutional.[2] Unless or until these rulings are reversed or mitigated by a future Supreme Court decision, the floodgates for political money will remain open.

Campaign-finance scandals have also revealed the political influence of money in Germany, Japan, France, the UK and elsewhere. In the UK, donors to the major political parties – that is those parties, chiefly the Conservatives and Labour, that get into government and gain the power to dish out rewards – are frequently given seats in the House of Lords, the country's appointed and hereditary upper chamber, which gives them great social prestige but also some chance to influence legislation and the workings of government.

In 2015 Lord (Michael) Ashcroft showed his wrath at the fact that his more than £1 million in donations to the Conservative Party had not also gained him a ministerial post from the then prime minister, David Cameron, in addition to his title and seat in the House of Lords, by publishing a scathing book of gossip about his former ally.[3] In 1997 the new Labour prime minister, Tony Blair, swiftly got into hot water over whether there were connections between a £1 million donation his party had received from the boss of the Formula One motor-racing business, Bernie Ecclestone, and the subsequent exemption of Formula One from a ban on tobacco advertising which was being introduced at that time by the EU. In response to the furore, Blair went on television to deny any connection between the donation and the exemption, claiming to have played no personal role in the British input into the EU decision, and saying, memorably, that he hoped the public realised that he was "a pretty straight sort of guy". He got away with it. More than a decade later, by which time Blair had stood down as prime minister, official documents were released showing that he had in fact instructed his ministers to seek a permanent exemption for Formula One.[4]

Nowhere does money guarantee electoral victory, not even in the US. Barack Obama and Bernie Sanders have both shown that it can be raised in spectacular quantities from supporters of more modest means. But it certainly smooths the way and leaves its recipients grateful to the donors and convinced of the need to keep the donations coming, for the next election is never far away. Money indubitably talks in politics, and as politicians' need for money has increased, alongside the availability of it, chiefly from wealthy individuals rather than public companies, especially outside the US, so its voice has grown louder.

This raises issues of direct corruption of the processes of government. We will see in Chapter 3 how much Google is spending on political lobbying and campaign donations in the US, all legally and legitimately, but all designed to have a beneficial effect for the company – and Google is naturally not alone in doing this. More widely, too, the growing role of money in politics has arguably affected tax policy in many ways. The general notion that lower top marginal rates of income tax help promote economic growth by stimulating investment and entrepreneurship forms part of the explanation for this. But so too does the desire not to displease generous supporters by dipping too deeply into their bank accounts, a desire that has increased over time. The idea that wealth acts as an incentive for risk-taking has been valuable, but its magnetic pull has also distorted our moral compass about how wealth should be treated.

This has applied especially to the rich individuals who run hedge funds and private equity firms and who have benefited from a big tax break by virtue of the fact that a large part of their income, so-called "carried interest", has been treated in both the US and the UK under capital gains tax rather than income tax and so at a lower rate.[5] From time to time – as in the 2012 presidential campaign, when Mitt Romney, the Republican candidate, turned out to have been a beneficiary of this tax break – public attention is drawn to the fact that these mega-rich people are paying lower rates of tax on their incomes than are their cleaners or janitors, but there has so far been little political will to do anything about it. The 2016 campaign was a first in featuring two leading candidates – Trump and Sanders – who pledged to end this tax break.

In his 2015 and 2016 annual budgets the British chancellor of the exchequer, George Osborne, at last responded to criticism by reforming the UK's rules on the taxation of carried interest, first to remove breaks that had allowed it to be taxed more lightly even than capital gains (28%), and then to tax it wholly as income (40–45%) for private equity or venture deals lasting fewer than three years. This improved matters but still left most such deals benefiting from a lower rate of tax than on most income.

Money not only gains you political friends and a louder democratic voice. It also gets better classes for your children, first by virtue of your ability to afford the fees of the best private schools, but second by providing better access to the best universities as well, in some cases, as higher public spending on education in the area where you live. In a revealing 2015 study of what it termed on its cover "America's new aristocracy", *The Economist* showed how "America is one of only three advanced countries that spends more on richer pupils than on poor ones" (the other two are Israel and Turkey, though the latter counts as "advanced" only because it is a member of the OECD).

It has always been true that the rich could afford better education, but normally public spending has acted to compensate for that advantage in the service of fairness and meritocracy. As universities have become more dependent on donations from their alumni (and from foreign potentates) and more competitive with one another for faculty and research but also for financial support, so a pre-existing temptation has grown bigger and more damaging: to give preference when admitting students to the offspring of generous donors. In the "new aristocracy" study, *The Economist* reported that according to a survey by the *Crimson*, Harvard's newspaper, 16% of the 2,023 students admitted in 2014 had at least one parent who was an alumnus. This does not mean that all won their places solely for that reason, but still alumni preference, or "legacy preference" as American colleges like to call it, has become controversial: it brings in money with which to subsidise poorer students, but the bias it represents is growing, and there is every incentive for it to keep on growing.[6] Jared Kushner, Trump's son-in-law and senior adviser, attended Harvard as an undergraduate; the fact that Kushner's father, also a real-estate mogul, had previously made a large donation to that university has not escaped the notice of others looking for evidence of system-rigging.

This sort of bias is not new. It would be naive to believe that the admissions policies of the likes of Oxford, Cambridge, Harvard and Princeton have ever been totally meritocratic, even if you set aside the selection bias that comes when elites choose people who resemble themselves. Countless princes and heirs to sheikhdoms have studied at top universities for reasons other than their intellectual talents, as have countless sons (and more recently daughters) of the wealthy. When Bo Xilai, a senior Chinese Communist Party official, was arrested and then jailed in 2012–13, the associated news that his so-called "playboy" son, Bo Kuangyi, was then studying for a masters degree at Harvard, having previously attended Oxford as an undergraduate, left few observers assuming that he had achieved these things strictly on merit, whatever the truth of the matter.

The more important question, though, is whether or not educational bias by inheritance is becoming entrenched and is growing. In most advanced countries the educational advantage provided by inherited wealth declined sharply during the 1950s, 1960s and 1970s thanks to the dramatic broadening of publicly funded education and the expansion of university systems. Some advantage remains inevitable given the impact of "assortative mating" – that is the tendency of well-educated people to marry each other, which is itself growing now that female access to education equals that of males – and of superior parenting, which includes not just the personal engagement of parents but also the resources they can devote to extra-curricular encouragement and training for their children. The combination of all these factors with growing income and wealth inequality is increasing the advantage of inheritance.

*

Traditionally, public policy has sought to lean against this advantage, both in the allocation of funds for public education and by the use of progressive tax policy. Political pressure from the wealthy has had some impact on education spending, but it has had a much larger impact on tax policy.

Some of this impact can be seen in lower income-tax rates, but by and large income taxes remain progressive, albeit with tax breaks that benefit the wealthy disproportionately such as that for carried interest, and, in the United States, the full deductibility of mortgage interest. The mortgage-interest tax break does not benefit the top 1% much since they tend to buy in cash, but it does benefit other top earners disproportionately. The rich, as revelations about Trump's tax affairs showed, are always able to get the best advice on avoiding tax and to use businesses to shield them from income taxes.

Inheritance tax, however, is a different and much less progressive story. Despite big rises in the wealth and income of the richest percentiles in the US, federal revenues from the estate (that is inheritance) tax have nearly halved from the equivalent of $38 billion (in 2015 prices) in 2001 to an estimated $20 billion in 2015, according to a report, *Estate and Inheritance Taxes around the World*, in March 2015 by the Tax Foundation, a non-partisan think-tank based in Washington, DC. This outcome sits oddly alongside the fact that the United States has the fourth-highest rate of inheritance tax in the OECD at 40%, the same level as the UK. The world's highest, at 55%, is in Japan, with South Korea at 50% and France at 45%.

In European aristocracies such as in the UK and France the system of inheritance concentrated wealth by handing control of it to a single heir, whereas the American system – adopted in deliberate contrast to Europe – tended to divide and recirculate capital through high rates of inheritance tax and the passing of legacies to multiple heirs. Although the latter remains true, the former does not. The US estate tax raises so little revenue because the size of estates that are exempt from it under the law has been raised repeatedly to high levels. In 2002 the exemption threshold was raised to $1 million; by 2006 it had been doubled to $2 million; by 2009 it was well over $3 million. Estate tax was temporarily abolished in 2010, but a year later, after well-publicised lobbying by a non-profit organisation called United for a Fair Economy backed by some wealthy individuals including Warren Buffett and Bill Gates, the tax was reinstated but with an exemption threshold of $5 million. By 2016 the exemption was $5.45 million. This compares with 2015 exemption thresholds of just $106,000 in France, $247,000 in Japan, $424,000 in Germany and $488,000 in the UK (conversions at 2015 dollar exchange rates).

The Tax Foundation concludes from this that the US estate tax ought to be abolished: it collects little revenue, and yet is costly to administer. Being levied essentially on the country's capital stock (chiefly property and securities), an inheritance tax might in theory harm economic growth. As the Tax Foundation points out, a lot of countries have no inheritance tax. Wealthy Americans do donate a lot of money to charities, encouraged by exemptions granted for gifts. Abolishing the estate tax was among the campaign promises made by Trump.

Yet an alternative conclusion would be that in the US above all the economic and political case for an inheritance tax with much lower exemptions is strong, for unlike Sweden (which abolished its inheritance tax in 2005), the country uses few other fiscal tools to govern, or at least influence, the level of inequality. And because of the open door to political donations, the effect of inequality on American democracy is growing. Entrenched educational inequality together with an automatic amplification of the political voice of the rich through donations makes social and political rigidity an increasing danger. That, at least, is what the clamour about the system being "rigged" is saying.

*

The political impact of inequality does not come only at the top end of the income scale. Nor is the top end the only source of system-rigging. This also occurs much lower down, but this time through unequal legal rights rather than incomes. These create a division between the lucky secure and the unlucky insecure, between what can be called "insiders" and "outsiders" to employment and the labour market, which often (though not always) overlaps also with divisions between the old and the young, and the educated and less educated. This can be seen most plainly in continental Europe and in Japan – but it is also present, in a slightly different form, in the US and the UK.

The clearest example of this division between insiders and outsiders is in Japan, a country once famous for its sense of equality and for the notion that employment was for life. During the 1980s, more than 80% of the population would typically tell market researchers that they were "middle class". Neither middle-class status nor lifetime employment ever meant quite what they seemed, but in a rapidly expanding economy during the 1970s and 1980s they accurately captured a widespread feeling of security, of improving living standards and of equality of treatment. The system was seen as fair.

Not now. In Japan today of the 127 million population, 33 million people are counted as "regular employees", which means they have permanent contracts, are entitled to benefits such as company pensions and are strongly protected against dismissal. Meanwhile, a little over 20 million people are now "non-regular" employees, which means they are on temporary and part-time contracts of various kinds, with no pension or other benefits and little or no protection against dismissal.

Such non-regular employees are typically paid wages that are much lower than those of regular workers, and unlike for regular workers their pay tends not to rise with age or seniority, since on temporary contracts there is no way to become senior. Two-thirds of non-regular employees are women. Most of the male non-regulars are young, though as the principal legal changes that made it possible to expand non-regular employment now date back 15–20 years, many such employees are moving into middle age.[7] As they do so, one of the chief characteristics of Japanese employment is thereby fading away: this was that even for university graduates, most professional skills were learned in the workplace, through experience but also through corporate training programmes. Now, despite the fact that young non-regular workers come from the best-educated generation of Japanese ever, they are neither being trained by employers nor gaining as much experience as did previous generations. Their "human capital", to use the economics profession's term of art, is not growing as it once would have.

This kind of division can also been seen in two European former bastions of hard-fought equality of labour rights, Italy and France. Italian workers enjoyed two decades of record-breaking economic growth in the 1950s and 1960s, and celebrated by achieving, through a huge wave of strikes and demonstrations, the Workers Statute of 1970, which gave workers on permanent contracts in any firm with 15 or more employees powerful protections against dismissal. In principle, employers can lay off workers if they need to but in practice that right is both costly and hard to exercise, as every dismissal is subject to judicial review in the country's incredibly slow-moving and often politicised courts. This rigid and costly form of protection has had two results.

One has been the growth of a large illegal, totally unregulated labour market, especially but not only in the south of the country: on some estimates this covers one-third of workers in the south, and about 20–25% of employment nationwide (this corresponds to estimates that the black or underground economy is worth around 20–25% of GDP). The second has been the introduction, under pressure from employers and from high levels of unemployment, of laws in 1997 and 2003 to permit employment on short-term contracts. Italians who work on these contracts, typically young adults who have graduated from school or university during the past 15–20 years, are known as *precari*, or precarious ones, and it is nigh on impossible for them to get a mortgage to buy a property if they are not on a permanent contract. According to the OECD, the share of Italian employees on temporary contracts had doubled to more than 13% by 2013–14 compared with 20 years earlier.

So if you add illegal workers to temporary workers the divide in terms of labour rights is stark and fairly similar to that in Japan: around 35% of workers, or 9.1 million people, either have no protections or rights at all or else have lesser protections and benefits. A little over 11%, or 2.9 million people, are unemployed. Meanwhile the remaining 54%, or 14 million people, either have permanent contracts or are self-employed.

The picture in France is similar. In 2012 Michel Sapin, then labour minister, was quoted as judging that in his country only one young worker in five could expect to move from a temporary contract to a permanent one, which he saw as a major explanation for a youth unemployment rate of 25%.[8] By 2015, according to the *Financial Times*, fewer than 16% of new contracts signed each year were permanent, down from a quarter in 2000.[9] (Note that a permanent contract is signed only once, by definition, whereas temporary ones have to be signed all the time, so permanent contracts will always be fairly small as a percentage of new contracts signed.) France's illegal labour market is much smaller than Italy's, so the accumulated total of precarious, low-rights or no-rights workers is smaller overall. But it is growing.

Germany has a similar story too, one that is partially disguised by the country's low level of unemployment and its economic success (relative to other Western countries) during and after the 2008 financial crisis. Legal reforms in 2003–05 recommended by a commission chaired by Peter Hartz, personnel director at Volkswagen, and hence known as the Hartz reforms, facilitated the creation of temporary and part-time jobs while also making unemployment insurance less generous. The reforms came at the culmination of a period of slow German growth and high unemployment, both of which were in part the legacy of the unification of West and East Germany in 1990. There are now around 6.6 million people in what Germans call "minijobs", on temporary contracts and exempt from paying tax or social-security contributions, and unemployment in Germany is remarkably low by the standards of the euro zone, at 4% of the labour force compared with the overall euro-zone figure of nearly 10%. So the Hartz reforms have been a success, especially in such difficult economic times. But they have created a divide, one defined by incomes and by legal rights.

In the United States, and to a lesser extent the UK, labour markets are already flexible. There is not the same deep divide in labour rights which then extends into other aspects of life. In the US, it is standard to be employed "at will", which means workers can be dismissed for any reason at all (and can resign for any reason), unless they are fortunate or powerful enough to have a contract that specifies otherwise. In the UK employees have more legal rights than those in the US and those rights are standardised between different sorts of employment. However, the big loophole is the so-called "zero-hours contract", under which employers take on no obligations about how many hours of work they provide to employees, a loophole that can make employment rights moot. Theoretical protections for such workers are standard; but they have no protection against having no work at all. This is hardly unprecedented in principle: after all, a film star might be considered to be working under a zero-hours contract too. But the difference is obvious: one is weak and vulnerable; the other is strong and generally wealthy.

Nevertheless, Britons and Americans who are used to thinking of their societies as especially unequal and of Germany as being much more egalitarian might be surprised by the following, from a report to the Policy Network think-tank by two senior officials at the German Ministry for Economic Affairs and Energy, both advisers to Sigmar Gabriel, the minister and leader of the Social Democratic Party:[10]

> *Wealth inequality is also greater in Germany than other countries in the euro zone. Almost nowhere else in Europe do the top 10% own more, namely two-thirds of total national wealth, while at the same time the bottom 40% of the population own nothing. What may surprise is that the disparity is greater even than in the United States. And those who are poor, all too often, remain poor because our educational system is not good enough at promoting social mobility ... People with lower incomes also pass on the pattern of lower education to the next generation, vote less frequently and are less actively engaged in the political processes.*

One reason for the inequality that is being described is recent economic circumstances. But the divide will not go away simply as a result of better economic times, and Germany's economic times have recently been better than most. For it has also arisen for other reasons, such as educational disparities and inequities entrenching inequality. But above all, in Japan, Italy, France, Germany and many other European countries the divide is becoming starker because of governments' decisions to leave intact the strong protections and rights held by permanent, often older, workers, for fear of the reaction in terms of votes and protests if they were to try to reduce those protections. Labour markets have been made more flexible by depriving other, often younger, workers of those rights. The longer this is left to endure, the more this inequality will become entrenched, for it affects almost every aspect of life: the ability to marry, to have children, to own property, to pay for education. It is not just a technical matter of labour laws. It is a widening rift that runs through the whole of society. It will be passed on from generation to generation.

*

The answer must be to restore equality of rights. The difficulty is that this needs to be done without simply recreating the economic problem that led to these dual labour markets in the first place, namely overly rigid and costly employment contracts that discourage companies from hiring people. The challenge is that the flexibility that firms and thus labour markets need can easily become a synonym in the public mind for total insecurity. Which, after all, is what the Italian, Japanese, French or other temporary contracts have represented. For some people, it doesn't matter. But for many, it does.

Such "insider" rights are therefore hard to change. The number of beneficiaries from them is large. But there is also another problem, which both Japan and Italy illustrate. It is that when reform to labour laws is contemplated, another interest group comes into play: big business. In Japan big business, both as individual companies and through the Keidanren business federation, is well connected to government and especially to the ruling Liberal Democratic Party. A similar story can be told in Italy of the Confindustria business federation. In both countries, each time a labour-law reform has come up for discussion, the business lobby has pressed, successfully, for it to offer as few protections and benefits as possible to those workers who will be covered by it. Hence the "outsiders" have gained employment, but the gap between them and the insiders has widened each time the law has been changed. The notion that flexibility just means total insecurity has been reinforced.

In 2015, this process was at last brought to a halt in Italy, as the energetic, reformist prime minister, Matteo Renzi, who had come to office a year earlier at the age of 39 as the country's youngest prime minister since unification in 1861, succeeded in proving that change is not impossible, even in a country so keen on holding onto legal rights. This was especially surprising coming from the leader of the centre-left Partito Democratico (Democratic Party), which had long stood firmly against any reform of the 1970 Workers Statute. Renzi introduced a new Jobs Act, which both trimmed back the privileges of full-time, permanent insiders and gave outsiders the chance to build up protections gradually over time. Insiders will no longer have a right to reinstatement by getting a judge to agree they were fired unfairly: they will get compensation instead, which is potentially still costly but removes the uncertainty that has long hung over employers. Outsiders will become entitled to a permanent job contract after three years.

It sounds revolutionary, and in a way it is. It should be a model for Japan and elsewhere. But if it proves to be revolutionary – and is not reversed by subsequent governments, which is eminently possible – the revolution will be fairly slow, for the Jobs Act applies only to new hires and only to the private sector. Still, it is a good start. To take on labour laws in Italy is often likened to confronting the Vatican: something not to be done lightly.

The poster-boy for gap narrowing, however, is Denmark, where labour laws began to be amended from 1994 onwards in pursuit of what is known as "flexicurity". This means a combination of relative ease of dismissal with active government help for dismissed workers to find new jobs afterwards. It is a more advanced form of what Italy introduced in 2015 and, in the end, a better way to convince citizens that flexibility need not mean a free-for-all, or the laws of the jungle.

Apart from pressure from the interest groups concerned, the main difficulty in moving to full flexicurity from the sort of dual labour markets seen in Japan, France and Italy is the public cost of active government help for finding new jobs. That cost, though, ought to be rather lower in Japan than in Italy, since the starting point in Japan is of a much lower level of unemployment – even though both countries are carrying huge public debts. Denmark's system faced its first severe test during the financial crisis of 2008–10 and it passed it fairly successfully: having entered 2008 with a low unemployment rate of 3.3% of the workforce (against a European average of 7.1%), Danish unemployment jumped swiftly to 8% during 2008–10 as its economy was hit hard.[11] But by 2015 unemployment had fallen back to 4.5%, less than half the rate in France or Italy. Change is difficult. But it is evidently not impossible.

*

The inequality that has recently been seen in the West is important chiefly because it is corrosive of the sort of social and political glue that holds countries together, ideally through thick and thin. But it is not corrosive simply because some people have a lot more money than others: the politics of envy still exist, of course, but they are not predominant. It is corrosive because inequality in all its forms deals a wounding blow to the fundamental principles of an open, democratic society, at the heart of which lie equality of voice and of civic rights.

Sharp differences between the rights held by one group and another, with no evident means by which to change group and improve your position, undermine faith in the whole system. At root, the issue of inequality, at this political and societal level, is about fairness: about whether the obstacles you encounter in your life, the inequities of rights and opportunities you face, feel to you to be unfair – not in the way that it feels unfair that one person is better at soccer than another, or a better violinist, but unfair in the sense that the system is stacked against merit and just deserts. However hard you work, neither you nor your children are going to be able to get a fair shake: that is the most undermining sentiment of all.

At many times in the past, in many countries that are now democracies, such basic unfairnesses have eventually been addressed and removed. Now, the same thing needs to happen again. What is needed, if the argument for an open society is to be won, is a new, or at least restored, vision of equality.

This better vision of equality can and should be one that is about rights, both legal and political. In many fields such rights have indeed been becoming more equal, not less: compared with 30–40 years ago, women's rights are more equal to those of men, and the rights of gay people have become more equal to those of heterosexuals. Every year seems to bring more progress towards equality of that sort. But the better vision also needs to be about an equality that produces freedoms – the freedom to choose, to speak, to know, and indeed to hope for new opportunities and better lives for each generation. Incomes and jobs are one crucial part of that freedom, but so are access to political influence and access on an equal basis to the best education. The failure of "elites" to deliver rising (or even stable) incomes and jobs means, quite justifiably, that anger about excessive political influence over the decisions made by those elites has grown. If solutions are not found to this inequality and this failure to deliver, popular anger will only grow louder and more destructive.

This vision of equality as being about rights and freedoms is the kind of vision outlined in documents such as the United States Constitution. It is a vision that can only be made real by a society that has some dynamism, some ability to change and evolve, and is thus one that embraces dynamism as a virtue. The closed, more authoritarian societies proposed by populist parties in Europe and the US are ones that would be likely to be relatively static, even, at their most extreme, frozen in aspic. Opportunities would be reduced, not increased. This gives the advantage to the open society. But still, the basis of that open vision needs to be an admission that all the Western democracies have recently slipped away from such an equality of rights, freedoms and opportunities, often absentmindedly while pursuing other goals. They need to return to it, and fast.

3

Democracy and the art of self-entrapment

Do I contradict myself?
Very well, then I contradict myself,
I am large, I contain multitudes.

Walt Whitman, "Song of Myself", 1855

Liberty depends on the division of power. Democracy tends to unity of power.

Lord Acton, 1882

"WE THE PEOPLE." It is a comforting phrase, the one that opens the preamble to the constitution of the United States of America, the greatest democratic document ever written. It conveys a reassuring sense of a shared, collective interest, of solidarity in citizenship, of a desire indeed to "promote the general welfare" as the preamble goes on to say. After the great financial calamity of 2008, that same idea lay behind the Occupy movement that originated in New York in 2011 and its slogan of "We are the 99%". We the people stand together, with a shared interest, the slogan was saying, assaulted by the selfish, destructive interests of "the 1%". It is a lovely image. The trouble is that it is an aspiration and not a fact. The effort to achieve such a shared interest lies at the heart of what open societies are all about. The effort to thwart it, however, lies at the heart of what individuals in open societies are all about. We are competitive creatures.

Democracy is supposed to be a counterweight to that individualism, a mechanism by which we translate individual interests into a public interest, reconciling our differences. Often it is. But that very mechanism also frequently works against the idea of the 99%, against this ideal of promoting the general welfare. Indeed, "the people" conspire against the very idea of being a "we", at least one defined by the nation. And not just the 1% or, in old class-war terms, the bourgeoisie: most of the people do so, most of the time, by seeking their self-interest in a spirit of competition, seeking to achieve an unequal hearing for their voice, often without thinking of it in that way.

Democracy, like many political principles, is rife with contradictions. The US Declaration of Independence, adopted a dozen years earlier than the constitution, stated:

> We hold these truths to be self-evident, that all men are created equal, that they are endowed by their Creator with certain unalienable Rights, that among these are Life, Liberty and the pursuit of Happiness.

Or, as it might have more accurately said had it been able to anticipate the workings of democracy, we all have the right to life, liberty and the pursuit of victory in the democratic contest. The equal right to try to become unequal – if that is what makes you happy. And it often does.

This tension between equality of voice and the competition to make your voice heard more than others' is an essential part of an open society but is also the greatest threat to it. For that reason, an open society also requires a constant effort to push back in the other direction, by promoting and making more credible the notion of the general welfare, of equal rights, equal treatment and equal voice, and shining a bright light on the harm that special interests and unequal voices do. Much of the time that battle happens naturally, out of the democratic battle of voices, but sometimes it needs extra help. The ideal will never be achieved, but it defines the right path, one from which democracy has an inbuilt tendency to stray, thwarting as it does so the successful and socially peaceful process of evolution that is the great achievement of the idea of the West. Basic liberal values have to be defended because they are so constantly in danger of being trampled on, not just by illiberal would-be fascists but by the unseeing and unknowing herd – ourselves.

Such idealism is exactly what documents such as the British Bill of Rights of 1689, the US Constitution of 1788 or France's Declaration of the Rights of Man in 1789 stand for. They were all efforts to make societies better than they were, political and social guidelines or lodestars to try to pull or push societies towards the right path, even though the authors knew full well that their societies were far from that condition and even though they have strayed from it many times since. So we should not be shy or embarrassed about aiming for political ideals, too, using political values rather as Christians do the Ten Commandments to deter us from straying from the true, sustainable path.

Indeed, that path also helps define the great opportunity that beckons before all the advanced open societies: success in clearing away the worst of such distortions, obstacles, inequalities and special interests promises always to bring back the dynamism and creative energy that have so characterised open societies in the past by releasing all sorts of underused and frustrated assets. Our societies are chock-full of such assets. We will never release all of them. But at certain times there is enough pent-up frustration and anger to enable us to release some of them, to clear away some distortions. This is one of those times. At such moments, there is a great risk that the anger will lead us further in the wrong direction, an anger and a direction epitomised by Donald Trump and Marine Le Pen. But behind that risk lies also great reward.

When Presidents John F. Kennedy and Lyndon B. Johnson forced through the Civil Rights Act of 1964, against fierce resistance, what they were doing was trying to end a violation of constitutional ideals that had persisted for nearly two centuries. And when Presidents Jimmy Carter and Ronald Reagan initiated deregulation in many sectors to eliminate cartels and revitalise competition in the 1970s and 1980s, they were also trying to move back towards an ideal, and end some serious distortions and frustrations that had set in.

Margaret Thatcher's battle with coalminers and other powerful trade unions in the UK during the 1980s was of the same nature, as were her determination to break the cartel of the London Stock Exchange and her programme of privatisation of what were then state-owned monopolies. Japan's failure to find new sources of vitality following its financial crash of the early 1990s has been chiefly a failure to take on this sort of battle, to face up to the risks in search of the rewards. So has the long stagnation in Italy, once one of the world's most dynamic countries. For we may believe we are tired, ageing, declining societies that have exhausted our energies, our assets. But in truth what we have done is to block those energies, to frustrate them, by building obstacles to their use. The construction of these obstacles has occurred by virtue of the very processes of democracy that we hold dear.

The effort to get back on the path towards equality of voice and rights can also be hampered by its own contradictions and hypocrisies. The methods that are needed to restore the fluidity, dynamism, adaptability and indeed openness of the open societies are generally forms of liberalisation, the removal of barriers and protections that have created privileges and benefits for particular groups. This process is frequently described in ugly economics jargon as "structural reforms". The process can also take on an ugly face, however, either by mistake or by being captured and subverted by other groups of beneficiaries, such as big business or the rich.

Those who dislike such liberalisation have invented (or, more strictly, commandeered) the label of "neoliberalism" as a means by which to denigrate it. Setting markets free does, as in any competition, create winners and losers, and the sustained rise in inequality of income and wealth that has been seen in almost all the advanced open societies over the past 30 years has been one consequence of such efforts, though liberalisation is not inequality's only cause. Higher inequality might, in principle, be a price worth paying if the result were rising living standards and expanding opportunities for everyone, a process known as "trickle-down" by its critics, or "a rising tide lifting all boats" by its fans. But this requires trust, and over time such reforms are likely to be greeted with suspicion if the promised higher living standards do not transpire and if reforms are not accompanied by measures to try to help losers adjust.

Moreover, there is further room for suspicion that arises from the direct political consequences of rising inequality: unchecked, it can enable the wealthy to gain an unequal political voice, which can be used to create new privileges for themselves and to entrench their advantages. Chapter 2 showed that this entrenching of political inequality is precisely what has happened in many Western countries but especially in the US.

The war against unequal privileges and special interests is a never-ending series of battles. And liberalisation alone – the "market fundamentalism" condemned by George Soros, as cited in Chapter 1 – is never enough. Defeating the self-entrapping habit of democracy by clearing away the unequal protections and privileges that have been won and the obstacles that have been built is necessary, but it needs to be accompanied by actions of reassurance, directed at the maintenance of social trust, by provisions of public goods and services that serve to level up the political and economic competition, actions that make the equality of voice and treatment at which liberalisation is aimed more believable, more broadly supportable, more genuine.

*

Enemies are easiest to confront and defeat when we can all recognise who or what they are. Currently, the most recognisable enemies to have built up political power by democratic means in order to create privileges that damage the wider public interest are – perhaps you have guessed – banks and other financial-services firms. Taken as a whole, bankers and other financiers have in the past decade been the biggest single cause of rising inequality, distortion of public policy, and generation of collective economic pain and anger at "the system".

There are plenty of other enemies of democracy, openness and equality in all Western countries, though unlike bankers following the crash they are not so readily recognisable. To name but a few, there are the Japan Medical Association; lawyers and other professions in Italy and many other countries; farmers everywhere; trade associations of all kinds; big business federations and even monopolies; trade unions in many countries; lobbies such as the National Rifle Association in the US; pensioners' lobbies all over the globe; and, as Chapter 2 explained, the tyrannous majorities of employees in countries such as Japan, France and Italy that fight to preserve their permanent, highly protected contracts at the expense of outsiders, especially the young, leaving them to make do with precarious temporary contracts. Elected politicians line up to hand out favours to all such groups, and groups spend their time lobbying for more, or else fiercely defending their past favours.

Moreover, we must not forget the simple biases that are inherent in democracy. The electoral cycle inevitably focuses attention on the short term, and politicians bidding to get into power can readily compete by bribing voters with promises of a disproportionate share of taxpayers' own money. This short-termism has been exacerbated by the ageing populations of all the rich, open societies, which have steadily driven up spending on health care and public pensions and crowded out other uses for the cash.

Chapter 9 explores the political ramifications of ageing societies in more detail, but for the present purpose let us focus on the broader effect rather than that particular cause. The effect can be seen most simply in the way in which public investment – that is, spending on long-term assets such as infrastructure – has gradually declined in the West relative to other forms of public spending. This decline may to some extent reflect maturity – plenty of roads and airports

FIG 3.1 **Public investment and consumption in the West, 1980–2014** % of GDP

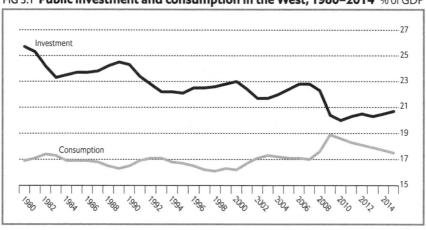

Source: Thomson Reuters (originally OECD)

have already been built. It may reflect changes in ownership, as what would once have been counted as public investment by state-owned companies has been privatised. But it is also a form of self-harm, one that rejects or defers projects that will bring benefits to future generations in favour of rewarding supporters with public spending in the here and now.

As Figure 3.1 shows, in 1980 in the advanced economies public investment averaged nearly 26% of GDP each year. By 2014 it was more than five percentage points lower at 20.7%, while public consumption climbed from 17% of GDP in 1980 to a peak of nearly 19% in 2008 before falling back to 17.5% under the pressure of recession and fiscal austerity.

In the UK the generations that are over 60 years old are more prosperous, relative to the rest of the population, than ever before: their pensions are higher, and the value of their assets, particularly property, is considerable, especially for those living in southern England. Yet, as will be explained further in Chapter 9, even during the post-2008 period when pressures on public finances were severe the UK government gave pensioners protections from cuts in their incomes that it denied to public-sector workers and to the rest of the population. After all, pensioners are more likely to turn out to vote than are young people.

This sort of bias is natural, unfortunately. It is what you would expect in any system in which votes bring power and power brings the ability to hand out public money and favours. It is democracy at work. The winning majorities that bring governments to power or throw incumbents out comprise many interests, many groups, many blocks of votes, sometimes with the same voters belonging to more than one group. These interests often balance each other out. The problem is that there is no reliable mechanism of self-regulation in the democratic contest either to prevent excesses or to prevent temporary advantages secured by interest groups from becoming permanent.

Just as you can do too well when competing in a market and so can create a monopoly, you can also do too well when competing in a democracy. This point is better recognised in economics than it is in politics, but it is even more consequential in the latter – and now in the US especially those companies that succeed in building monopolies have learned that they can best protect those dominant positions by deploying their resources in politics, in lobbying and in campaign finance. The results of democratic overachievement by interest groups can be felt in a country's economic performance, in the functioning of open societies' political systems and in their social cohesion – or lack of it. As a result, it can even affect countries' international power, influence and prestige. Which is what has been happening to the open societies of the US, Europe, Japan and the rest of the West over the past couple of decades.

In economics, there has long been a healthy debate about monopolies, cartels and the threat they pose to open markets and welfare, and about the wisdom of governments using antitrust laws to combat them. Adam Smith, the father of modern economics, wrote a sentence in his 1776 book *The Wealth of Nations* which has become one of his most quoted:

> *People of the same trade seldom meet together, even for merriment and diversion, but the conversation ends in a conspiracy against the public, or in some contrivance to raise prices.*

The high priest of self-interest and the invisible hand was identifying the dangers of selfishness going too far, of hands joining together in their mutual benefit. One might adapt this to politics thus:

> *People of a shared interest seldom meet together ... or act in even unknowing concert ... but the conversation ends in a conspiracy against the rest*

of the public, or in some contrivance to distort public policy and win a
disproportionate share of resources or rights.

Milton Friedman, a leading light of the great University of Chicago school of free-market economists that emerged from the 1950s onwards, agreed with Smith in condemning cartels but was much more reluctant to condemn monopolies, and was positively hostile to the antitrust laws that have been mobilised against them since the late 19th century in the US and Europe. Friedman saw monopoly as an ultimate reward for business success and therefore an ultimate incentive for risk-taking and hard work. To damage that incentive would itself have damaging results, he reasoned. More often than not, he argued, the development of a profitable monopoly would in due course lure in new competitors and new ideas. Unless government collaborated with the monopolist to thwart the market through laws or the use of its own vast resources, the monopoly would eventually be undermined.

Other economists argue that this is far too sanguine: monopoly power too often enables a company to use its profits and other market power to erect high barriers against the entry of new competitors which can endure for long periods. In the meantime consumers lose out by paying high prices, drawing resources away from more productive uses and deterring innovation. This was essentially the debate that surrounded the antitrust cases brought against Microsoft first by the US Department of Justice in 1998–2001 and then the European Commission, which were given added controversy by the fact that Bill Gates's software company was operating in a field of rapid innovation.

I flinch a little when recalling my meetings with Gates during that period in which he, as a self-confessed devoted reader of *The Economist*, would berate the publication's then editor-in-chief for its support for the department's antitrust action against him and his company, demanding to know "on what principles" we based our stance. (They had in fact been explained clearly, as he surely knew well; he just didn't agree with them.) Microsoft was in constant danger of "being replaced", he asserted: it did not have a dominant position that it could abuse. With hindsight, it is true that Microsoft has now indeed been replaced in some respects. But recollection of its high prices and profits over a long period, and of its destruction of the small start-up web-browser company Netscape – which at the time was as much a pioneering star of Silicon Valley as, say, Google, Facebook and Twitter became in the 2000s – tempers the memory.

Technology is a highly competitive field. But regulation, including antitrust regulation, can make a huge difference to a firm's prospects and freedom of manoeuvre. Today's equivalent to Microsoft as a holder of a dominant position is Google, which renamed its parent company as Alphabet in 2015. Its command of digital advertising revenues clearly gives it dominance, along with the ability to see off potential competitors in all sorts of subsidiary or innovative markets rather as Microsoft did with Netscape. But no interest was shown by the Obama administration or the Department of Justice in any antitrust investigation of Google. Only the European Commission's competition department has moved on Google. Why? Since the firm's name is now Alphabet, we can readily spell it out: according to the Centre for Responsive Politics, Google/Alphabet made political donations to 162 members of the US Congress in the 2014 electoral cycle; and according to another non-profit watchdog, Public Citizen, in 2014 and 2015 it spent more money than any other corporation or trade association on federal lobbying. The firm donates to campaigns through its own Political Action Committee, which Public Citizen reports now donates more each year than does Goldman Sachs, a financial-services company, and senior executives also make personal donations.

Google may not always succeed in avoiding antitrust scrutiny in the United States, but it has done well in doing so thus far. It has also lobbied US officials to attack the European Commission's investigation, denigrating it as being an effort by Europe to weaken a foreign competitor rather than reflecting a genuine antitrust concern.

Google is just one powerful example. Other political overachievers are highly visible as individuals: these are the mega-wealthy who are able to buy political influence directly through campaign donations. Others are large interest groups that gather together people and entities, whether wealthy or of a humbler nature, many of which defend their privileges – such as low taxes, or high subsidies, or in the case already cited of banks, "light-touch" regulation, or immunity from dismissal, or protection from competition – with righteous indignation as if they had arisen as divine rights.

Such outcomes could in principle be considered to be simply rewards of success in legitimate political competition, much as Friedman viewed market monopolies. If any turn out to be abusive or undesirable, they could in theory be undone by debate, by legal challenge, by the next election. As with the free market, it is possible to argue that competition and innovation can be relied upon to produce a better outcome in dealing with these outcomes than any sort of governmental interference, especially in an environment in which there is not only freedom of expression and information but also rapidly improving technologies for the collation and dissemination of that information. A democracy powered by the internet and the smartphone – by Google, in other words – might be imagined to work better and better all the time, with an inbuilt mechanism for ensuring that one man, one vote really does bring equality of influence. Well, it is a nice idea, and perhaps one day it will happen. But for the time being, there is no sign of it.

*

The reason interest groups develop and tend to succeed in open societies in creating such economic and political distortions was explained most clearly by an American economist, Mancur Olson, in a series of books written well before the internet was born, beginning with *The Logic of Collective Action* in 1965 and continuing, most appropriately for the present purpose, with *The Rise and Decline of Nations* in 1982. His essential point was that while it is not easy to get people and firms to band together as an interest group, the incentive to do so is nevertheless much stronger than the incentive to fight against that interest. The gains to farmers from getting public subsidies, or to doctors or taxi drivers from restricting entry to the profession, or to Wall Street investment banks from keeping regulation soft, public safety nets secure and taxes low are of great value to all of those in the interest group, whereas the cost of those gains is typically spread thinly across thousands or millions of people or entities. A group is hard to form, but once formed it is hard to break.

As an economist, Olson's chief interest lay in the economic consequences of interest groups. In his 1982 book he argues that those consequences can be grave, producing rigidities and misallocations of resources that sap the economic dynamism of a country. Olson, perhaps as befitted the pessimistic, somewhat declinist mood of the 1970s and early 1980s, took a view of distorted economies and social rigidities that was equivalent – if less widely read and noted – to that of Oswald Spengler and his *Decline of the West* in 1918. On the Olsonian reading of things, Western economies and democracies were doomed. As interest groups inevitably built up as thick layers of barnacles on societies' hulls, so these countries' would find it harder and harder to make progress.

The rest of the 1980s and the 1990s must have given him some comfort (Olson died in 1998). This may be why his last book, published posthumously in 2000, had a more positive flavour: it was called *Power and Prosperity: Outgrowing Communist and Capitalist Dictatorships*. The collapse of the Soviet Union and its communist satellites confirmed the vital importance of markets as part of what helps societies evolve. The reforms promoted in the UK during the 1980s by Margaret Thatcher and in the US by Ronald Reagan showed that it was possible in a modern democracy to disrupt and dismantle interest-group power and tackle the economic sclerosis that such power had caused. Thatcher's reforms to trade union law and her fight with the mineworkers' union were aimed at exactly that, as was Reagan's defeat of the air-traffic controllers' organisation in 1981. Similarly, the retreat of governments around the world from state ownership in the 1980s and 1990s had the benefit of not just introducing more competition and greater efficiency but also reducing the number of opportunities for interest groups to coerce governments.

In his final book, Olson also observed that no country in the post-war world that had satisfied two simple conditions had failed to prosper. The first was the existence of secure and well-defined individual rights. This is the rule of law, and equality of rights within it, made universal throughout a society. The second condition "is simply the absence of predation of any kind". By predation he meant the arbitrary threats to persons and property that arise from war or authoritarian, confiscatory governments, but also the lobbying and subversion of legislation by interest groups of all kinds that leave individual rights intact in theory but in practice prey upon those rights through legal and democratic means. He wrote: "I believe that [this sclerotic process] occurs in all long-stable societies."

*

One long-lasting form of stability in the US and Europe from roughly 1993 until 2007 was what is known as "the great moderation": a period of low inflation and steady economic growth that led politicians and pundits to believe even that the economic cycle might have been conquered. It certainly had not been, but a vastly powerful interest group arose to exploit the stability: the banks, or to give them their wider name, the financial-services industry.

The Occupy movement chose big finance as the chief enemy of what it called "the 99%". The "1%" are not only financiers. But it was no coincidence that the most prominent occupation began in New York City's Zuccotti Park in 2011, nor that it was emulated by a movement across the Atlantic aimed at the City of London. The Occupy movement had correctly identified the fact that the single biggest source of inequality of voice and treatment, of distortions of public policy, in both the United States and western Europe, has been the rising power of the financial industry and of those who lead it.

Half a decade later, the Occupy movement had not succeeded in its aims – which were anyway somewhat inchoate. Rather than broad attacks simply on "capitalism", which are rather like attacking "life", those aims ought better to have been the cutting down to size of the financial sector and the removal of the exorbitant privileges that have enabled banks to make profits at the expense of the rest of society and that, after the crisis, seemed to grant impunity to senior bankers. If the movement's aims had been that clear and straightforward, it might have garnered widespread popular support – as was demonstrated five years later by the strong backing for Senator Bernie Sanders in the 2015–16 Democratic primaries against Hillary Clinton, largely on the basis of his anti-Wall Street position.

What has been seen, instead, has been proof of the continuing political power of this financial-sector interest group, in both the US and Europe, just as was seen in Japan during the 1990s after that country's market crash. But the story is not over. The case for cutting bankers down to size remains stronger than ever. The popular mood against banks is, if anything, growing, especially in the United States but also in Europe.

Sometime in the late 1990s, I recall being invited to breakfast in London with the then chief executive of Goldman Sachs, Jon Corzine, during one of his visits from New York.[1] To break the ice, or rather to wind him up, I asked him "for how long do you think the current period of excessive profits for investment banks will last?" He looked at me as if I was an alien from another planet. He genuinely couldn't understand the question. When his successor-but-one, Lloyd Blankfein, made the mistake of joking in November 2009 to a visiting reporter from the *Sunday Times* that he "was doing God's work", he was exhibiting a similar sort of incomprehension.

Blankfein was also, however, probably responding to accusations by authoritative, thoughtful observers such as Adair (now Lord) Turner, then chairman of the UK's Financial Services Authority, that much of what financial firms like Goldman do is "socially useless". Turner first made that accusation in September 2009 in a roundtable discussion for *Prospect* magazine, "How to tame global finance", and then expanded upon it in a speech at London's Mansion House on September 22nd of the same year, in which he acknowledged that the private pursuit of profit generally produces good economic results, followed by a resounding "But":

> But it's possible to say all of that, and also recognise that not all financial innovation is valuable, not all trading plays a useful role, and that a bigger financial system is not necessarily a better one. And, indeed, there are good reasons for believing that the financial industry, more than any other sector of the economy, has an ability to generate unnecessary demand for its own services – that more trading and more financial innovation can under some circumstances create harmful volatility against which customers have to hedge, creating more demand for trading liquidity and innovative products; that parts of the financial services industry have a unique ability to attract to themselves unnecessarily high returns and create instability which harms the rest of society.

Paul Volcker, a highly respected, even revered, chairman of the US Federal Reserve Board who slew inflation during his term in office in 1979–87, was also typically blunt in a speech in New York later that same year as Turner's. The last useful piece of financial innovation that he could remember, Volcker said, was the ATM (automated teller machine). He told a story about being at another conference listening to a hyperbolic talk from a young investment banker about financial innovation:[2]

> I found myself sitting next to one of the inventors of financial engineering who I did not know, but I knew who he was and that he had won a Nobel Prize, and I nudged him and asked what all the financial engineering does for the economy and what it does for productivity. Much to my surprise he leaned over and whispered in my ear that it does nothing. I asked him what it did do and he said that it moves around the rents in the financial system and besides that it was a lot of intellectual fun.
>
> Now, I have no doubts that it moves around the rents in the financial system, but not only this as it seems to have vastly increased them. How do I respond to a Congressman who asks if the financial sector in the United States

*is so important that it generates 40% of all the profits in the country, 40%
after all of the bonuses and pay? Is it really a true reflection on the financial
sector that it rose from two-and-a-half percent of value added according to
GDP numbers to six-and-a-half percent in the last decade? Is that a reflection
of all your financial innovation or is it just a reflection of how much you pay?*

These are excellent questions, to which there are no good answers. One that
might in other circumstances suffice could be: so what? We do not worry about
whether other sorts of innovations – in dentistry, smartphones or consultancy,
say – are socially useful: we just leave it to people, that is the market, to decide.
Nor do we normally worry on any but grounds of monopoly about whether
or not profits are "excessive". We think that if they are indeed excessive then
eventually either new competition will arrive to drive them down – which was
the point of my late-1990s gibe to Corzine – or that customers will be alienated
and stop buying from the profiteers, or that the Department of Justice,
European Commission or other antitrust authorities will step in. But the "so
what" question no longer works in finance, if it ever did.

We have seen where that innovation which Turner and Volcker were
lamenting led: to the credit crunch that began in the summer of 2007 and
then the full-scale financial collapse that was marked by the bankruptcy of
the Lehman Brothers investment bank in New York in September 2008. Most
important, what that calamity demonstrated was the true basis of the sector's
success: it was taking bigger and bigger risks, confecting financial products
of greater and greater complexity (the profit margins of which may well be
related to the difficulty for customers in understanding them), while being
supported by a massive public safety net – in effect, a subsidy – consisting of
official deposit insurance and the sure knowledge that the bigger that financial
institutions became, the more that governments would consider them "too big
to fail" and step in to rescue them if they ran into trouble. And that is exactly
what they did, on both sides of the Atlantic.

As Volcker said, there was no correlation with any gains in productivity
while this was happening. But also, over roughly the decade leading up to the
2008 crash, the entry of more competitors simply drove the "innovation" and
the boom in the creation of complex credit instruments even crazier, rather
than driving margins down. Afterwards the public subsidy stayed in place in
the form of ultra-cheap lending by central banks, and in many cases consisted

of publicly funded or publicly underwritten schemes to remove dud assets from banks' books.

Nice (God's) work if you can get it. How have bankers got away with it? They have combined direct political lobbying, aided by lavish campaign-finance contributions, with broader (and more legitimate) campaigns of public persuasion. And they have exploited the natural interest politicians in many countries have had in the continued flow of tax revenues from financial firms and in taking credit for those firms' apparent contribution to economic growth. What the financial sector achieved now looks extraordinary: regulatory permission to take bigger and bigger risks, while keeping many of those risks hidden from public view or even from the regulators themselves. Most notorious, in the US at least, was the successful lobbying in 1998 by Wall Street of the treasury secretary, Robert Rubin, and his deputy, Larry Summers, to block regulation of the trading of complex derivatives products which had been proposed by the then head of the Commodity Futures Trading Commission, Brooksley Born.[3]

The US was not alone in failing to do anything about the dangers of financial innovation: neither did the UK and nor did Germany, whose banks became among the biggest customers for the derivative securities that it spawned. What has been even more extraordinary, however, is what has happened since the financial calamity of 2008: in effect, not much.

After the crash the financial sector used its lobbying resources, along with the fear that unless bank lending was maintained, economic recovery would be threatened, to avoid suffering any substantial penalties or tightening of regulations. Certainly, there has been some stiffening of the rules surrounding finance in both the US and Europe, but it has not made a fundamental change to the way banks and their executives are able to behave.[4] There have also been fines in cases of evident malpractice, borne by shareholders though not by bank executives themselves. The stiffening of rules, the levying of fines and the furious response from bankers on each occasion has largely been Shakespearean: "A tale ... full of sound and fury, signifying nothing."

This is a huge but unfortunately not surprising failure. It means that the basic causes of the worst financial collapse and economic slump the rich countries have seen in more than 80 years have not been remedied. The same thing could happen again, once memories of the 2008 collapse have faded. There have been measures that deal with symptoms, such as taxes on bank profits, or limits to the size of bonus payments to bankers in Europe, and some measures that increase capital requirements, but none that truly make the banking system significantly safer. Bank shareholders have suffered, but few bankers – the managers who took the risks and created the crash – have done so, either financially or through the justice system.

In the UK, even Sir John Vickers, a mild-mannered academic economist who chaired an "Independent Commission on Banking" for the government in 2010–11, displayed his anger and dismay at this failure in an article in the *Financial Times* in early 2016.[5] He lamented the fact that the Bank of England's proposed capital requirements for UK banks were much lower and more lenient than those his commission had recommended, or than those recommended by Anat Admati of Stanford University and Martin Hellwig of the Max Planck Institute in the most respected analysis of the crash so far published, *The Bankers' New Clothes*.

The result is that banks remain vulnerable to potential shocks. Moreover banks are still permitted to put at risk huge sums while being able to keep many of those risks off their balance sheets, hidden from the view of regulators, shareholders and, most crucially, counterparties, in businesses that are riven with complexity. It was the evaporation of confidence between financial counterparties, the vast global network of firms that lend to each other, that brought about the 2008 crash. Dud subprime mortgages in the United States started the trouble, but the reason it became so catastrophically large was the loss of confidence between those many layers of counterparties.

One of the most devastating delusions during the decade that led up to the 2008 collapse was the notion that a process called securitisation was spreading risk around, putting it where it could most efficiently and safely be held, making the global financial system less risky than in the past. Securitisation is the process by which packages of loans – most notoriously subprime mortgage loans to poor people in the US, but also many others – are assembled by financial firms, often sliced up into their component parts, and sold on as so-called "derivative securities" (that is, paper that was derived from an original debt) in more and more complex forms, supposedly so as to make the slices of rights thereby concocted more appropriate for particular species of buyer.

The consequences were twofold. Many buyers had little understanding of the real nature of what they were buying, just that its apparent yield was higher than the dull alternatives on offer in what was a disinflationary, low interest rate environment. And many banks decided, fatefully, that rather than passing on all these derivatives to others – a business model that was known as "originate and distribute" – it would be more profitable to hold onto large bundles of derivatives themselves, placing them out of regulators' sight in special off-balance-sheet entities. By these and other means, risk that was supposedly being spread out ended up being concentrated. "Originate and hoard" would have been a better description. The reason this was able to take place, at such ultimately devastating scale, was that most of it was hidden from view. No one, literally no one, knew the full picture of what was going on.

In the aftermath of the crash, the pressure to maintain bank lending was hard for governments to resist: their economies were on life support, so making radical changes to bank regulations at that time could have risked cutting off the flow of blood. The crash had been caused by too much credit, but what was needed above all to help economies survive was more credit, chiefly provided by public borrowing but also by persuading banks to keep on lending to the private sector. Nevertheless, it ought surely to have been easier and uncontroversial to deal with the lack of transparency that in 2008 had proved so catastrophic. That obscurity, as captured by the term "shadow banking", ought to have been a relatively straightforward target for improvement.

Seven years on from the crash, the chief economist of the Bank of England, Andrew Haldane, made a speech in which he essentially said that in finance it was still true, to borrow an old Hollywood phrase, that "nobody knows anything":[6]

> Even among the world's largest banks, data on their bilateral exposures to one another remains partial and patchy, especially for off balance sheet positions and securities holdings. That means large parts of the core of the international banking map remain, essentially, uncharted territory. These data gaps are even more acute when moving beyond the banking system. Large parts of the non-bank sector remain in the shadows from a data perspective.

So whatever the rules governing banks' capital, the leverage they are allowed to deploy, or anything else, the fact remains that those whose job it is to supervise the banks basically have no real idea of what is going on and nor do other financial institutions that are lending to them. Shadow banking lives on, and the shadows are as dark as ever.

One reason why this has happened is that finance is global, which means that to change disclosure requirements in any meaningful way requires a wide international agreement, since otherwise operations could just be moved to less demanding jurisdictions. Politics, however, is local, so national governments are easily persuadable to protect their banks' interests. Another reason is that governments have sometimes connived in keeping the true condition of banks secret: notably, at exactly the time (2010–12) when international negotiations on shadow banking were under way, the crisis in the euro zone over sovereign debt, much of it held by banks, was also under way, so neither France nor Germany was keen on clearing the fog surrounding their then rather precarious banks. Similar connivance in disguising banks' true condition had occurred in Japan during the 1990s. But the third, and overarching, reason is simply that banks are enormously powerful politically.

Bankers' strongest argument against stiffer regulation no longer holds much sway: neither the US nor the UK economies are any longer on life support, and the euro-zone economy is also in a bit better shape than it was. Countries on both sides of the Atlantic can now better afford the risk that reforming or restructuring finance might in some way load costs on to other parts of the economy. This is what banks and their lobbyists claim would happen, though it is far from obvious that it is true.

Admati and Hellwig say that this argument that tighter regulation would come at an economic price was always self-serving nonsense. We have learned the hard way that riskier banks come at a huge price, so safer banks must surely come at a lower price from the point of view of an economy as a whole. During the emergency conditions of 2008–12, the trade-off was at best unclear, since lending was fragile. But the emergency has now passed. The US and European economies, like Japan's before them, still carry the wounds and scars of their immense crash, but what they now need is not emergency blood transfusions but deeper fitness regimes.

Curbing the financial sector, as Martin Wolf, chief economics commentator of the *Financial Times* has written,[7] ought to be a vital part of that new fitness regime, rather like cutting out an injuriously fatty part of your diet to avoid the recurrence of cardiac arrest. The fitness formula favoured by John Kay, a distinguished British economist, a professor at the London School of Economics and the author of a 2012 government review of the UK financial sector, is to reduce complexity by stripping deposit insurance and the public safety net from all investment banking, retaining it only for retail banking and corporate wholesale banking.[8]

Economists at the Bank for International Settlements, known as the central bankers' central bank, have confirmed that such remedies would do no underlying economic harm: in a 2012 study they showed that beyond a certain point (one that advanced economies passed long ago) a larger financial sector harms both productivity growth and overall economic growth.[9] You can, as they say, have too much of a good thing. It is time, to put it more bluntly, to have less of that bad thing. Not, unfortunately, that America's new president or his team at the Treasury would agree: they favour loosening the constraints on Wall Street, returning it even closer to the conditions that brought about the 2008 crash, rather than cutting it down to size.

4

Setting America straight again

Moloch! Solitude! Filth! Ugliness! Ashcans and unobtainable dollars!
Children screaming under the stairways! Boys sobbing in armies! Old men
weeping in the parks!

Allen Ginsberg, *Howl*, 1956

For 240 years it's been a terrible mistake to bet against America, and now
is no time to start.

Warren Buffett, annual letter to Berkshire Hathaway shareholders, 2016

AMERICA HAS LONG SEEN ITSELF, in the words of Abraham Lincoln,
as "the last best hope of Earth". Whether or not that is so, there can be no
doubt that on every dimension explored in this book – geopolitical, military,
economic, technological, social, demographic – how or whether the United
States of America succeeds in dealing with those issues will play a decisive
role in determining the fate of the West and of the ideas it encapsulates. It is
the quintessential open society, one in which equality of rights is intrinsic
to its very concept of itself and in which freedom is the highest value of all.
The US is not the West. But the West would be severely diminished, even
finished, without the US. If it were to abandon central tenets of Westernness
and its alliances with other Western countries, even if just for a few years, the
barbarians who are at the West's gates would applaud and conclude that the
modern equivalent of the Roman Empire was about to collapse.

The ideas advocated by Donald Trump represent the beginning of exactly
that sort of abandonment. His ideas have clearly found substantial support
even if many who voted for him in 2016 may also have done so simply because

they disliked Hillary Clinton even more. These ideas will, if carried forward as anything more than a negotiating threat, mean a repeat of earlier periods of American history during which high barriers to foreign trade were erected and strict controls on immigration imposed, often ones that discriminated between different categories of immigrant. Doing so would detach the United States substantially from world affairs, withdrawing it from decades-old military alliances or else weakening its commitment to them, and placing it in confrontation with multilateral treaties and organisations that it designed, built and led. An even more extreme implementation of Trump's ideas would entail the abandonment or at least serious erosion of some of the country's own fundamental constitutional principles, including freedom of speech and the rule of law.

To describe the ideas in that way, in other words to take them both seriously and literally, is also to show why it cannot be in America's interest that they be implemented in anything like their stated form. If "America First" means anything, it ought to mean protecting basic national values, the values enshrined in the constitution, of equality before the law, of free speech, of religious freedom. Domestic resistance to any encroachment on such values will be strong. Different forms of patriotism will compete fiercely with one another. After all, the 2016 election was no landslide: just the opposite, for the winning candidate lost the popular vote and squeaked ahead to win crucial Electoral College votes by modest margins in Florida, Michigan, Wisconsin and Pennsylvania. The Trump administration will be acutely conscious of that background, looking ahead to the 2020 election, as will be Republicans in Congress, looking ahead to their own mid-term polls in 2018.

Moreover, while old "America First" campaigners were true isolationists, battling in 1939 to prevent the country from entering the second world war, and though even the Founding Fathers shunned "foreign entanglements", a cold look today at American national interests must inevitably retain quite a strongly global view. The business of the US, whether high-tech or low-tech, is inescapably global in its scope. This is even true of President Trump's own real-estate and golf-course portfolio. Trade protection will please a few protected firms and industries but it will harm and annoy many more, both because their costs will rise but also because they will be subject to retaliation by their overseas markets. Moreover, the security of the US depends on the ability to deter or defeat rivals and enemies, big or small, far from the country's coasts, for their ability to harm American interests and hurt American citizens and American assets is also global in presence and even in reach: North Korea may soon have missile systems capable of hitting the US mainland, perhaps with nuclear warheads. President Obama had already, during his eight years in office, been withdrawing the US from frontline military interventions and security responsibilities, seeking to fight wherever necessary by using unmanned drones. He had been, in the phrase made notorious by his approach to the Libyan civil war in 2011, "leading from behind". Greater detachment is already the trend, for good or ill. Isolationism is not an option.

What is at issue, however, is how reliable the US will in future be as an ally to the many countries tied in with it in military, security and economic pacts, and what effect any change in that reliability could have on countries' relationships with other great powers, notably China and Russia but also Iran, India, Brazil and so on. In play, also, is the status and strength of international law and of the multilateral institutions that try to shape and enforce it. These themes are explored in Chapter 10. The even more basic question – indeed, the question the answer to which is likely to determine the US's international behaviour – concerns what is good for the country's own economy and society.

Despite an economic recovery from the 2008 crash that has been more rapid and stronger than those across the Atlantic, and despite having so far avoided the deflationary stagnation that has held Japan back, US incomes and expectations have remained depressed. Anger may today be an overused word, but dissatisfaction and alienation, a kind of social dyspepsia, are clearly widespread. The way in which the US chooses to try to cure that social dyspepsia will be crucial both for its long-term future and for the idea of the West.

That there is a problem is incontestable. Like any problem, it must first be understood before it can be solved. Earlier chapters have sketched some of the reasons for discontent and dysfunction. The effect is stagnant incomes and dying communities. The cause lies in policy blunders and in the unfair, manipulated, overly rigid decision-making that stands behind them. We have seen how entrenched inequality of income and wealth is creating a new aristocracy that is distorting the political system and subverting equality of rights. We have seen how Wall Street has captured the regulatory system and not just made individuals rich but preserved the right to take huge risks while landing the costs of those risks on the public purse. We have seen how technology giants such as Google have been able to see off antitrust investigations and preserve their dominant positions.

For the US is not only the epitome of openness. It is also the epitome of how both democracy and free markets become sclerotic and rigid by their own natural workings, as winners in the democratic and market contests succeed in entrenching their positions and privileges, with consequences that can be dire or merely degenerative but that either way build up frustration and loss of faith. Such an inherent tendency towards sclerosis can never be cured in any country, but it needs to be treated vigorously every so often, every couple of decades at most, if it is not to cripple political, economic and social systems.

In the past, the US has been good at achieving such regular self-treatments, defying forecasts of decline, an ability that in turn has helped to give it credibility and legitimacy in international affairs. However hypocritical the country may seem, however heavy-handed its methods can be, in most countries' eyes the US has remained a better friend to have than the alternatives. American power is far from alone and not particularly "hyper", as a French foreign minister, Hubert Védrine, sought to define it in 1999, whether military, commercial, cultural or technological.[1] But American power still exceeds everyone else's and still represents the avant garde. *The Shock of America* is what David Ellwood, a professor at Johns Hopkins University in Bologna, called it in his 2012 book about the US's disruptive but invigorating impact on Europe over the past century. The shock truly would be if the US were to start delivering its main shocks not to other countries but to itself.

The question is therefore whether the United States remains capable of reviving itself in the same way as in the past, of restoring the openness and sense of equality that lie at the heart of what it is to be American. Or could it have become so polarised in its politics and its society that it will be unable to reach agreement on the need for such a restoration, let alone on how to do it?

*

External threats are easy to spot. Internal ones are more hidden, more insidious. So we need to do a very American thing: lift the hood and peer underneath to get an idea of why the great American machine is not firing on all economic and social cylinders. As any mechanic would, we should begin with the country's main power-train, what President Calvin Coolidge – one of the country's previous businessman-presidents – said in a speech to the

American Society of Newspaper Editors in 1925 was "the chief business of the American people": business. We can then move to what is the chief activity of the American people: work. In both, we will find that the US is not quite as we think it is: bit by bit, it has become less open, less competitive, less free and notably less equal in terms of rights and opportunities than it is generally assumed to be.

Where the United States certainly remains the world champion is in innovation and commercial disruption. In no other country could the "fracking" revolution in energy production have happened at anything like the same pace and scale as it did in the US in the early 2010s. Seemingly from nowhere, American companies, many small and entrepreneurial, shocked and impressed the world by turning the country from a declining producer, and big importer, of crude oil and natural gas into one of the world's biggest producers of both, and soon a major exporter of liquefied natural gas. One measure of their achievement is how well-established the two technologies of fracturing deep seams of rock and of horizontal drilling to extract oil and gas now are, and how universally it is accepted in the energy business that US "unconventional oil and gas" producers have taken over the global role of swing producer from Saudi Arabia. But just half a decade ago this was predicted by virtually no one.

It was all about price, technology, finance and enterprise: a very American formula. When international crude oil prices were at $100–150 a barrel, the success of fracking created a bonanza in states such as Texas and North Dakota, the rush of investment and well-paid employment in the new, wildcat energy industry helping to drive the economy's overall recovery. The ability of American business to smell an opportunity, to grab an emerging technology and improve it, and to compete fiercely for profits was proved yet again. One vital asset was the breadth and depth of financing that is available through the venture capital industry and also more crucially the capital markets. Another was US law, under which mineral and extraction rights belong to the owners of property rather than the state, as is common in other countries, generating a strong and direct incentive for landowners to accept and even encourage fracking. Environmental concerns – contamination of ground water by chemicals used in fracking, images of gas bubbling out of residential taps, earthquakes – that have held up the technology in Europe, and indeed in New York state, were swiftly overcome in the less populous and more experimentally minded states of the American west.

Saudi Arabia, used to exercising some control over the international oil market by virtue of the huge reserves of low-cost crude oil that it can turn on and off at will, knew an unbeatable opponent when it saw one, and from 2013–14 onwards decided in effect to surrender and drive the oil price down by maintaining high levels of output even amid a glut. The surrender may have been a tactical one, intended to drive out marginal fracking producers and establish a new, but still high, equilibrium price once oil supply had fallen. If it was, it did not succeed. Although the plunge in oil prices from 2013–14 onwards (at one point to less than $40 a barrel, a roughly 75% drop) did hurt the fracking industry and caused big worries about many companies' debts, firms proved more resilient, adaptable and inventive than expected. Far from buckling at $75–80 a barrel as the industry consensus expected, fracking firms managed to reduce their production costs and develop their technology further. They are not about to go away.

The energy industry even managed the seeming impossible, namely to overshadow for several years as the US's leading innovators the world-beating technology companies associated with Silicon Valley, such as Google, Facebook, Twitter and Apple, young (or, in Apple's case, born-again) companies that themselves now look like veterans compared with nimble and richly financed upstarts such as Uber and Airbnb. To these could be added many leaders in health care and biotechnology, often now known as "life sciences", as well as companies working in artificial intelligence, robotics and other forms of automation. Enterprise and innovation are alive, well and kicking.

This is all very encouraging for the country's future prospects. But such shock at the new can distract from the bigger picture, which is a less positive one. Despite all that innovation, the intensity of competition in the US has actually been decreasing in recent years. The country has been becoming less dynamic, not more.

Many industries have become dominated by larger and larger firms, thanks to mergers and takeovers, which are able to obstruct newcomers and extract high profits. A 2016 report from the White House Council of Economic Advisers, *Benefits of Competition and Indicators of Market Power*, showed that in the majority of industry categories surveyed by the US Census Bureau, the revenue share held by the 50 largest firms increased between 1997 and 2012. Not surprisingly, the council report shows that this applies to banking too: the loan-market share, nationwide, held by the top ten banks increased from

30% in 1980 to 50% in 2010, and the deposit-market share held by the top ten banks rose from 20% to almost 50% in the same period. Concentration is not the same as monopoly. Yet market power does bring greater profitability: the biggest publicly traded firms now earn returns on their investments that are more than five times that of the median firm, whereas in the early 1990s the ratio was closer to two.

And what about all those start-ups? Don't they challenge the excess profits being earned by the commercial elephants? Despite all the attention given to Silicon Valley, there are not in fact as many start-ups as there used to be. According to US Census Bureau data cited by the council, the rate of entry of new firms has declined steadily over time whereas the rate at which firms exit the market has remained steady. Until 2008, the rate of new entry always exceeded the rate of exit, but since then it has generally been the other way around. Moreover that decline in business dynamism has spread to all sectors since the turn of the century, even information technology.

Gary Hamel, a management writer and visiting professor at London Business School, and Michele Zanini, his colleague at a Silicon Valley-based non-profit advisory firm called The Management Lab, identified in an article in *Harvard Business Review* one probable consequence of this rise in market concentration and decline in competition. They reckon that "more people are working in big, bureaucratic organisations than ever before", including a total of 23.8 million managers, first-line supervisors and administrators in the US workforce in 2014, that is one manager and administrator for every 4.7 employees in all Those categories, they say, made up 17.6% of the US workforce in that year and received nearly 30% of total compensation. This rather puts in the shade all those predictions that intelligent automation is destroying millions of supervisory jobs. If only that were true, would be Hamel and Zanini's response.

Using as their comparison the management practices of companies that they see as using a leaner, "post-bureaucratic" model, Hamel and Zanini argue that the ratio of managers and administrators to all employees could be halved from 1:4.7 to 1:10. That would, they reckon, free up 12.5 million people to do more creative and productive work. Adding to that direct gain the indirect savings that could come from eliminating a lot of wasteful internal compliance activities, the authors arrive at the deliberately provocative estimate that excess bureaucracy costs US companies $3 trillion a year, which is equal to 17% of annual GDP. Even if just half of that burden could be shed over the course of a decade, they claim, the annual rate of growth in productivity in the US economy could be doubled.

The important point such analysis reveals is that although scale and concentration in industries increases profitability by allowing companies to raise prices, the associated increase in the bureaucratic complexity of giant corporations brings huge inefficiencies of its own, an unproductive burden that is being made possible and encouraged by the excessive profits being earned because of market domination. The clearest proof of this has been seen in banking, where the creation of mega-banks such as Citigroup and JPMorgan has produced huge organisations which no one, whether regulators or executives, can really understand. And banking also illustrates the broadest explanation for this phenomenon: lax regulation from financial supervisory bodies, Congress and the antitrust authorities, which have looked the other way as gigantic corporations have been created and competition has been diminished.

The business of the American people is nowhere near as competitive as the image of start-ups and disruptive innovation would lead us to believe. Nor, however, does the way in which Americans work, whether in the private or public sectors, fit the popular image.

That image is one of being free, easy, flexible and somewhat ruthless. In the laws of all American states except for Montana, the default expectation is that workers are employed "at will" unless there is a contract that specifically overrides that status, meaning that employment can be terminated at any time without the need to give a reason. Employers are therefore restricted in their ability to hire and fire only by their own decision to enter into contracts with employees individually, or collectively through a trade union, say, and by laws that prohibit discrimination such as on grounds of race, creed, age, gender or sexual orientation. Like it or not, the labour market in the US looks as open as a cattle market.

Except that it isn't. One way in which it isn't is that an increasing number of jobs now require applicants to hold a special "occupational licence" for that particular profession, generally provided and regulated by the states. According to a report released by the White House in 2015, nearly 30% of the US workforce now needs a licence from state, local or federal governments.[2] Measuring just state-licensed jobs, the report says that the proportion has increased fivefold since the 1950s and has been rising in every decade in that time. Part of this is explicable by the rise of service industries and the relative decline in importance of manufacturing. Some of the licensing brings benefits to consumers: everyone would want their doctors, dentists, teachers and so forth to hold qualifications appropriate to their role, and in many cases to be subject to periodic checks. As Italy shows, however, licences, often guarded jealously by medieval-style professional guilds, can easily become privileges, barriers to competition and innovation that raise costs unnecessarily and make it harder for people to find and get the jobs that they aspire to. This is precisely what the White House report says is happening.

Only about one-third of the increase in the percentage of workers requiring state-level licences has occurred as a result of the changing composition of the workforce, according to the report. The other two-thirds comes from an increase in the number of professions that now require licences. The report cites newly licensed professions such as sales, management and craft sectors, including construction or repair. Again, this is not necessarily all bad: it can reflect an increase in the professionalisation of a particular job, with new and better training. But one of the drawbacks, arising from the decentralisation of government to state level in the US, is that licensing requirements differ hugely between states. So people able to qualify easily in one state for a profession can be excluded in the state next door, hampering the mobility of labour for which the country was once renowned.

In Michigan, for example, it takes three years of education and training to become a licensed security guard while in most other states it takes 11 days or fewer. It is estimated that more than 1,100 occupations are licensed in at least one state, but fewer than 60 are regulated in all 50. In Louisiana a licence is even required to become a florist, although thanks to legal challenges the steps required to get that licence have at least been reduced. According to Morris Kleiner, a professor of public affairs at the University of Minnesota, in his state it takes more classroom time to become a cosmetologist than to become a lawyer, and the hours of instruction to become a manicurist are double those needed by a paramedic. This spread of licensing represents a creeping sclerosis in the American way of work. It has also contributed to the decline in the rate of entry of new firms to many sectors that was noted in the Council of Economic Advisers' study on market concentration: licences raise the cost of creating a new business, as do requirements for the firms themselves to obtain permits of various kinds.

Another source of rigidity and inefficiency in the workplace is the treatment of ex-prisoners and other felons – which is also affected by licensing rules. In half the 50 states applicants for jobs can be denied an occupational licence if they have a criminal conviction of any kind, regardless of the offence's relevance to the particular licence or how long ago it occurred. According to Nicholas Eberstadt, a specialist on demography at the American Enterprise Institute in Washington, DC, one adult male in eight in the civilian population, or 15 million men, is either an ex-prisoner or a felon who did not have to spend time in jail, to which can be added the 2.2 million that are currently behind bars.[3] The rate of incarceration in the US is one of the highest in the world – with 5% of world population, the country is home to 25% of the world's prison population. This rate of incarceration raises its own issues, but for our purpose the chief importance of this large pool of convicted criminals is the part they play in one of the most puzzling phenomena in American life: the number of people, chiefly men, who have disappeared from the workforce. That is Eberstadt's main concern too.

Americans are known for working harder, and longer hours, than their counterparts elsewhere. They are also known to have suffered from meagre growth in wage rates and household incomes over the past 20 years, but especially since 2008. Normally, you might expect that more members of each household would be looking for work, so as to make family ends meet. That is what has been happening in the UK, for example. But in the US the opposite is true: the proportion of adults who are taking part in the labour force has been declining steadily. This applies in particular to men.

In 1967, fully 96.6% of adult American males aged between 25 and 54 were in the labour force, by which is meant that they were either employed or looking for work. By 2014, the share of these prime-age men in the labour force had fallen to 88%. Participation by men of that age in Switzerland in that year was 96%, in Japan 95.5%, in Spain 92.6% and in the UK 91.7%. So although there has been some decline, or at least ups and downs, in prime-age adult participation in many Western countries, especially when welfare benefits have made it easier to subsist without working, the decline in the US stands out as exceptional.

What cannot be known at any one time is how much of this loss is temporary – the result of recession, say – or permanent. The decline in participation has been secular, but it accelerated after 2008. Indisputably, on Eberstadt's figures there are 7 million men of prime working age not just jobless but not even looking for work. That is equivalent to about 9% of the country's male labour force of 80 million or 4.4% of its total labour force of around 160 million, figures that don't even take account of older workers who the country also needs to be in work.

Why are so many men not even bothering to look for jobs in a country that is not exactly famous for the generosity of its welfare benefits? Eberstadt's answer comes in two parts: first, the barriers to employment for felons leave many of this big pool of often young men as outcasts; second, government disability and means-tested benefit programmes are bigger and more useful to recipients than you would think, once you account for all the different schemes that are available. Indeed, disability benefits in the US exhibit a classic law of unintended consequences as well as the power of incentives. Welfare reforms during the 1990s under the Clinton administration took millions of people off welfare schemes, which are typically run and financed by states, but provided states and, most particularly, lawyers, with an incentive to get people qualified instead for disability benefits, which once acquired can be more or less permanent and are financed by the federal government instead of the states.

The income that disability benefits provide is enough, Eberstadt argues, to discourage work at a time when the federal and state statutory minimum-wage rates with which the least-skilled men will compare them have been allowed to sink so low. In inflation-adjusted terms, the federal minimum wage of $7.25 an hour was reckoned by the Congressional Research Service in 2014 to be 32% lower than it had been at its peak in 1968; admittedly, 29 states mandate minimum wages that are higher than the federal minimum, with District of Columbia the highest at $11.50 and others ranging between $8 and $10. The federal minimum wage was last raised in 2009.

A 2016 report on the topic of non-working men, *The Long-Term Decline in Prime-Age Male Labor Force Participation*, prepared by the Council of Economic Advisers, disagreed with Eberstadt about the role of benefit programmes, judging their contribution to be marginal at best. To blame welfare schemes would not be attractive to a Democratic president. The council report agrees, however, that high incarceration rates along with the legal bans in many states on hiring ex-prisoners for many jobs play a big role: as it points out, "by one estimate between 6 and 7 percent of the prime-age male population in 2008 was incarcerated at some point in their lives", and the proportion will only have grown since then. But it places most of its emphasis on falling demand for low-skilled workers, perhaps caused by automation and globalisation, with accompanying wage levels that make many men feel that it is not worth their while working.

The government's emphasis on the role of low statutory minimum wages in discouraging work is plausible (and not incompatible with a big influence from benefit programmes), even though it also reflected President Obama's effort at that time to persuade Congress to raise the minimum wage. That effort failed, but meanwhile several places, including New York City, District of Columbia, California and Oregon, have passed laws mandating rises in their minimum wages to $15 an hour at differing paces from reaching that level in 2018 (New York City) to 2022 (California).

If, however, low demand for unskilled workers were to be the heart of the problem, raising the wage rates that such workers are legally required to be paid would be likely to reduce such demand, not increase it. In any event, it is difficult to believe that low demand for unskilled labour is the main explanation for a decline in participation that has been so continuous, so secular rather than cyclical, over a period of more than 40 years.

Any explanation for the decline in participation needs also to take account of the illegal economy, especially that involving the production and trade of narcotic drugs. Such an illegal, drugs-based economy exists in European countries and Canada too, but the most extreme case of it is found in the United States, since that is also the largest market for illegal drugs. Plenty of those who have been incarcerated will have lost their liberty through drugs offences, and the drugs business has grown steadily (and strongly) over the past four decades. A country which creates, broadcasts and enjoys the TV series *Breaking Bad*, about a middle-aged chemistry teacher who turns to "cooking" and dealing in crystal methamphetamine both as an excitement and as an income supplement preferable to washing cars, cannot deny the growing role of illegal business in American society and the economy.

The US's long-running "war on drugs" has created a vicious cycle, in combination with restrictions in the labour market. Young men deal in drugs, are caught, convicted and incarcerated, and then when they are released they often return to the same trade for lack of other options. Just as in Italy with its organised crime, the illegal economy contributes to the American economy by enabling participants to spend the money they make, but it yields no direct tax revenues – the need for which is increased by the costs of incarceration – and imposes clear social costs.

Fighting the war on drugs through military assaults on the supply of drugs in Central and South America, and, especially in the case of crystal meth, a large drug enforcement operation inside the US itself, has been costly and ineffective. The legalisation of trade in narcotic drugs, which would open up the chance both to regulate supply and to try to moderate demand through taxation and education, makes more and more sense.[4] In the case of marijuana, decriminalisation has spread at state level thanks chiefly to arguments for the drug's medicinal use. But fuller legalisation that would stand a chance of cutting the $40 billion–50 billion the US spends on drug enforcement each year and reducing the number of people incarcerated for often minor drugs offences remains far away.

Like prohibition of alcohol in 1920–33, the war on drugs has increased crime and gun violence, enriched criminal groups big and small, spread corruption at all levels, and yet has failed to deter people of all social classes from using drugs. When the drugs trade and its impact on incentives to work are being celebrated in popular culture, it must surely be time to break with a bad and failed strategy. In politics, attention is given constantly to illegal, or to use its euphemistic term "undocumented", immigration but only rarely and spasmodically to the undocumented economy that is being led by drugs.

The American way of work is not motoring as well as it should. Official unemployment rates are low, but those statistics conceal a lot of underemployed people as well as a vast army of men who have stopped bothering to look for work or are creating work of their own through the illegal economy. Yet, as the Council of Economic Advisers' report stresses, the US spends much less money than other countries on helping and encouraging unemployed or underemployed people to find new jobs or assisting with retraining. Combining all levels of government, it spends merely 0.1% of GDP each year on such active labour-market support, just one-sixth of the average for OECD countries as a whole. This neglect will have done cumulative damage, since it is well known that the longer people stay out of work, the harder it is for them to re-enter the labour market.

The good news that emerges from all these examples is that it is clear what needs to be done to get a sizeable chunk of Eberstadt's missing millions back to work and to improve the wider ways of the US labour market. Some is already being done at state level through the rises in minimum-wage levels already mentioned, which should draw some people back into work. The system of occupational licences needs to be reformed through collaboration between states to improve the compatibility of differing state requirements and to abolish unneeded licensing. Increased spending by local, state and federal government to help equip prime-age men to find new jobs, whether in their own town or state or, in the classic American manner, elsewhere, would take time to make a difference but would do so eventually.

This is, moreover, just what those who complain of the damaging impact of globalisation on manufacturing jobs in rustbelt cities have long been calling for: direct assistance to enable people to adjust to change. Provision for such assistance has been included in recent trade legislation, such as the North American Free-Trade Agreement between the US, Mexico and Canada that took effect in 1994. That money, however, has often been diverted by politicians and interest groups to their own pet causes, and has anyway been inadequate to the task. More money is needed for this purpose and it needs to be better directed. Dealing with the missing male workers may not be rocket science, but it is political science – which in a democracy can prove harder. Hence the common instinct to create or protect jobs through subsidies and trade barriers, which are costlier in the long term but seductively easy in the short term.

The same applies to the other scleroses listed, of declining competition and increasing business bureaucracy. Stronger antitrust enforcement is the main necessary cure: the Trump administration would be well advised to make the Department of Justice at least as active and interventionist as it was during the 1990s. This broad antitrust effort will need, however, to be supplemented by direct interventions in specific industries by other government agencies – such as the breaking up of mega-banks by regulators, or the introduction of rules governing the sharing and portability of consumers' data to prevent companies holding that big data from using it to restrict competition (a suggestion made in the Council of Economic Advisers' report on industrial concentration). If swamp-draining is truly the desire, this is the way to do it.

*

Having policy prescriptions is important, but it is not enough. The foregoing analysis, incomplete as it necessarily is of subjects as vast as the American economy and the social impact of labour conditions, indicates that to make a big difference what is needed is not a revolution but a persistent evolution; not a fancy new engine for the great American machine but rather a servicing and tuning-up of the one that is already there. Annual GDP growth has averaged 2.1% since 2010, but that compares with an average rate of 3.3% a year taking the whole period from 1950 to 2006.[5] Demographic change – no baby boom as in the 1950s and 1960s, an ageing society – means that the US cannot expect to return all the way to that average. But it needs to gets nearer to it – more like a consistent 2.5–2.75% – if living standards are to rise in the way that they used to, and if some of the social ills that the country recurrently suffers from are to be eased for the present generation.

There is no reason why this should not be possible. A new programme of public investment in infrastructure, as advocated by President Trump, but also education would help, and would probably boost economic growth sufficiently also to boost tax revenues. But will this happen? And will it be managed in a way that will avoid it stoking inflation, which would risk undermining the whole exercise and raising borrowing costs again? These are questions about politics and leadership.

If there is one word typically associated with American politics beyond "money", it is "dysfunctional". At both national and state level, politics has become more polarised between the two parties and more distorted as parties have exploited state laws and majorities in state assemblies to redraw – gerrymander, to use the political slang – constituency boundaries so as to increase their electoral control, a process which has reduced the proportion of seats in the House of Representatives that are able to change hands during elections. Any political system that presents a choice for the presidency between the dynastic and highly distrusted Hillary Clinton and the bombastic serial liar Donald Trump is not one that can be described as in good health.

The de facto monopoly that two highly dysfunctional political parties, Democrats and Republicans, hold over the electoral process at both federal and state level is one part of the problem, and has long been so. This is not a freely competitive system shaped for the digital age, but a legacy of the 19th and early 20th centuries. The traditional parties are poorly organised and dysfunctional in all ways except those required to entrench their own power, such as using majorities in state assemblies to gerrymander congressional constituencies and to keep a grip on voter registration processes so as to suppress likely votes for opponents. Another big part of the problem is the vast role of money in political campaigning at all levels, a role which helps perpetuate the two-party monopoly as channels for fund-raising.

The Supreme Court's "Citizens United" decision in 2010 to define campaign donations as a form of free speech means that the money–politics floodgates will remain open until a future court decision reverses the verdict. In this case, four of the nine justices tabled a dissenting opinion, so the decision was not a slam-dunk. In that opinion, which was led and read out by the soon-to-retire Justice John-Paul Stevens, it was argued that the ruling "threatens to undermine the integrity of elected institutions across the Nation" and that "A democracy cannot function effectively when its constituent members believe laws are being bought and sold". Another decision by the Supreme Court, in 2015, brought more cheer to reformers as it endorsed the right of states to empower independent redistricting commissions to counter gerrymandering of congressional districts, as has been enacted in Arizona, California, Idaho, Montana, Hawaii, New Jersey and Washington state. Arizona Republicans had sought to get the redistricting power returned to the state assembly. Again, the court split by five justices to four.

During the new presidential term one vacancy on the Supreme Court has already needed to be filled, but there will probably be more, given the age of some of the current justices. This will give President Trump the chance, subject to congressional approval, to shape the Supreme Court for the next several decades. Whether this will lead to the campaign-finance decision being revisited, however, remains to be seen. The fact that Trump financed his own campaign and did not rely on donors is some cause for optimism. Reducing the power of big donors would at least fit with any genuine agenda of swamp-draining.

Turnarounds are possible in the American political system, rigid and dysfunctional as it can often seem. They have happened many times before, most notably the major turnaround that occurred in what is known as "the progressive era" of the 1890s to the 1920s, when leaders such as President Theodore Roosevelt responded to the inequalities and mounting sclerosis of the "gilded age" with reforms such as antitrust laws, direct election of senators and female suffrage. But there have also been more incremental but still seminal turnarounds such as those of the 1930s, with President Franklin Delano Roosevelt's "New Deal", or the 1960s when Presidents John F. Kennedy and Lyndon B. Johnson brought in the Civil Rights Act of 1964 and the so-called "Great Society" initiatives of Medicare for the elderly and Medicaid for the poor.

Could there be another turnaround? The sort of protest movements exploited by Trump and Bernie Sanders in the 2016 election campaign are not very different from the one that marked the end of a previous gilded age of wealth and inequality at the turn of the 20th century. Their equivalent protest leader then was William Jennings Bryan, a populist Democrat from Nebraska, who failed to be elected president in three attempts in 1896, 1900 and 1908, but still had a big influence on the political agenda and campaigning style of the time, from his attacks on "money power" and the gold standard to his assaults on monopolist corporations and big banks. A similar pressure for radical change is building up following today's gilded age.

For practical, recent evidence of how turnarounds can occur in the American political system it is necessary to go to the states, for this is where many initiatives have begun that have later gone national. Whether or not there are now federal initiatives for real change, innovation can and will continue at state level. One state that has often been a pioneer, in bad ways as well as good, is California. Currently, California is passing through quite a turnaround, one that has confounded political forecasters just as much as the rise of fracking confounded energy pundits, and in more or less the same space of time.

In the early 2010s, and for the decade running up to that, California was notorious as a deadbeat debtor, a state whose politics had turned dysfunctional and whose finances were so crippled that public services were disappearing, fast. The election as state governor of Arnold Schwarzenegger, "the Terminator", in 2003 was not the cause of that dysfunction but the choice of such an unconventional outsider was probably a symptom of it.

One cause of the disease was something that is often proposed as a way to improve democracy but actually ended up damaging it in California, namely referendums or, in their local form, ballot initiatives. Referendums generally hold legislatures to account or give them instructions, but initiatives go straight into the law if they are passed. Starting with the infamous Proposition 13 in 1978, which cut property taxes, ballot initiatives in the state have brought out the worst aspects of democracy: short-sightedness and selfishness. Voters regularly choose to cut their taxes but never to cut public spending, with predictable results for which no one needs admit responsibility. And the process of bringing forward ballot initiatives has become dominated by lobby groups and other forms of money politics.

Another cause of California's woes is the fact that one-third of its tax revenues come from a single, highly volatile source: capital gains made by initial public offerings, stock-option awards and the like, from the state's famous start-up scene. In the good times, such revenues seduce politicians into thinking they have no need to make hard decisions on spending or imposing taxes on other groups. But in bad ones, revenue drops like a stone: in 2009 following the Lehman shock of the previous September, state GDP fell by 4% but budget revenues plunged by 25%. The state's finances had also taken a big hit when the dotcom bubble of the late 1990s burst in 2001 and the Nasdaq technology-stocks market plummeted. On that occasion unemployment did not rise too sharply, but it did in 2008–09, since manufacturing and construction, both big features of the state economy, were hit hard. Only in 2016 did California's unemployment rate fall back to its pre-2008 level and close the gap with the national average.

The annual state budget has anyway been a particularly hard piece of legislation to pass through the state assembly, for its passage has required a two-thirds majority as does any measure to raise taxes through the legislature (thanks to a clause in Proposition 13 back in 1978). The result has been deficits, debt and in hard times a constant process of spending cuts even on the neediest targets, such as education. Moreover the state's "three-strikes-and-you're-out" law, passed following a ballot proposition in 1994 and under which a felon faces mandatory life imprisonment following conviction on three serious felonies, has meant that the share of state spending devoted to prisons in 2010 was almost double that on universities, taking up 10% of general fund spending.

In 2011 *The Economist* pointed out that California was known not just as dysfunctional but as "ungovernable" and even a "failed" state.[6] It quoted Nathan Gardels, a journalist who works for a new think-tank in Los Angeles, the Berggruen Institute, as saying, compellingly and accurately, that California had become a "diet-Coke civilisation of consumer democracy, of services without taxes, like sweetness without calories, of rights without duties". During the 2012 presidential election campaign the Republican candidate, Mitt Romney, speaking in Iowa, warned that "at some point America is going to become like Greece, or like Spain or Italy, or like California – just kidding about that one, in some ways".

In these respects, joking or otherwise, the state had become an extreme case of the democratic habits of self-entrapment that have featured in this book: short-term thinking, money politics, capture by interest groups, bust public finances, an inability to invest in long-term purposes such as education and infrastructure. Even the use of direct democracy, which works so well in its homeland of Switzerland as a check on centralised power, had been captured and turned into a counterproductive, even destructive weapon, a source of irresponsibility rather than assurer of responsibility.

By 2016, the picture looked very different. The state budget was balanced and a "rainy day fund" had been set up (passed by a ballot initiative) to store up surpluses and use them to pay down debt. This was helped by a reform in 2010 making a simple majority in the state assembly sufficient to pass the annual budget, not two-thirds as before. But it was helped even more by two important political events: first the formation of a non-partisan reform body, the Think Long Committee, which proved to have clout with both major parties and with many interest groups; and second the election in 2010 as governor of Jerry Brown, or Edmund G. Brown to give him his full name, for his second spell in the office. His first had been in 1975–83, when, having been elected at age 36, he was the youngest California governor since 1863. On his election in 2010 he became the oldest California governor ever, at age 72.

The combination of two spells in office and Brown's current age have helped. He has experience, including of his own mistakes during his 1970s term and of failed presidential bids in the meantime. Now he has the advantage and credibility of having little to lose because he is not likely to have a tilt at the presidency in 2020 when he will be 82. This has enabled Brown, who has always been a fiscal conservative, to be tougher on spending and taxes than his predecessors, and to gain some bipartisan support.

Hard times, as often in the case of turnarounds, have also played a big part. Had the 2008–09 financial crash not caused that 25% drop in tax revenues, change might well have taken longer or not have happened at all. Instead, it exposed a stark public interest in curing some of the long-running diseases that have been enfeebling California. This is what Brown gambled on, in any case. Taking office with unemployment above 10% of the state labour force, a deficit on the annual state budget of $26 billion and state debts of more than $35 billion, he cut spending hard on higher education, health care and other services, and tabled a ballot initiative of his own, Proposition 30, to raise state sales tax and income taxes on the rich. It passed, on the election day in 2012 on which Mitt Romney lost, and has raised an extra $6 billion a year in revenues.

Beyond such fiscal gap-plugging, one of the biggest successes so far, initiated and promoted by the Think Long Committee, has been reform of the rules governing ballot initiatives for the first time in 80 years, signed into law in 2014. The Think Long Committee is essentially a gathering of California's great and good, including two former Republican secretaries of state (George Schulz and Condoleezza Rice), a former Democrat head of the White House Council of Economic Advisers (Laura Tyson), a former state chief justice (Ronald George), the chairman of Google (Eric Schmidt), the man who formed and financed the committee, a French-born businessman turned philanthropist (Nicolas Berggruen), Arnold Schwarzenegger's predecessor as governor (Gray Davis), a trade union executive (Maria Elena Durazo), and others from business, law and politics. Although such gatherings bring no guarantees of either coming to a conclusion or carrying weight with the public or current legislators, this one has so far managed to score one big success with the initiative reform, and is pressing for more.

According to Gardels, an adviser to the committee, one key to its success in forming a public consensus for ballot initiative reform lay in bringing together about 30 lobbies, including trade unions and civil liberties groups, all of which have a stake in the initiative process being made to work, both because they want to stop others harming their members by abusing it and because they want to be able to use it themselves. The reform consists of a new procedure designed to blend the institutions of representative government with those of direct democracy.

In the old system, once a minimum level of signatures petitioning for a proposition had been reached, the initiative automatically qualified for the ballot and could not subsequently be amended. In the new system, once 25% of the signatures required to qualify a measure have been secured, public hearings have to be held by the state legislature about the measure. Sponsors of the initiative are then allowed to make changes to their initial filing to reflect what has emerged at the hearings, or to negotiate a compromise version with the legislature and governor in an effort to secure their support. Crucially, sponsors can withdraw their initiative altogether if this process of hearings yields an agreement to introduce legislation that meets the objectives of the initiative. Finally, there now has to be public disclosure of everyone who is financing either side of any initiative campaign.

As Gardels writes in *The Great Transformation*, this reform had an immediate impact in the debate over raising California's minimum wage to $15 an hour.[7] Unions had put forward ballot initiatives to raise the wage to this level in scheduled steps by 2020. However, it became clear that the state itself would be one of the employers hit most by the rise, notably for in-home health-care workers the state pays for under a programme called MediCal, costing the state an extra $4 billion a year. So Brown and the unions negotiated a compromise allowing the state to delay wage increases if a recession were to cause tax revenues to plunge again. The unions then withdrew the initiative from the ballot and it was passed instead by the legislature in April 2016.

There is much still to be done. The state's tax base needs to be broadened so that it can become less volatile. At present, capital gains tax and personal income tax account for 67% of state revenues. Until Proposition 13 in 1978, most of the brunt was borne by property taxes. To provide a broader base, sales taxes need to be levied not just on goods as now but on the services that form the bulk of the state's economy. This means that lobby groups for all the industries and professions whose services are currently not taxed need to be won over, which will be far from easy, even for a modest sales levy of perhaps 2%. Money needs to be found to increase public spending on infrastructure, such as water supply and public transport, including a San Francisco to Los Angeles high-speed rail link much favoured by Brown, and to reverse the huge decline in public spending on higher education.

It is not hard to list the difficulties, from local intransigence about permits for new housing in the congested Bay Area cities, to teachers' unions that cut up rough against schools reforms, to all the difficulties in dealing with drug crime and the huge prison population, to the fact that nobody likes higher taxes. California's basic problem now is whether a natural constituency can be found that will support public-finance and other reforms so as to pay for the stepladders and moving walkways of social mobility, in a state that is not only the largest, with 39 million residents, but also one of the most unequal in the nation. Now that over 60% of the state's population is non-white, with Latinos having overtaken whites as the largest ethnic group in 2014, the chances of forming such a constituency (that is, getting elected by it) must be high, and rising year by year.

*

In California, as in every one of the revival or turnaround stories that appear in this book, success is never complete and new problems will arise. California's turnaround is new and still tentative. But it points in a positive direction and encourages optimism about the prospects for reform and revival in the United States as a whole. The 2016 election cycle surely demonstrated that there is now a big natural constituency in the US for measures that moderate inequality, that reduce the damage the financial sector can do, that seek ways to get the hidden millions of non-working men into work, and that get the visible millions of disgruntled lowly paid men and women into higher-paid work.

This means that the 45th President of the United States has a chance to emulate some of the achievements of the 26th President, Theodore Roosevelt, whose two terms in office from 1901 to 1909 followed and dealt with many of the excesses of the previous "gilded age" of inequality and monopoly. President Trump's anti-establishment mandate, fuelled by resentment at inequality and at the power of big international corporations, would justify new efforts to enforce antitrust laws and to break up concentrations of power, including on Wall Street, as well as efforts to reduce the role of campaign-finance donations and lobbyists. It would more than justify sincere and sustained efforts to retrain or otherwise help the under-employed or discouraged to find jobs. The question is whether one should be encouraged or discouraged by his choice of business leaders and billionaires from outside traditional politics for so many jobs in his administration: they could prove refreshingly free of old ties and traditional thinking; or they could prove dedicated to crony capitalism.

The rhetoric about American national interests could cut either way. The United States now does need to wake up to its national interest in dealing with these scleroses, and to the need to make its great economic and social machine work far better. Faster economic growth can be obtained in the short run by pressing on the fiscal accelerator through public investment, but if that growth is to raise incomes for ordinary Americans in a sustainable way, it will need to be supplemented by strong efforts to improve competition and the jobs market, as well as by further direct intervention in the labour market to raise minimum wages. Dynamism is needed, but so is a fresh focus on equality. There is, moreover, a direct contradiction between the need for dynamism, for the lubrication of the mechanisms of competition, and the idea of taking shortcuts through the imposition of trade tariffs or provision of corporate subsidies. Such measures reduce competition rather than increasing it, handing greater profits to big corporations without increasing their incentives to invest.

The biggest dangers will come as and when unexpected events bring about downturns or even recessions. At such moments there will be plenty of pressure to close borders, doors and minds, especially on trade, just as there were during the Reagan administrations of the 1980s. But there is now the opportunity to use the populist pressure for change as a lever to force bipartisan efforts to take place on reform, just as occurred under Theodore Roosevelt. A National Commission on Fiscal Responsibility and Reform, commonly known as the Simpson–Bowles commission and set up by Barack Obama, tried to achieve consensus on fiscal reforms in 2010 and only narrowly failed to get its way. With populist wolves at the door of both political parties, the chances of success in the next effort at bipartisanship, in a kind of Think Long Committee for America, have surely risen. The formation of such bipartisan commissions is one way in which congressional Republicans could seize the initiative away from the White House, or, to put it in less adversarial language, guide it in the right long-term direction.

The battle over that direction remains to be won, but there are good reasons to be optimistic that it can be. The United States has far more often in its history been an embracer of the new, a country eager for the next cycle of evolution and change, than a rejecter of it. It has been a world champion of evolution, grasping moreover with both hands during the decades after 1945 the idea that in modern times its national interest encompasses a powerful interest in global security, in global rules of the game, in a wide network of alliances and in global prosperity. The task of setting America straight again, of enabling it to remain the world's evolutionary champion, will begin at home, as will the fight to ensure that any reforms embrace both openness and equality. But it will not stop there.

5

Britain, their Britain

I must admit I find the English are
extraordinarily difficult to understand.

A.G. Macdonell, *England, their England*, 1933

Be strong, Maggie told us all. Get educated. Get away.
That's what she said. I listened.

Damian Barr, *Maggie & Me*, 2013

IF WE LOOK BACK AT BRITAIN in the 1970s and 1980s, the big migration issue then was what was known as "the brain drain" – the movement of talented Britons chiefly to the US, but also to other European countries, Canada and Australia. Tension over immigration to Britain was focused on arrivals from Commonwealth countries, former colonies such as India, Pakistan, Bangladesh, the West Indies and parts of Africa. The Immigration Act of 1971 imposed tighter controls on inflows from the Commonwealth. Membership in 1973 of the European Economic Community, later known as the European Union, produced no concern in Britain about immigration from other European countries, for the flow was largely expected to go the other way. One popular TV comedy was *Auf Wiedersehen Pet*,[1] a series that from 1983 onwards depicted a group of construction workers from north-east England who go off to work in Germany – thanks to free movement under the EU treaties. Britain was known to be the sick man of Europe. Why would any educated, skilled European have wanted to move to a country in decline, one so stuck in its past?

Why indeed? But two decades later that is exactly what hundreds of thousands were doing and by their choice they were identifying Britain as a dynamic story of revival, a country with a future in which to make their own futures. According to the Migration Observatory at the University of Oxford, the number of foreign-born people living in the UK more than doubled from 3.8 million in 1993 to about 8.3 million in 2014, making up 13.1% of the population. London alone had more than 3 million foreign-born residents among its population of 8.7 million. The newspaper headlines have focused on migrants from Poland and elsewhere in central and eastern Europe, that is, "Polish plumbers" and others from the former communist countries that joined the EU in 2004 and came when the UK joined Sweden and Ireland in being the only countries of the then 15 EU member countries to permit immediate access to come and live and work, rather than imposing a seven-year transition period. But hundreds of thousands also came from Ireland, Italy, Portugal, France, Germany and others during the decade up to the EU referendum. The UK was where the jobs were, where the buzz was, and where talented, often well-educated young Europeans could make their mark – and their money – much more quickly and easily than at home. The brain drain had become a brain gain as well as a brawn gain.

The UK is a revival story which is now in need of a new revival thanks to new obstacles and anxieties, but which nevertheless can be seen as a cause for optimism for the rest of the West. Following three decades of decline and industrial strife after the second world war, decline that coincided with (but was not provoked by) the dismantling of the vast British empire, the country in the 1980s and 1990s transformed itself economically, socially, culturally, politically and in terms of its status in world affairs. The revival, which Tony Blair's supporters termed "cool Britannia" when he swept into office in 1997, lasted for something like 20 years, but then following the 2008 global financial crisis the country fell into a new slough of despond.

Within three or four years it again seemed to be recovering from the financial crash and deep recession as it was by then outpacing its European neighbours who had become mired in their own euro-zone sovereign-debt crisis. The UK's relatively smooth recovery – it had a banking crisis thanks to the City's international shenanigans but no property crash – enabled unemployment to fall rapidly and maintained the country's attractiveness to immigrants from other EU countries, especially those with heavy sovereign-debt burdens. Yet neither the economic nor the social climate was altogether sunny, since wages had taken a big hit in the recession and failed to show any real revival until

2015. Since the supply of labour had increased through immigration, the belief that migrants were one of the causes of depressed incomes was hard to refute.

And so it was that in 2016 the UK found itself in a fresh political and constitutional crisis following its 51.9% to 48.1% vote in a national referendum to become the first country ever to leave the EU. In a tightly fought campaign, the presence in the UK of so many EU citizens, willing as they had been to say *"auf wiedersehen, Mutti"* or *"arrivederci, tesoro mio"* in order to come to a land of opportunity and dynamism, proved one of the decisive issues, though it was far from the only motive for voting to leave. This was despite the fact that EU immigrants are on average better educated than the average Briton and have made a positive contribution to economic growth, tax revenues and entrepreneurship.

No wonder that Archie Macdonell, a Scot born in India, said in his 1930s satire, *England, their England*, that he found the English hard to understand. Now the English, along with the Welsh (who like them voted to leave the EU) and the Scots and Northern Irish (both of whom voted to stay), are finding it hard to understand where leaving the EU is going to take them and what it will do to the United Kingdom of Great Britain and Northern Ireland. Are they going to become more closed or more open, poorer or richer, safer or unsafer, less influential around the world or more? All of these questions will take years to gain clear answers. Unlike the election five months later on the other side of the Atlantic of Donald Trump, the Brexit vote in June 2016 was not, at least in the minds of most of its advocates, a vote against open trade or Western liberal ideas in general, but that does not preclude it from ending up that way. And it was certainly not a vote for a stable, predictable future.

*

The story of the UK's unstable past, and its escape from that long post-1945 decline and its image as Europe's sick man, is as inspiring as it is well known. During the 1980s Margaret Thatcher, the prime minister dubbed "the Iron Lady" by the Soviet Union, took on and defeated a series of powerful interest groups, most notably coalminers and other trade unions, but also industrial cartels, state-owned companies and the City of London. She also, however, simultaneously mounted an attack on the UK's recurrent problem of inflation by imposing tough monetary controls, budget cuts and high interest rates which, in inadvertent collaboration with a rising value for the pound owing to high oil prices during what was the heyday of North Sea oil production, caused a deep recession and raised unemployment to the highest level seen in the UK since the 1930s.

American economist Mancur Olson wrote *The Rise and Decline of Nations* (1982) during Thatcher's first months in government. This theorist of interest-group sclerosis recognised clearly the nature of the British problem:

> *[C]ountries that have had democratic freedom of organisation without upheaval or invasion the longest will suffer the most from growth-repressing organisations and combinations. This helps to explain why Great Britain, the major nation with the longest immunity from dictatorship, invasion and revolution, has had in this century a lower rate of growth than other large, developed democracies. Britain has precisely the powerful network of special-interest organisations that the argument developed here would lead us to expect ... The number and power of its trade unions need no description. The venerability and power of its professional associations is also striking. Consider the distinction between solicitors and barristers ... Britain also has a strong farmers' organisation and a great many trade associations.*

The story of what came to be called Thatcherism is in large part a story of Olsonism, of breaking the power of such special-interest groups and reopening British society and the British economy to new ideas, new freedoms and new entities. As happened at the same time in the United States, the UK also defeated its old enemy of inflation. Probably its biggest achievement in doing so was to reform the supply side of the economy, in other words to open up many activities to competition, through privatisation of state-owned monopolies, through deregulation of all sorts of industries, especially ones directly serving the consumer, and through reforms to trade union law.

The slow response of producers whenever demand rose had made the UK more prone to inflation during the 1970s than Germany or France. Producers responded slowly in part out of fear of the fast response of trade unions, striking for higher wages, which made new investments and production expansion risky. Moreover, the impact of clearing away obstacles and creating new competition, new openness, to help speed up this response was not just an economic one. Thatcherism was not always liked, but it had a big social impact: old groups, old loyalties, old conventions became fractured. New freedoms came along with the end of old certainties. There was destruction but also creation, just not always in the same places.

A Scottish writer, Damian Barr, described this especially eloquently in a personal memoir, published in 2013, about growing up in Scotland during the 1980s, which he called *Maggie & Me*. His story is of life as a child in a small industrial town in Scotland, near the huge Ravenscraig steelworks, which was eventually closed in 1992. To his broken family and to the community in which he grew up, Thatcher was akin to the devil. Yet to him she was a kind of hero, a role model not in her political views but in her attitudes, her willingness to stand up to people, to defend what she stood for, to fight as a woman beset by prejudices and surrounded by enemies. The young Barr plots his escape from the poverty, squalor, prejudice and self-defeating attitudes he sees around him, with "Maggie" as an inspiration. She fought prejudice as a woman, Barr as a homosexual. He writes:

Yes, Maggie, you did all that [snatched milk, smashed the miners, closed the Craig, made millions unemployed then cut their benefit] ... You also saved my life. You were different, like me, and you had to fight to be yourself. You were the only woman among all those men. You fought wars and won them, even managing to carry off a headscarf at the helm of a tank. You led by example. You made a hero of the individual, a cult of the striver and I did my homework to impress you ... You hated where I was from and I did too so you made it OK for me to run away and never look back. You offered me certainty, however grim, when I had none at home. You threw me an escape ladder.

How was the escape ladder thrown? The standard narrative is one of a national crisis in 1978–79 followed by the election of a heroic-cum-ruthless politician who bulldozed her way through opposition in order to beat up the interest groups and open up British society. Those who dislike Thatcher adapt the narrative to make it consist of the malicious tearing up of a supposed "1945 settlement" between workers and employers, and the heartless tearing apart of communities in the areas that suffered most from her assault on coalmining trade unions or from the assault of tight money and a strong pound on old manufacturing industries – especially in Scotland and the north of England.

The truth about 1978–79 is that such crisis as did occur was political rather than economic. The UK had no big financial catastrophe comparable to that of Japan in 1990 (see Chapter 7) or of Sweden in 1991 (see Chapter 8). What it had was a series of strikes during late 1978 and early 1979, chiefly by public-sector trade unions, including most embarrassingly by gravediggers in Liverpool and part of Manchester and by refuse collectors, in response to an effort by the then Labour government to impose a maximum annual pay rise of 5% in the public sector so as to help curb inflation. This became known as "the winter of discontent", which helped in May 1979 to bring about a general election victory for Thatcher's Conservative Party, in which she achieved the biggest swing (5.2%) of votes away from the incumbent governing party seen in any general election since 1945. It was an impressive victory even though the parliamentary majority the Tories won – an overall margin of 44 seats – was far from overwhelming. Plenty of political pundits could be found who believed that had Labour's prime minister, James Callaghan, had the guts to call a general election during the previous year, before the winter became so Shakespearean in its discontent, he might have won and British history might have been different.

In reality, however, what the 1979 election represented was the culmination of nearly two decades of constant strife, a crisis that was of governance rather than of finance. In the 1970s the UK did have a couple of financial dramas, but they were not cathartic. In one, in 1973–75, a sudden plunge in house prices sent many smaller financial institutions, known in the parlance of the day as "secondary banks", into near-bankruptcy, forcing the Bank of England to bail out about 30 of them. The second was in June 1976 when the Labour government had to borrow £2.3 billion (then $3.9 billion) from the IMF to tide itself over and prevent a forced devaluation of the pound. It seemed humiliating at the time for the government of a developed country to have to go to the IMF, but the euro sovereign-debt debacle in recent years puts this in a rather different perspective.

The UK's troubles were more like a long chronic illness, one that was summed up best by the question that Thatcher's predecessor as Conservative Party leader, Edward Heath, posed when as prime minister he called a general election in 1974: "Who governs Britain?" Not you, was the voters' answer. They had suffered through a series of industrial conflicts, during which long strikes by coalminers had forced Heath's 1970–74 government to impose a three-day working week for industry to curb electricity consumption and thus coal demand, and had forced households to return to the candlelit era. So voters brought back Harold Wilson's Labour government instead, a government that had in 1969 tried, and failed, to reform trade union law through a package of proposals called "In Place of Strife". The core proposal in that package, that unions be required to hold a ballot of members before a strike could legally be called, was eventually adopted by Thatcher's Conservative government in its 1984 trade union law. Labour did not dare to reintroduce the proposal during its 1974–79 term in office, a period during which the problem of huge numbers of working days being lost to strikes just got worse and worse.

The simplest way to depict the UK's decline and recovery is through the statistics on the average number of working days lost each year through strikes. During the 1950s, the annual average loss was 3.3 million days. During the 1960s, the decade which led Labour to try to replace such strife, the annual average rose to 3.6 million. But in the 1970s, under both the Conservatives and Labour, the annual average loss soared to 12.9 million working days, with 1979 a particularly extreme year, with 29.5 million working days lost.

Then in 1984 Thatcher fought a long battle against the National Union of Mineworkers (NUM) that she eventually won, thanks to good preparation and, by then, to having won a second general election fuelled by victory over Argentina in the Falklands war, this time with a huge parliamentary majority of 144 seats. Industrial strife in 1984 and in some preceding years inflated the decade's annual average, but that average nevertheless dropped to 7.2 million working days, thanks to the victory over the NUM and to Thatcher's legal reforms, which introduced secret ballots for union members and outlawed the disruptive practice of secondary picketing, by which strikes and blockades were extended to companies not directly involved in the original dispute. In the 1990s the annual average plunged to a mere 700,000 working days lost. Which is where it has stayed. This places the once strike-torn UK at a mere half of the EU average for strikes in that decade, when made proportionate to the size of the workforce.

Some of this change can be attributed to a decline in membership of trade unions, from about 40% of the workforce at the time of the miner's strike of 1984 to 25% now, which in turn is related to the shrinking role of manufacturing in the economy. The most unionised workforce now is in the public sector, where about 55% of employees are members of a union. Such declines have, however, also occurred in most Western countries, often more precipitately: in Germany,

18% of employees are in a union; in France, the figure is an astonishingly low 8%. Sweden is truly the outlier, with 70% of employees in unions, though even that has declined from a peak of 86% in 1995.

Although manufacturing shrank considerably as a share of the British economy (from 27% of UK GDP in 1970 to 10% in 2013), one particular sector demonstrates a more positive picture. In the 1970s, the British car industry ranked alongside coal and steel as a heartland of industrial strife. British Leyland was the main British-owned car company, the result of a merger of old, famous names including Austin, Morris, Jaguar and Rover, but it was hit by a series of strikes in the early 1970s, many organised by a shop steward called Derek Robinson, a Communist Party member who became known to the press as "Red Robbo". The firm was saved from bankruptcy only by nationalisation in 1975. It accounted for about 40% of the British car market, rather as Fiat dominated the Italian market at that time. Neither British Leyland nor Fiat was in a fit state to compete in an open market with either the increasingly competitive Japanese imports or the other European makers, against which both firms would have to battle on more equal terms once the EU banned state subsidies and then created a genuinely single market in cars, which it did after 1993.

Yet the British car industry has survived that European challenge rather better than the Italian industry. In the early 1970s production of cars and trucks in the UK and Italy was at similar levels, but in 2014 the UK produced more than twice as many vehicles (1.6 million) as Italy (700,000). The main reason is the change in British trade union law and in industrial relations, which in turn lured Japanese carmakers to open factories in the UK to serve the European market, beginning with Nissan near Sunderland in 1986, soon to be followed by Toyota and Honda. Japanese companies led the way in achieving higher productivity, higher quality and competitive costs in making cars in the UK for export, principally to elsewhere in Europe, and have been followed in that success by German companies (BMW's purchase of the former British Leyland Mini) and India's Tata Motors (Jaguar and Land Rover, also formerly part of British Leyland). Italy achieved no such labour-law reform until 2015, and has attracted no foreign car producers at all.

The end to industrial disruption represented an end to the ability of relatively small interest groups to hold the country to ransom. But there was also a brighter side to the transformation of the UK under, and after, the Thatcher era. It too can be summed up by a statistic: in 2014 the share of annual British GDP that came from what the Department for Culture, Media and Sport (DCMS) defines as "the creative economy" reached 8.2%, placing it ahead of financial services (which some might call "the creatively destructive economy") at around 8%, and not far behind the whole of manufacturing, which provides 10%.

The DCMS's definition of the creative economy consists of a list of what it deems the creative industries – design, software, IT, publishing, film, television, advertising, communications, architecture, music and performing arts – plus an estimate of the contribution of people in the same creative occupations but working for other industries, that is, designers working directly for a manufacturer rather than selling it services from outside. Companies in the creative industries have grown faster than in other big EU countries and account for a larger share of employment. According to *Creative Economy Employment in the EU and the UK*, a study by Nesta,[2] 7.9% of employment in the UK in 2013, just over 2.3 million people, was in the creative industries, compared with 5.3% in the 28 EU member countries as a whole. A further 2% of employment consisted of creative jobs embedded in other sectors, making 2.9 million, or 9.9%, in all.

The Nesta study showed that the EU country in which creative industries and the embedded creative economy account for the highest share of employment is Sweden, at 11.92%: as Chapter 8 will describe, another revival story. Second on that measure comes the Netherlands at 10.9% with the UK third at 9.9%. In Germany the share is thought to be 8% and in France 7.5%. To put this into a global context, a later study, *Creative Economy Employment in the US, Canada and the UK*, estimated the US creative economy in 2013 to account for about 9.75% of its employment, and that in Canada in 2011 an even higher 12.9%.

So much for the 1970s image of the UK as a drab country that had lost the moment of creative celebrity it had been given in the 1960s by the Beatles, the Rolling Stones and their sort. By the 1990s, the UK had become one of the creative centres of the Western world. This is one reason why, by the 2000s, it was proving a magnet for hundreds of thousands of talented, well-educated immigrants from European countries previously thought of as much more creative than the UK, including Italy, France and Spain. Tate Modern, which opened in 2000 in a converted power station in London, has become one of the most visited contemporary art museums in the world, part of a nationwide revival of museums and art galleries. All that creativity is heavily centred on

London and south-east England, but is not only found there: Nesta produced a further study, *The Geography of Creativity in the UK*, showing how creative employment is distributed around the UK. It found that such jobs and firms are principally urban, thus in Manchester, Leeds, Bristol, Edinburgh and Cardiff as well as in London, but also that one-fifth of what it calls "creative clusters" are to be found in the north of England, with others in Scotland, Wales and Northern Ireland.

A notable example of one of those clusters is in Manchester, and it is based on science rather than the arts or software. In 2010 a team of scientists at Manchester University won the Nobel prize in physics for their discovery of graphene, a substance derived from carbon and popularly known as the new wonder material, as it is the strongest and thinnest material ever known. This achievement has led to the creation at Manchester University of the National Graphene Institute. The discovery, moreover, was a typical story of the modern, open, post-Thatcher UK: it was made by a team led by two immigrant scientists originally from Russia, Andre Geim and Konstantin Novoselov, one of whom had come to the UK via a university in the Netherlands.

*

But did the UK really escape from its long and not always genteel post-imperial decline? The question is unavoidable, thanks to three big, destabilising events. The first was the 2008 global financial crisis, which hit the British economy harder than any other big Western economy, except for Italy. The second was the referendum in 2014 on Scottish independence from the United Kingdom, in which although the status quo won by a ten-point margin, it was nevertheless shocking that 44.7% of voters favoured departure from the UK. This does not fit well with the notion of a country that has fully recovered its dynamism and is feeling good about itself as "Team GB", to use the name used for the British contestants in the Olympic Games. Then in June 2016 there was the vote to leave the European Union.

That vote represented the rejection, albeit by a narrow margin, of what had been the centrepiece of British foreign policy for more than half a century. It was a rejection that was driven by many different, often contradictory, feelings. Although an "in–out" referendum might sound like a decision over a single issue, the issue of membership of an institution as complex and multifaceted as the European Union inevitably meant that the 33.5 million people who voted must have made their choices for a wide variety of reasons.[3] The campaign was a distinctly unpleasant affair, in which the "Leave" campaign relied on its open-ended but smart slogan of "Take Back Control", supported by a series of demonstrably false statements about the EU,[4] while the "Remain" campaign's slogan was a poorly argued claim of "Stronger In", reinforced by rather apocalyptic speculations of the economic consequences of Brexit. Such speculations relied in particular on a forecast from the Treasury that stretched implausibly forward to 2030 and purported to find that the average British household would be £4,300 per year worse off by then if the country were to leave the EU than if it were to stay. This was absurdly precise, given that this was a 14-year forecast comparing two potential outcomes, the nature of both of which was unknowable.

In the end, though, polling analysis showed that the factor shared by the widest number of voters was a desire to put limits on immigration, and one unarguable fact was that under the EU's treaties it is not possible for a member to impose limits on the freedom of movement to their country of other EU citizens. The vote was not as such a rejection of the British elite, since the elite themselves were sharply split both over immigration and over the EU, especially within the Conservative Party but also in the trade unions. Such deep divisions, both elite and popular, and the vote's rejection of mainstream policy, of one of the great international institutions of the post-war era and of immigration do not suggest a country at peace with itself. Nor may the vote leave the country at peace: it, and the process of leaving the EU, could lead to all sorts of conflicts, social, regional, political and constitutional.

The decision to leave has shocked many of the country's international friends, especially those like Japan whose companies had invested in the UK as a base from which to serve EU markets under a consistent set of laws and regulations. Security relationships, in NATO and with the United States, are unlikely to be much affected, unless the UK proves unable to afford to maintain its armed forces at a strong enough level to meet the country's international commitments. But the economic waters will be choppy for several years to come.

Nevertheless, it also wouldn't be right to see the vote as indicating that the UK is, behind the bonhomie and prosperity of London, an angry, alienated place. If it were, why would the country have re-elected David Cameron and his

Conservative Party to government in the general election of 2015, even giving him a surprise absolute majority in Parliament, albeit on only 36.9% of the vote? Indeed, part of the narrative that was used to back the campaign to leave the EU was a distinctly positive, upbeat, confident one.

A key difference between the UK's first referendum about EU membership in 1975 (which was also the country's first ever national referendum) and the one in 2016 was that in 1975 the British felt economically weak and defensive, and saw themselves as having to choose whether or not to join their more prosperous, more successful European neighbours as part of a self-rescue plan. In 2016, the European neighbours were seen as relative failures, thanks to their debts, their slower economic growth and their struggle to manage the flow of refugees across and around the Mediterranean. Voluble pro-Leave campaigners such as Daniel Hannan, a Tory member of the European Parliament, and Douglas Carswell, the UK Independence Party's sole Westminster MP, relished every chance they found to liken the UK's EU membership to being "shackled to a corpse". A key part of the Brexiteers' psychology was one of a renewed confidence in the UK's ability to stand on its own, just as part of the Scottish National Party's argument for independence in 2014 was one of confidence in Scotland's resilience and its unity. Both the Scottish nationalists and the EU leavers may have been arrogant and even deluded, but they were not lacking in confidence.

There was also, though, a sour side to both votes. The sourness was partly economic: in Scotland's case a lingering resentment dating back to the 1980s at the demise of old industries such as coalmining and shipbuilding; in the UK's case a legacy of stagnant or falling household incomes ever since the global financial crisis began in 2008 which could not be blamed on the EU but perhaps could be blamed on the elites that favoured EU membership. This national legacy can be traced both to the grossly negligent regulation of the City of London that gave rise to the crash of 2008 and its costly and painful consequences, and to economic and social failures during the decades that preceded it in some of the country's poorer regions.

John Lanchester, an author, writing in *London Review of Books* after the Brexit referendum, gave his view of Britain's divisions and sourness:

> *To be born in many places in Britain is to suffer an irreversible lifelong*
> *defeat – a truncation of opportunity, of education, of access to power, of life*

expectancy ... the vista instead is a landscape where there is often work ... but it's unsatisfying, insecure and low paid. This new work doesn't do what the old work did: it doesn't offer a sense of identity or community or self-worth ... What, over the last few decades, has been the political "offer" to these people? In truth, nothing much.

The Lanchester view, in other words, is that those like Damian Barr who escape down Thatcher's ladders from small industrial towns in Scotland are exceptions, not rules. His description of the geographical differences in perceptions of opportunity, social mobility and health could, rightly or wrongly, be applied to a number of other Western countries too, certainly the United States but also France and some places in Germany, especially in the former East Germany. Most pertinently, however, his reference to the lack of a political "offer" goes on to imply that something else must be rotten in the state of the UK beyond raw economics, something that helps to explain why not much of an offer has been made, in the form of either mitigation of the blows dealt to incomes and economic prospects by industrial change, or concerted efforts to enable the replacement of old industries with new ones.

This lingering resentment at the inadequacy of the political offer is related to the steady, long-term breakdown of the British electoral system, and with it the sense of a reasonable equality of political rights and voice across the whole nation. What had been, principally, a two-party system that corresponded chiefly to class and income has become a fragmented, multi-party system, made more complicated by regional parties in Scotland, Wales and Northern Ireland but also featuring a decline in the old class identification with the Conservatives or Labour. Despite this, the electoral system under which winners take all in first-past-the-post constituency voting remains one that implicitly assumes that there are two dominant political parties. In the old days, there was a strong incentive for such parties to make a political offer to poorer voters, as their votes were needed for victory. This is much less true today.

In 1970, the Labour and Conservative parties between them collected 89.5% of the vote in the general election held in that year, an election in which 72% of the electorate turned out to vote. In 2015, the combined share of Labour and the Tories had fallen by 20 percentage points to 67.3%, and the Conservatives achieved a working majority in Parliament with just 36.9% of the vote, on an

FIG 5.1 **British general elections, 1945–2015** Turnout and winning party's share of the vote, %

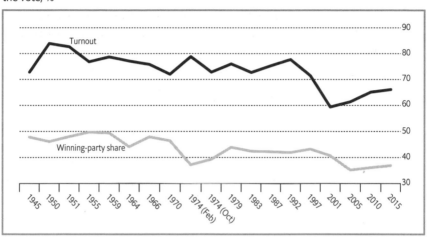

Source: UK Political Info

electoral turnout of 66.1%. When Thatcher came to power in 1979 she did so with 43.9% of the vote, on a turnout of 76% (see Figure 5.1).

Out of long historical habit and a liking for decisive, rapidly formed governments, the British still purport to favour single-party administrations over coalitions, even though the fragmentation of the party system has made coalitions the more logical and legitimate solution. A referendum in 2011 to make the electoral system more proportional was defeated heavily. The coalition between Conservatives and Liberal Democrats that governed the UK in 2010–15, the country's first formal coalition government since 1945, was unloved, and in the 2015 election the smaller coalition partner was almost wiped out from Parliament, its share of the vote slumping from 23% to 7.9%. Yet coalition government and a more proportional electoral system look increasingly desirable from the point of view of equality of political rights, as well as from that of stability. It is the old system, one that in 2015 chose a government through the votes of little more than a fifth of the overall electorate, that now looks unstable.

As a system for national elections, the current one has long looked unfair to the Scots, especially as the Conservative Party's representation in Scotland has dwindled to almost nothing, and given that the Scottish Labour Party too took a beating in the 2015 elections. Those elections handed a single party, the Scottish National Party, 56 of the 59 Scottish seats at Westminster on a vote share of 50%. The big grievance behind the 2014 independence referendum was already one of another sort of political inequality: a belief that Scottish voters had too little voice over policies being decided in Westminster but implemented in Scotland, despite the establishment of a devolved parliament (elected by proportional representation through what is called an "Additional Member System") and government in 1999. This grievance is likely to grow.

Some of the same sentiment – dislike of decisions being made by powers far away – lay behind the EU referendum vote. But so too did another set of grievances about unequal political rights. Pressure inside the Conservative Party for a referendum to be held, and the move to centre-stage of what had once been a fringe, single-issue movement, the UK Independence Party (UKIP), reflected a feeling that opinions against the EU and against immigration were finding no hearing thanks to the first-past-the-post electoral system.

There was a constitutional argument too for the issue of EU membership to be decided by referendum, which is also why the country's first ever referendum took place, the one in 1975 to confirm the membership to which the UK had signed up two years earlier. As the UK has no written constitution, its sole constitutional principle is the sovereignty of Parliament. But a basic principle of parliamentary, that is representative, government is that while the people thus delegate the power of decision-making over laws to MPs, they do not thereby empower those MPs to decide to transfer that lawmaking power to anyone else. In 1975 it was argued that to have legitimacy, a transfer of powers to the European Community needed a direct mandate from the people, and that was the underlying argument for 2016 too.

Analysis of the result by Geoffrey Evans, a fellow in politics and sociology at Nuffield College, Oxford and co-director of the British Election Study, suggests that the roots of the Brexit victory can be found in the alienation of working-class voters from general elections since the 1990s.[5] Their turnout levels, which had previously been similar to those of middle- or upper-class citizens, had plummeted: in 2015, Evans says, turnout among degree-level middle-class voters was 83%; that among lowly educated working-class voters was 48%. To become electable in the first-past-the-post system, Labour had under Blair's leadership (1994–2007) chosen more or less to ignore working-class voters' concerns and to focus on appealing to middle-class voters instead. It was a successful strategy – Labour won three successive general elections – but one with consequences. Moreover, many traditional working-class voters live in constituencies which are safe Labour seats, so may have felt their votes did not really matter. They assuredly did not influence Blair's policy of allowing citizens of the new EU member countries to begin migrating to the UK in 2004. But finally, on June 23rd 2016, those working-class votes counted. Turnout among such voters in the referendum was much higher than in the general election a year earlier.

What those votes may also have reflected, however, is that in the UK perceptions of being "working class" are different from the definitions used by socio-economic analysis. Another study, the annual British Social Attitudes report, which was released just after the referendum, revealed a surprising finding that 60% of British people consider themselves to be working class. Based on the objective measures of income, expenditure and occupation that are normally used by social researchers the figure is 25%. Among those 60% were even included 47% of those demonstrably in the professional and managerial classes.

This could be dismissed as just a cultural quirk, a relic of a society that was once sharply defined by class not just in perceptions but also on objective measures. This may be true, but it matters politically in so far as it may mean that working-class values – including suspicion of both immigration and of cosmopolitanism – extend more widely in the electorate than general election results and political parties' policies may have suggested.

One of the big questions for politics and government now is how far this balance of views, manifested in the referendum, can and should influence public policies, party programmes and even the agenda for constitutional reform. Much of the debate in the UK over the past decade has been about income inequality, even though measured in the traditional way by the Gini coefficient[6] family incomes in the UK are far more evenly distributed than in the United States and inequality levels are similar to those in other countries in Europe. According to World Bank research, the UK in 2014 had a Gini coefficient of 32.6, while that in the US was 41.1, in France 33.1, in Italy 35.2, in Sweden 27.3 and in Switzerland 31.6. Measured in this way, inequality in the UK has even declined a little since the 2008 financial crisis, though that fact has not made the continued success of the country's richest citizens, especially bankers, any easier for those on the left to stomach. But, as Chapter 2 argued for the West as a whole, the inequality grievance is no longer simply a matter of incomes. It is now more importantly a matter of the inequality of political voice and influence over public policy that big differences in wealth can bring.

Political parties could, in principle, decide to view the referendum as having been a one-off, an exception not a new rule. However, the huge gap it revealed between opinions as expressed in the 2015 general election and those in the 2016 vote will be hard to ignore. Any government, indeed any major political party, that decides that the strength of feeling against immigration shown in 2016 can be taken lightly or even disregarded will be taking a big risk, especially as British politics is looking more volatile than for many years.

UKIP is heavily discriminated against by the electoral system, as 2015 showed when it won 12.6% of the vote but just one seat in Parliament. Research by Evans and Jonathan Mellon (also from Nuffield College, Oxford) for the British Election Study, *Are Leave Voters Mainly UKIP?*, found that between February 2014 and May 2016, 35% of respondents to their survey admitted to having voted UKIP at least once at an election at some level, that is local, devolved, mayoral, national or European. Having achieved the party's principal aim of Brexit, UKIP might now fade away. But equally, it could become a home for any voters who end up feeling betrayed by post-Brexit policies or party programmes. In a first-past-the-post electoral system, if that were to happen UKIP could even, in theory, suddenly jump from one seat in Parliament to becoming the second-biggest party, or even to holding an absolute majority. The fear of that prospect might, alternatively, lead the Conservatives or Labour, or both, to adopt UKIP's stance against cosmopolitanism and immigration.

It ought also to make those two old, mainstream parties take seriously at last[7] the case for two big political reforms. The first is electoral reform, to bring in a more proportional voting system, one that accommodates and provides a framework for the fragmentation of the party system rather than remaining in denial of it, as now. A properly multi-party system, with coalition governments the norm, would have the merit of restoring a greater sense of equality of political rights and voice to a larger share of the population. Such reform would have been desirable regardless of the Brexit vote. The case for the second has been increased by Brexit: constitutional reform to make the government of the UK formally federal, with either a separate English Parliament or several English regional assemblies, with devolved powers of both expenditure and taxation arranged far more equally than now across the whole UK. Without that, a new referendum for Scottish independence seems inevitable. It may come anyway, if the terms for exiting the EU find enough disfavour in Scotland. But the UK could survive such a vote, if the devolved, federal system could meanwhile be made more coherent and more durable.

Britain revived the idea of the West triumphantly during the 1980s and 1990s by restoring openness. This helped create new personal and social freedoms, as well as defeating the selfish forces that were harming its democracy. But it paid too high a price in terms of equality, developing a new inequality of political rights and voice, the consequences of which were seen especially in the 2008 financial calamity and in the alienation that followed it. Now, in its time of introspection, it needs political reforms so as to recreate the *isonomia*, the equality of political rights. Such reforms need also to be accompanied by a renewed emphasis in public spending on education, to maintain the sense of equality of opportunity, and on infrastructure, to reduce the wide gaps in productivity and modernity that exist between the wealthy south-east and the rest of the country.

For Britain to turn inwards following Brexit, to close its borders and become isolationist, feels almost as inconceivable given the country's history and culture as it would be for a smaller trading nation such as Sweden or Switzerland. This is a country that has a Canadian citizen heading its central bank, a Portuguese citizen managing its most famous football team, Manchester United, and foreigners of countless nationalities running its biggest companies. But to remain open, now that the country will be outside the EU and outside all the constraints that membership imposed on the protectionist, subsidising instincts of national politicians, Britain is going to have to restore equality of voice by giving its political system at least as big a shake-up as Thatcher gave its economic system. Without that equality, British openness cannot last.

6

European paralysis

Change? Why change? Aren't things bad enough as they are?

Lord Salisbury, 1830–1903

Everything needs to change, so that everything can stay the same.

Giuseppe Tomasi di Lampedusa, *The Leopard*, 1958

UNTIL BREXIT, advocates of the European Union could always shrug off its many troubles by pointing out that things could not be all that bad since this was a club that nobody had ever chosen to leave and which countries were queuing up to join. The same could be said of the EU's most ambitious project yet, the euro single currency, which was launched in 1999 by 11 of the then 15 EU members and which, despite a horrendous series of sovereign-debt dramas from 2010 onwards, had by 2016 expanded its membership to 19 countries.[1] Greece had looked likely to leave the euro and probably the EU after its referendum in July 2015 rejected its creditors' financial rescue terms by the huge margin of 61% to 39%. But when the creditors didn't budge and the Syriza party's left-wing government peered over the precipice on which they realised their country was standing, they decided not to jump and gave in to the creditors instead. No one would ever leave, it seemed. Until, in their referendum a year later, the British chose to do exactly that. The curtain had been pulled aside, and the Wizard of Oz had been revealed to be human.

In truth, the magic had long gone. What the Brexit vote made clear was that countries are members of the EU out of self-interest, and their views of how their interests are best served can change, rightly or wrongly. What it also represented was a decision by British voters to at best weaken the EU, at worst kick it in the teeth, at a time when it was anyway in a rather sickly state. Few are heard to dispute the view that Europe is in decline, a judgment which most analysts believe applies both to many of the individual countries of western Europe and to the supranational institutions that they began to create in 1951 with the European Coal and Steel Community, which begat the European Economic Community in 1957, which in turn became known as the European Union in 1993. The EU's political influence is in decline, its institutional coherence and sense of solidarity is in decline, its economic strength is in decline, and thanks to the effects of that economic weakness on most countries' public finances, its ability to maintain the welfare system that has long been an integral part of the European way of life is also in decline. Look a few decades ahead at the impact of ageing and in Germany's case declining populations on those welfare costs, and you may be even more convinced that the EU's best days are behind it. The question for this chapter, however, is whether this is necessarily true for all time, or whether some of the stuck European countries could in future look less like the Wizard of Oz and more like the great escapologist Harry Houdini.

The picture is far from pretty, the traps and chains tight and forbidding. For much of the past decade, European governments have been wriggling desperately in the grip of successive, sometimes simultaneous dramas and panics, of which Brexit is just the latest, though the most directly institution-shattering.

The 2008 global financial crash was the first, a crash which originated in the US but which quickly exposed the fragility of many European banks, sent unemployment rising a lot higher in the EU than in the United States and caused property markets to collapse in Spain and Ireland. Then two years later it emerged as a second crisis, a full-blown sovereign-debt panic in the euro zone, with several mainly southern European countries struggling to avoid insolvency. The UK's humiliation of 1976, of a rich country having to go cap in hand to the IMF for emergency loans, was repeated in the euro-zone bail-outs (jointly financed by the IMF and solvent euro-zone countries) for Greece, Ireland, Portugal and Cyprus.[2] It all seemed so unfair: the original crash was an American mess-up, and yet it was now hurting Europeans much more than it hurt Americans.

Russia's annexation of Crimea in 2014 and fostering of conflict in Ukraine was the third drama, though it was a story that had long been foretold by the Russian-Georgian war of 2008, which had pulled two breakaway provinces,

Abkhazia and South Ossetia, definitively out of Georgia and into the Russian camp. It also followed an unseemly tug of war between the EU and Russia over which of them Ukraine should sign a trade and investment deal with, a deal that Russians believed could if struck with the EU be a path to full membership and perhaps even to joining NATO.

EU countries did at least achieve a quite impressive unity from 2014 onwards over the imposition of economic sanctions on Russia, a unity that they signally failed to achieve over the fourth and most politically destabilising challenge, the flow of millions of refugees and economic migrants into the EU fleeing from wars in the Middle East and North Africa, and from poverty or discontent further afield. Unnervingly, this fourth challenge coincided with and became inevitably conflated with a fifth, that of terrorism in European cities, an outgrowth of the civil wars in Syria and Iraq from which the migrants have been fleeing. Mass killings in Paris, Brussels, Nice and Berlin, and smaller but still horrifying attacks in other European cities, produced a political atmosphere of emergency and extreme insecurity.

It has been the migrant crisis, above all, that has done most damage to the whole idea of the EU, including encouraging Britons to vote to leave. After all, if the EU has any purpose it ought surely to be to enable its member countries to collaborate to solve collective problems arising in their common neighbourhood, which is exactly what the migrant issue is. No single country would have been able to deal easily with tens of thousands, then hundreds of thousands, of refugees arriving in boats on their shores or trudging across their borders, and many would just have been tempted to divert as many migrants as possible to neighbouring countries.

Such a problem cries out for a collective solution, but efforts to achieve one in order to police the EU's combined external border or to manage the asylum-seekers once inside have left national governments crying out in rage against each other, even more than during the euro crisis, which is saying a lot. One of the great symbolic achievements of the EU, the Schengen Agreement on borderless, passport-free travel and trade, which was first agreed in 1985 and by 2016 comprised 26 European countries (including Switzerland, Norway and Iceland but not the UK and Ireland), has in effect been suspended, with borders reimposed "temporarily" by seven countries.[3] Above all, the migrant crisis has made Europe look feeble and dysfunctional and given back respectability to the idea of controlling your own borders and your own immigration policy.

In the thick of these crises, British Brexiteers shouted that the EU does not want to be reformed, ignoring the way in which the migrant and terrorist challenges in particular were rocking every part of the EU and many of its member states. They wanted to discredit the efforts by their own prime minister, David Cameron, to prove otherwise through his pre-referendum "renegotiation". The accusation missed the point twice over.

The EU has no mind of its own on whether to reform or not: any changes in its rules or the way it works are decided by its 28 national governments, so any such decision is the sum of the minds of those countries' leaders and of their domestic political circumstances at the time, circumstances that in 2015–16 were dominated by the migrant challenge. But second, and even more important, the EU's malaise is not principally or even largely an institutional or supranational one. It is a malaise with its main economic, social and political origins at national level. This is where the chief resistance to reform is found, just as it was in the 1970s in the UK.

What has changed in recent years is that in the past, EU institutions, laws and intergovernmental agreements acted as a means through which governments could ease their national problems or overcome national political constraints and rigidities. The EU was a solution, not a problem in itself. This process is no longer working, partly because of the enlargement of the EU from 15 to 28 countries of which the UK was one of the most enthusiastic advocates, and which has made supranational decision-making harder. But chiefly it is no longer working because of the euro.

Europe's single currency was born in 1999 of many motives, some political and some economic, but prominent among them was the belief that the pressure and discipline of a common currency and monetary policy would force countries to shake themselves up internally, to restore their own dynamism by removing interest groups' privileges and dismantling obstacles to enterprise and innovation. It would be the latest and most powerful of the long series of EU or intergovernmental tools that acted to make countries more open, less rigid and more dynamic than they would be if left to their own devices. Unfortunately it didn't.

If anything, it did the reverse, by making it much cheaper for people, companies and governments in previously inflation-prone and economically unstable countries such as Ireland, Spain and Greece to borrow, cutting their interest rates to German levels and creating artificial economic booms. In highly indebted Italy, euro membership lowered the cost to the taxpayer of servicing public debt and so reduced the pressure to control or repay it. There was less discipline, not more. Then, when the credit bubble burst after 2008, EU countries' underlying economic weaknesses and rigidities were laid bare.

In 2012 a new, more disciplined framework of rules was agreed in response to the sovereign-debt crisis, chiefly to restrict national fiscal deficits, but it has acted more like a prison than a self-improvement tool. Despite the fiscal restrictions and the associated requirements for austerity, euro-zone sovereign-debt burdens have risen rather than fallen, from an overall 91.3% of GDP in 2012 to more than 93% in 2015, according to the IMF. This overall debt ratio conceals a telling difference between countries: Germany's public-debt ratio fell during those years but the ratios in France, Italy and Greece all rose, while those in Spain and Portugal only barely stabilised. Ireland is the sole example of a bailed-out, austerity-constrained euro-zone country that has succeeded in lowering its public-debt ratio markedly, from a peak of 120% of GDP in 2012–13 to 94% in 2015.

Some say this insistence on fiscal austerity was unavoidable because financial markets had become too spooked by the spectre of sovereign defaults among the euro zone's biggest debtors. Others believe that it reflects a German misdiagnosis of the currency area's sickness as being one of public profligacy rather than private excesses (including notably by Germany's own banks). In all the bailed-out countries bar Greece, public-debt levels before 2008 were low and under control: they rose after the Lehman shock only when governments stepped in to support economies and their banking systems. Italy and France had high public-debt levels throughout the period, but they have not gone bankrupt and so have not had to be bailed out. Others, more sympathetic to the German position, hold that the only way to keep pressure on national governments to open up their economies has been to deny them the fiscal scope to keep on putting off their rainy days. Probably, a fair reading would be that it has been a combination of all three. The outcome, however, has been poor.

Two of the most troubled countries, Ireland and Spain, have achieved impressive economic turnarounds, and both have introduced a number of liberalising reforms. But the euro zone as a whole has not succeeded in reviving itself, so that unemployment edged below 10% of the workforce only in the late autumn of 2016. Greece, the sickest case, has made little economic progress, though it has implemented many reforms demanded by its creditors.

Austerity might have been necessary for those debtors that were in need of bail-outs, on the principle that when you are in a hole it is best to stop digging, but the trouble is that it has been applied to every euro-zone country, hole-dwellers and those on moral high ground alike, with consequently depressing effects on overall demand. Even the IMF, which traditionally is a champion of fiscal austerity for sovereign bankrupts on the stop-digging principle, has turned against the idea in the euro zone. On its analysis, creditor countries, essentially northern European ones including Germany, should have been following a more expansionary fiscal policy in order to maintain demand, even as the bankrupts made their necessary cuts. The IMF also believes that the most unsustainable sovereign debts – essentially those of Greece – need to be written off and/or restructured rather than refinanced, just as they were for Latin American debtors during that continent's sovereign-debt troubles of the 1980s and early 1990s. Private-sector lenders to Greece have written down their debts, but public-sector ones – which now, led by the European Central Bank, account for almost all Greece's sovereign debt – have not. They have lowered Greece's interest costs but not tackled the debt itself.

This is an argument about economic policy, but one that has political consequences. These fiscal restraints and the consequently slow economic recovery have made countries fractious with one another, vulnerable to populist political parties, and wobbly in facing up boldly to other pressures, such as those from Russia or Islamic State. Terrorist attacks are unnerving at the best of times, for that is their intention, but when your nerves are already frayed by economic woes, their impact can be even greater.

*

That is the short-term picture, if a term that has lasted over eight years since the global financial crisis can be called short. But several simple facts show that the decline of western Europe is also a long-term, deep-rooted affair, originating in nations rather than in the EU. Let's start in grand, basic science: during the 1980s, intellectuals working in countries that are now in the EU or European Economic Area won 29.1% of all Nobel prizes, behind the United States with 54%.[4] During the 1990s, however, Europe's share fell to 23%, while the US took 68%. In 2000–16, Europe again won about 23% of Nobel prizes while the US took 43% (and China entered the scene, winning 1.7%).

Or look at technology: in France's Minitel information and messaging service, launched nationwide in 1982, Europe then had what was in many ways the pioneer of what is now the world wide web, and indeed the web itself was first invented by a Briton, Sir Tim Berners-Lee, working at CERN, the European high-energy physics research lab on the Franco-Swiss border near Geneva. Now, none of the giant firms that lead in using the internet or digital technology is European. The Skype internet telephony service was invented and developed by Swedes and Estonians, but is now owned by Microsoft. For nearly 15 years up to 2012 the world's leading maker of mobile phones was Nokia of Finland. But Nokia's failure to keep up with the development of smartphones meant it lost out to Samsung, HTC of Taiwan and the makers of Apple's iPhones. In 2013 Nokia sold its handset business to Microsoft, which then flogged it on at a big loss to Foxconn of Taiwan in 2016. This slide in technology is reflected in broader data: the EU as a whole devotes 1.9% of GDP to spending on research and development, both private and public, compared with 2.9% in the US and 3.3% in Japan. In 2000, innovators in the EU registered 12% of the world's new patents; a decade later their share of new registrations had fallen to 5%. China's had risen from 2.5% to 17.3% in that period, three times that in the EU.

Next, look at the main economic data that underlies living standards and social health. From 1950 until the mid-1980s, unemployment rates in western European countries were always below those in the US (see Figure 6.1). Since the mid-1980s, they have always been higher, apart from a brief period after the 2008 crash which hit the US so hard.

Moreover, from 1950 until the early 1990s, productivity levels in western Europe were always narrowing the gap with the country that was by then at the world's productivity frontier – the United States. Freer trade globally and inside the EEC, improvements in public education, stable governments and a big flow of foreign direct investment by US companies helped the Europeans catch up, enjoying the strongest and most sustained period of economic growth during the three decades to 1980 that they had ever had – what in French became known as *les trentes années glorieuses*, the 30 glorious years.

The best, most comprehensive recent study of the European economy is the World Bank's 2012 *Golden Growth* report. The authors described the EEC/EU as having acted as a "convergence machine", using open trade and the transfer of ideas, people and funds to drive poorer countries to catch up with richer ones,

FIG 6.1 **Unemployment rate, 1955–2015** % of civilian labour force

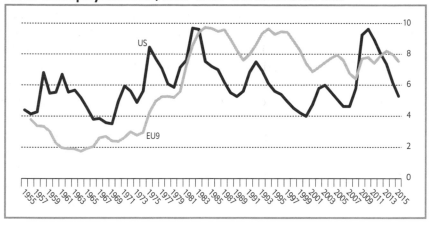

Source: OECD

maintaining the rich countries' growth too, and allowing the whole of western Europe in turn to close the gap with the United States.

Those *années glorieuses* took place despite the fact that the European continent was divided by an Iron Curtain. The fall of that curtain, of the Berlin wall and of the Soviet empire in 1989–91 ought to have given the continent a new economic lease of life, a new period during which the convergence machine could work its wonders. And it did to some extent, as many of the former communist countries of central and eastern Europe first achieved freer trade with the EU during the 1990s and then became full members in 2004. But that effect was not sufficient to prevent a more ominous development: since the early 1990s, west European productivity has been falling behind US productivity again as European companies and governments have proved slower at implementing and exploiting information and communications technology. Figure 6.2 is based on data in the *Golden Growth* report.

It is not that western Europe's overall economic performance has been dire: looked at over the course of the past two decades, and measured by GDP per head rather than simple GDP growth so as to reflect population changes, it has not been all that much different from that in the US. But it needed to be better in Europe, for two big reasons: to reduce western Europe's chronically

FIG 6.2 **EU productivity relative to the US, 1950–2016** US = 100 (weighted)

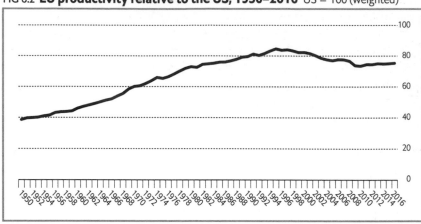

Source: World Bank

high levels of unemployment, which threaten social division; and to finance European welfare spending, which is so much higher than in the US.

Here can be brought in what have become known as German chancellor Angela Merkel's favourite facts, which she tended to use during euro sovereign-debt talks to lecture other governments on what needed to be done. She was said to enjoy producing from her bag a piece of paper carrying three numbers, which she repeated in a 2012 interview with the *Financial Times*:[5]

> *If Europe today accounts for just over 7% of the world's population, produces around 25% of global GDP and has to finance 50% of global social spending, then it's obvious that it will have to work very hard to maintain its prosperity and way of life.*

According to Eurostat, the 28 EU countries' share of global GDP (at market exchange rates) in 2013 was 23.7%, compared with 22.2% in the US. Thanks to the rapid growth of China and other emerging economies, the share of both the EU and the US has long been falling. Just a decade earlier, in 2003, the EU-28's share had been 30.7% and that of the United States 29.7%. In that ten-year period China's share nearly trebled, from 4.3% to 12.1% in 2013. Such trends are inevitable and not particularly worrying as long as the global pie is itself growing. Similarly, between 1960 and 2013 the EU-28's share of world population fell from 13.4% to 7.1% and that of the US from 6% to 4.4%, as EU and US birth rates declined a lot faster than those in poorer parts of the world. Yet these output and population numbers are not the most important part of Merkel's message. It is the social spending.

Her phrasing is a bit misleading. Although EU countries are big aid donors, the social spending (pensions, disability benefits, unemployment insurance, and family and housing benefits) she refers to is money paid out domestically, not globally. So in reality, her favourite fact indicates that European countries spend far more on their own social welfare systems than any one else does on theirs, which most relevantly means far more than other rich countries such as the US and Japan do. To put this in context, data in the *Golden Growth* report show that in 2004–09 European countries accounted for 58% of all spending worldwide on social protection while the United States accounted for 43% of all military spending worldwide in 2010. Which would you rather be, the biggest spender on guns or the biggest on social welfare? It is not so bad to be the world's welfare champions.

The real question, as Merkel points out, is whether you can afford it. But also there is a second, related issue, which is the effect of this spending on your own economic performance. To an important extent, the problem is circular: the more a country spends on welfare the less able it is to afford to spend so much on welfare. And then, following the argument of Chapter 3, we should note that democracy's habit of self-entrapment is particularly strong with this sort of public spending, for once flows of welfare benefits have been captured by a group of voters, that group will resist fiercely any attempt to reduce their payments and politicians will be loath to force them to. This is why such welfare payments have become known as "entitlements".

There are two ways in which this economic trap can be set. One arises when high levels of taxation have to be imposed to finance the welfare spending. This could in the past have been described as the Swedish problem until that country's reforms in the 1990s (see Chapter 8). Now it might be termed the French problem, with public spending in France at over 55% of GDP, more than five percentage points higher than in Sweden and ten higher than in Germany. France has run a budget deficit continuously since 1974, so this is also why its public debt keeps on rising and is now nearly 94% of GDP. Italy created its own public-debt problem by running a budget deficit averaging nearly 10% a year from 1973 to 1995, spending the money in particular on public pensions. Which is why Italy's public debt to GDP ratio is now more than 130%, second only in the euro zone to Greece (175%). It does not leave much room for manoeuvre.

Some countries are more willing than others to accept high levels of taxation in return for public services such as welfare, depending principally on whether citizens believe the money will be well spent. Yet even in such countries, of which Sweden is one, there is a cost, for high taxes have some disincentive effect on work and on entrepreneurship, and lead some high earners to emigrate. They also act as an incentive to avoid taxes. It is hard to believe now given Sweden's law-abiding image, but in the 1970s Gunnar Myrdal, a winner of the Nobel prize in economics, bemoaned the fact that steeply progressive income taxation had turned his country into a nation of tax-evaders. A nation of tax-evaders typically becomes a nation in which the burden of taxation is increasingly borne chiefly by those unable to evade it, which means ordinary employees, whose ability to consume and save becomes correspondingly crimped. We could now call that the Italian problem.

Even more significant than those incentive effects is the issue of what the welfare money is spent on and what impact that spending has on economic activity. Unemployment insurance can have a disincentive effect of its own if the level is set too high, discouraging some people from working. But these days the much more important impact comes from publicly funded pensions. Not only are these more and more costly to the public purse as the proportion of the population that is elderly increases, but also the rules of eligibility and of retirement ages are having a bigger and bigger impact on people's choices about whether to work or retire. And the fewer people that work, the fewer there are to pay income taxes and the fewer hands there are to produce the output an economy needs.

Looking at western Europe, this can be seen as a lifestyle choice, one which is hard to object to in principle, but the real question is how practical it is. According to the *Golden Growth* report, in the 1950s western Europeans worked more hours every year than Americans did; by the 1970s their annual hours were about the same as Americans'; in 1990–2009 they worked fewer hours than Americans. Europe's problem is that this is not compensated for by higher productivity. But its even bigger problem is that in many countries Europeans' working lives are now shorter than those in the US or Japan, while their life expectancy is nearly at Japanese levels. This too may be seen as a lifestyle choice, but it has to be paid for, by somebody. The average labour-force participation rate for people aged between 55 and 64 in 2005–09 was 67.1% in Japan and 64% in the US. In western Europe (that is, the EU's pre-2004 15 member countries) it was 49.6%.

So western European countries have set a trap for themselves. To afford the welfare spending to which they have become accustomed and which is an important contributor to social trust, they need people to work more productively and for longer proportions of their lives, but the welfare spending and associated labour rules are leading Europeans to work less and for fewer years. This has been a political choice as well as a lifestyle one. Governments, notably in Italy, France and Greece, have often bought off short-term pain by using public pensions and early retirement as a substitute for unemployment insurance when big industrial restructurings have been needed or as a way to reward groups of voters.

Just to show that such political pandering is not only a feature of southern Europeans, this was done even in Germany by Merkel herself in 2013 when she formed her third cabinet. As that cabinet had to be a "grand coalition" of her Christian Democrat and Christian Social Union parties with the Social Democratic Party (SPD), she chose to accept the SPD's demand to lower the retirement age for some longer-serving[6] employees to 63, which the SPD wanted in order to pander to some of its trade union supporters. This was, admittedly, a smallish softening of a broader measure under which the official retirement age was being raised from 65 to 67, but still it was a move in the wrong direction at a time when Germany was lecturing other EU countries to tighten their fiscal belts. That said, France, one of Germany's favourite lecture targets, had made a similar backward step in 2012 when it also cut the retirement age for selected workers from 62 to 60.

To get social spending back under control requires governments to annoy some interest groups – notably pensioners, present and prospective. It also requires governments to make broader efforts to encourage people to stay in the workforce, even part-time, well past traditional ideas of retirement age, into not just their 60s but also their 70s, as this will keep them contributing to tax revenue and paying for the services of which they are among the chief beneficiaries (or, in the case of health care, soon will be). Chapter 9 shows how South Korea and Japan have become pioneers in the continued employment of the elderly, with proportions of the over-65s in their labour forces often four or five times higher than in western European countries.

If Europe could successfully match Japan in that regard, its social spending would quickly look a lot more affordable. Yet to muster the political will to alter the pension rights and retirement expectations of millions of citizens is far from easy at a time when slow growth, austerity and terrorism form the background. As Chapter 8 shows, Sweden's example from the 1990s demonstrates that welfare reforms are more palatable if at the same time growth is being revived and jobs created through liberalising measures. The two need to go hand in hand.

There can also be a tension between the increased openness that comes with liberalising measures and the desire to maintain equality, especially when welfare has to be cut. But in Sweden faster growth enabled that tension to be eased and welfare cuts to be moderated. In the case of pension reforms and later retirement ages, the chief inequality is between the young and the old, not the rich and the poor. Since the old are the parents and grandparents of the young, it ought to be easier to win the argument about this than it would be about other entitlement cuts. It ought to be, that is, as long as jobs are being created and economic hope is being restored.

*

Europe's most critical test cases for this are France and Italy – the continent's second and third biggest economies, countries which were once, even recently, two of the richest, most creative and most dynamic in the world. They are test cases in part because a dynamism that has been lost so recently ought to be able to be regained: only if something fundamental has changed should the situation be irreparable. But also they are test cases because the loss of hope and confidence that their recent troubles have caused – troubles which, in France's case, have been added to by repeated terrorist atrocities – has put their openness and even their membership of the EU at risk.

These are the two EU countries which have the highest chance of an anti-EU political party getting into government or gaining a strong influence on government in the near future, for in both places such parties have sustained scores of 25–30% of the vote in opinion polls over the course of several years. Elsewhere – the Netherlands, Sweden, Denmark, Austria, Germany, even the UK with its UKIP – populist parties have risen and have even become the largest parties on some measures but have not got fully into power. In France, the rise of the anti-EU, anti-immigrant Front National led by Marine Le Pen has been the biggest cause of concern. In Italy, the danger comes from a more middle-class insurgent anti-establishment party, the Five Star Movement founded by a comedian, Beppe Grillo, which is not formally anti-EU nor anti-immigrant but does insist that Italy should hold a referendum on its membership of the euro. If that were to happen, the impact on financial markets would be no laughing matter.

France was once the byword for novelty, innovation, even daring, whether in art or science, fashion or society, literature or music. Young people, especially young Americans, flocked to Paris a century ago to breathe in its air of freedom and experimentation, exaggerated though the idea of Parisian libertarianism might have been, and still in the 1950s could be intoxicated by the idea of sitting next to Jean-Paul Sartre or Simone de Beauvoir in the café Les Deux Magots or being a fashionable radical in 1968. Italy had been one of Europe's poorest countries before the second world war, but in the decades that followed 1945 it grew richer and richer, not just in wealth but also in culture, all aspects of design, and even in social and corporate organisation. To drive an Italian car, to wear an Italian suit, to watch an Italian film were all measures of sophistication, of being on the frontier of thought and achievement.

France and Italy are still marvellous places to visit and to study. They are still among the world's richest nations. What they are not, however, is dynamic – at least not by their own past standards. Paris is no longer the creative hub of Europe: that title has moved during the past two decades to London. Paris could be considered the 21st-century Venice, beautiful, redolent with history, but no longer really going places. Worse, this modern Venice is surrounded by troubled, impoverished suburbs – while the English word is generally taken to imply areas of leafy middle-class calm, of houses with gardens, the French word, *les banlieues*, signifies dreary housing estates on the edge of the city, with high levels of crime, poverty and unemployment, often dominated by immigrant populations from North Africa and the Middle East, and prone to periodic outbursts of violence.

Italy really went places during the 1950s and 1960s, a period during which it ranked as the third-fastest-growing economy in the world, behind Japan and South Korea, recording an average annual growth rate in real GDP of 5.8% a year. But it moved off the frontier of thought and achievement during the 1970s when it was riven by strikes and terrorist violence, and only a surge of public spending and borrowing during the 1980s kept up its *Bella Figura*. Since its combined political and financial crisis of the early 1990s, the country has stagnated, exhibiting the medical condition described in the title of the 2013 documentary film about Italy (co-authored by me and the director Annalisa Piras), *Girlfriend in a Coma*.[7] In 2016 its economy remained 10% smaller than it had been before the 2008 crash while others – Germany, the UK, the United States – had more than made up the ground they had lost. And it had been doing badly during the decade before then too.

France's economic performance has been merely mediocre, not as bad as that in Italy. In France, persistently high unemployment is the clearest sign that neither the economy nor society has been functioning well. Another is the preponderance of companies with 49 employees or fewer. This is because an array of laws and regulations – 34 in all, according to the 2008 official commission on growth chaired by Jacques Attali, an intellectual and former political adviser – governing labour and much else comes into play when a company reaches 50 employees. France has plenty of successful multinationals but a vast empty space where you would expect medium-size companies to be found, thanks to all those laws, social-security taxes and the like.

In Italy, unemployment has also been high, but the clearest indicator there of dysfunction can be seen in household incomes. McKinsey Global Institute, the consultancy's think-tank, published a study in July 2016 called *Poorer than their Parents? Flat or Falling Incomes in Advanced Economies*, which identified a phenomenon shared across the whole of the West: in 25 advanced economies 65–70% of households had incomes in 2014 that were the same as or below the level of 2005, in real terms, before taking account of taxes and public transfers. After taxes and transfers, the number suffering stagnation or decline fell to 20–25%. The worst country of all, however, on this measure was Italy. There 97% of households had flat or falling incomes before taxes and transfers in that ten-year period, or 100% once such government interventions are taken into account. Usually, especially in welfare-conscious Europe, you would expect government interventions to ease the pain for households. In Italy they made it worse.

They did so mainly because of the long legacy of Italy's financial crunch in 1991, when investors lost faith in the government's ability to service its public debts, because those debts were huge – by 1995, nearly 120% of GDP, one of the highest ratios in the EU at the time – and because a big corruption scandal had discredited the two political parties that had governed the country for much of the past few decades, the Christian Democrats and the Socialists. A run on lira assets drove the currency out of the EU's Exchange Rate Mechanism, the precursor to the euro. Most Italian governments since then have felt obliged to keep their borrowing under tight control for fear of a new financial crunch and of rising borrowing costs. This constraint also helps explain why Italy was so keen to join the euro at its launch in 1999, even having to make some short-term budget cuts in order to qualify: joining promised a fall in interest rates and thus in the costs of servicing all that public debt.

Such fiscal restraint has held back economic growth. But lower interest rates after joining the euro ought, in principle, to have boosted the economy, countering that contraction. They did not, because the other reason for the country's long record of slow or no growth is that so many obstacles have been placed in the way of both enterprise and work that companies, whether Italian or foreign, have not wanted to invest their capital in the country. The then governor of the Bank of Italy, Mario Draghi, now president of the European Central Bank, put it well in a speech in 2011 at a Bank of Italy conference examining the country's economic record since unification 150 years earlier in 1861:

> In the Venice of the sixteenth century or the Amsterdam of the seventeenth, societies that were then rich, a long period of great dynamism was followed by the weakening of the commitment to compete, to innovate. The forces once directed at the pursuit of growth became redirected towards the defence of small or big privileges that had been acquired by various organised social groups. In a stagnant economy, these defensive mechanisms and the promotion of special interests become reinforced.

No one present had any doubt that in these phrases Draghi was describing contemporary Italy, in terms with which Mancur Olson would have been familiar.

One of the proudest claims that one hears in Italy is that "Made in Italy" remains an admired and valued brand, worldwide, representing an image of artisan craftsmanship, high quality and good design. It does, but a slogan that would more truthfully sum up the country would be "Obstructed in Italy". For this is a country full of strengths, ideas and excellence, many of which are obstructed by regulatory barriers imposed by local and central government, by professional and trade associations and cartels, by trade unions, by a slow-moving and dysfunctional justice system, by political interference and by organised crime.

Many Italian companies, even ones that have worldwide reputations, remain small by international standards because it can be costly and risky to become big: labour laws penalise you if you employ more than 15 workers; politicians and criminals (sometimes the same people) start to demand favours the larger you get; the cost of enforcing contracts in the courts becomes more significant; and, in some sectors, you may need a separate licence to operate in other cities and regions of the country, let alone abroad. Keeping your head down and staying small is a safer option. Yet it wasn't always like that. In the 1950s and 1960s Italian entrepreneurs were ambitious and often gung-ho, with firms like Olivetti cutting a dash in office machinery and with early computers.

Massimo Banzi, a young inventor who co-developed a piece of open-source hardware, a circuit board called Arduino (or Genuino outside the US), which has played a part in the development of 3D printing and other new technologies, put the contemporary problem nicely in a 2014 interview for *Girlfriend in a Coma*. If he were to invent something outside Italy, he said ruefully: "People will say 'Wow'. But in Italy, they just try to stop you." Indeed, the Ivrea Interaction Design Institute in Italy where he and his colleagues developed Arduino had itself been stopped in 2005 when its sponsors, Telecom Italia, decided not to renew its funding.

This is the vicious circle in which Italy has caught itself. It needs innovation, investment and growth if it is to afford the nearly 16% of GDP that it is currently spending every year on public pensions. Yet to release that innovation and investment requires privileges and protections to be given up by all sorts of companies, professions and groups that have been made more determined to hang on to their entitlements by the years of stagnation.

Italy is not alone in facing this sort of self-imposed trap. As public spending on pensions is the single best measure of the burden of welfare entitlements and the impact they have on the public finances, it is worth listing the top five countries in the OECD on this measure.[8] At the top is Italy (15.8% of GDP), followed by Greece (14.5%), France (13.8%), Austria (13.2%) and Portugal (13%). All the top 10 countries in the OECD in terms of public spending on pensions are EU members, but these five stand out as having a particular problem.

The best international assessment of the rigidity or fluency of countries' regulatory systems is the World Bank's annual "Doing Business" rankings, which measure how easy it is to start a business, pay taxes, enforce contracts, get connected to electricity and information technology, acquire land and so forth. In other words, how easy it is to do business. The top-ranking countries are not laisser-faire, free-for-all capitalist wonderlands but are simply efficient. They are New Zealand, Singapore, Denmark and South Korea. On the list, the 28 EU countries fare very differently from one another, giving the lie to claims (for example by Brexiteers) that it is EU regulations that tie up businesses in red tape. National systems count for far more. In the 2017 report, which covers 190 countries, Denmark ranks third, the UK is seventh and Sweden is ninth. Then France is at 29, Spain at 32, Belgium 42 and Italy 50. Greece is at number 61.

If you were to comb the bookshelves of an economics ministry, central bank or leading think-tank in France or Italy, you would find plenty of tomes, whether books or the reports of learned commissions, that say what needs to be done to restore these countries' dynamism. It is not complicated. If the UK and Denmark can make it so easy to run businesses there, to hire workers and to enforce contracts in courts, the same could be done in France or Italy. Similarly, are Germany (public pensions spending of 10.6% of GDP) and Japan (10.2%) hard-hearted and mean to their elderly? There is no reason in principle why countries like France and Italy should not be able to emulate them and get their public-pension spending under control. The question is whether either of these things can be done, politically.

In both of our test cases, they are beginning to be done or at least to be contemplated, albeit slowly and tentatively. In Italy, a crucial threshold, which was crossed during the euro crisis in 2011–12, was the ending of a sense of denial. Silvio Berlusconi, prime minister on three occasions in 1994–95, 2001–06 and 2008–11, owner of a near-monopoly of commercial television, had spent most of his time in office swearing that everything was really fine. Under the three prime ministers that succeeded him – Mario Monti (2011–13), Enrico Letta (2013–14) and Matteo Renzi (2014–16) – the message changed and the process of reform was started. The most seminal reform came in 2015 with Renzi's so-called "Jobs Act", which made it easier for employers to fire workers by restricting employees' ability to appeal against their dismissal in the country's slow-moving courts and in return made it easier for employees to get open-ended, permanent contracts rather than temporary ones. Yet this will make little difference until economic growth accelerates and with it demand for labour. Other necessary reforms, especially to the justice system and to regulations on businesses, are unlikely to occur until or unless general elections in 2017 or 2018 bring in a new government with a stable parliamentary majority. Renzi is a radical simply by virtue of his youth: in 2014 when he took office he was, at 39, the country's youngest prime minister since unification in 1861. But he struggled to get major reforms through Parliament, and failed spectacularly in a referendum in December 2016 to win public support for constitutional reforms designed to make government stronger, following which he had to resign. He has not left politics, however: he hopes to win a second chance to reform his country.

Similarly in France there is a new political language of reform. The Socialist government of Manuel Valls (2014–16) pushed its own reforms to labour laws, as well as supporting pension reforms. The economy minister, Emmanuel Macron, launched in April 2016 a movement called "En Marche" (on the move) dedicated to restoring openness and social mobility and then ran as an independent, centrist candidate for the presidency. His opponents on the centre-right also offered liberal solutions. The debate among all the main figures apart from the Front National's Le Pen has centred on how to bring liberalisation while preserving or restoring both equality and national values. It is in that debate that the future of Europe will be shaped.

*

European countries are far from basket cases, with the notable but small exception of Greece. But their domestic politics has brought a degree of paralysis in the face of the social and economic pressures that they have encountered over the past two decades. Entitlements that were generally granted in the 1960s or 1970s, especially to high levels of job security and to state pensions for retirement at ages that once presaged a decade or so of leisure and now presage three decades or more, have proved costly. This in turn has drained resources and energy away from other vital uses, such as investment in scientific research, in universities and in infrastructure, with the result that when an economic or political meteorite has hit – the Lehman shock of 2008, Russia's intervention in Ukraine, refugees, Brexit, terrorism – the Europeans have been in a poor state to cope, let alone respond.

It is perhaps surprising how little social and political unrest there has been in the worst-hit countries such as Greece, Spain and Ireland, or in those suffering longer and slower pains such as Italy or France. Social trust has held things together. But endurance, cushioned by past affluence, cannot be relied upon indefinitely. Patience could break suddenly. Clearly, the progress that has been seen in Ireland and Spain in recovering from property collapses, and the glimmers of liberalising reform in France and Italy, need to be reinforced and accelerated.

If the insurgent political parties can be kept at bay, these countries ought to be able to write their own revival stories. The other big question, though, is whether the EU and its own political dynamics will be a help in that process or a source of meteorites of its own. As stated earlier, during its six decades of history it has usually functioned by making member countries work better than they would have done on their own – by stopping them imposing trade barriers against each other, subsidising industries, devaluing currencies against those of their neighbours, or being deliberately laxer on pollution, for example. The hope with the euro was that it would pull off the same trick, but as we saw it didn't. And since 2012 the collectively agreed fiscal rules have generally made things worse, not better.

The second problem for the EU is that it has become harder for 28 governments to agree on collective actions than it was for 15, and that was hard enough. Decision-making based on qualified majority voting between countries has eased this problem, but it has not gone away. Moreover, the move nearer to being a continental-sized system of collaboration and common rules has worsened the feeling among citizens that there is a huge gap between them and the locus of decision-making. This is more than the famous "democratic deficit" of the EU. It is that a 28-country process feels alien and even incomprehensible. If Scots resent decisions being made in London, which has been their de facto capital for more than three centuries, it is not surprising that Hungarians, Danes or the French suspect EU decisions are being taken against, or in disregard of, their interests.

The euro is the easier of these issues to sort out. We cannot know what things would have been like in 2008 if the euro had not existed. In some cases, countries might have been in a better state to withstand the shock because their banks might not have lent so much money across borders in previous years. But the experiences of the UK (outside the euro) and Iceland (outside both the euro and the EU) show that life wasn't easy. Non-euro countries had also done huge amounts of cross-border financial trading, and currency devaluation was no panacea. EU countries trade so much with each other that volatility in the value of the Irish punt, the Italian lira, the Spanish peseta and the French franc could have brought about some nasty systemic consequences of its own.

What could and should have been better was the policy response by euro-zone countries. Compared with the US and the UK they were slow to intervene to shore up and then shake up banks. And the universal rule of fiscal austerity imposed in 2012 has made the recession deeper and much longer than it needed to have been. Domestic politics, especially in the creditor countries led by Germany, made the response less generous or, to use a more neutral word, less far-sighted than the solidarity and collective interest required in a genuine currency union.

Many economists, especially in the UK and the United States, have responded by arguing that the euro should therefore be dismantled, or perhaps divided into two different currency zones for northern and southern Europe. Many politicians, especially in Brussels and some euro-zone countries, have said that the answer must be "more Europe", by which is meant more integration of banking regulation, of tax systems, even of finance ministries, all leading towards a centralised federal government for the currency system.

Practical politics – that is, the small matter of what citizens will actually accept – dictates that neither of these paths should or will be taken. Dismantling the euro would be so financially disruptive and risky that it would probably cause a new recession and much higher unemployment. "More Europe" is simply anathema to most voters in virtually every EU country, since they already blame the EU for many of their problems, rightly or wrongly. They want less of it, not more.

The better approach would be not "more Europe" but "more European collaboration" directed at creating the sort of virtuous cycle of growth and restored political confidence that will make national reforms easier. This should mean relaxing the fiscal restraints to permit co-ordinated public spending, ideally on capital projects, to help boost demand in the whole euro zone. Two, three or four years ago this would have been impossible for German voters to accept, since it would have seemed as if German taxpayers' money was being used to support spendthrifts elsewhere. But now that the financial situation has stabilised and some turnaround can be seen in Spain and Ireland, the politics of this should change. The pressure of refugees and of terrorism makes it essential that it does. Europe needs to feel stronger and more positive.

The main way in which European collaboration could assist that positive feeling would be by building electricity grids, roads, railways or broadband networks together, creating connectivity and sharing of capacity, but also creating jobs. Instead of centralising power, EU countries can and should pool their borrowing capacity to finance a big co-ordinated programme of public investment in infrastructure, both digital and physical, a modern version of the post-war Marshall Plan that the United States financed. As happened with the Marshall Plan, such reflation of European investment and demand, through collective borrowing at what currently are the lowest interest rates for sovereign borrowing seen by European countries for two centuries, would not just boost growth and jobs but also tax revenues. The fiscal rules of the euro zone could be confined to controlling the current spending of governments rather than capital investment, and perhaps be kept tough only for countries whose public debts exceed 100% of GDP. In this way, 14 of the 19 members of the euro zone could readily chip in.[9] It would not just be German money, but Germany would have to lead it.

The EU, on the basis of its current trajectory and policies, is heading towards disintegration and eventual demise. It needs to change direction, which means its member countries need to change direction. Slow growth, high unemployment and high levels of immigration from the Middle East and North Africa are a deadly combination. Such migration is largely outside the control of either the EU or European countries. Slow growth and high unemployment are not. The main solutions are domestic, but collaborative public spending could help. There is little time to spare.

Europe is in many ways in a similar economic condition to that of Japan following its financial crash of the early 1990s, and it shares many of that country's demographic characteristics too. What it cannot depend upon is the same sort of popular patience – endurance or *gaman*, as it is called in Japanese – from which Japan and its conservative elites have benefited.

7

The Japanese puzzle

Taking medicine
It is as bad as having
Frost on the pillow

Matsuo Basho, 1644–94

A hangover
Is nothing as long as
There are cherry blossoms

Matsuo Basho

HOW MANY FALSE DAWNS can the Land of the Rising Sun have? That is the question that has to be confronted when thinking about this ultra-modern, highly developed democracy that for more than 30 years until 1990 always surprised on the upside and since 1990 has tended to disappoint. There are reasons aplenty for pessimism: its population is shrinking, it is being overshadowed by China politically and by South Korea industrially, and in many ways its people seem to have become more insular and less globalised while the rest of the world has gone (not always willingly or happily) in the other direction. And yet, having been writing about Japan for more than 30 years since being transferred to Tokyo as a young foreign correspondent for *The Economist* in 1983, I can never quite shake off an underlying optimism about the place.

Mancur Olson's analysis of how the entrenched power of interest groups can make a country sclerotic for a long time is as good an explanation of Japan's disappointing rigidity since 1990 as it was of the UK before Margaret

FIG 7.1 **Growth in real GDP per head, 1990–2015** annual average, %

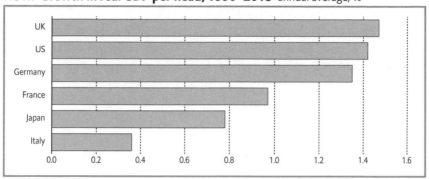

Source: OECD

Thatcher, which also means that as in the UK the power of such groups can in principle eventually be broken. Despite such sclerotic conservatism, the country nevertheless is replete with young innovators trying to do new things, against heavy odds, which suggests that the balance between progress and regress, between renovation and decay, could at some stage be tipped. It will not happen in a "big bang", or with a big Thatcher-style confrontation, for that would not be the Japanese way. But it could happen stealthily, step by step, such that we will suddenly notice that more things have changed than we realised.

Japan has often disappointed for understandable and forgivable reasons. Its population structure has been ageing more rapidly than that of any other large Western country. It has suffered extraordinary natural disasters such as the 2011 earthquake and tsunami in eastern Japan that killed at least 16,000 people, or the Kobe earthquake in 1995 that killed nearly 6,500. Just as it had been getting stronger and even used to some social and economic renovation, Japan was hit hard by a 2008 global financial calamity which it had played no part in producing.

But still it has disappointed, often for its own reasons. It has disappointed not just outside observers but also its own expectations, which are high given its stellar decades before 1990, and by comparison with its own needs, given the pressures of its ageing population, of the strategic threat from China, and of the huge size of its public debts. The ultimate irony may even be that complacency over these public debts has permitted the country to avoid dealing properly with the rigidities that have caused it to disappoint.

A common notion has been that Japan is a place that needs a catastrophe to fully transform itself. A crisis did the trick during the 1860s when Western pressure led to a civil war that overthrew the long-standing dictatorial regime of the Tokugawa Shogunate and replaced it with a more open, outward-looking, modernising regime under Emperor Meiji. Then defeat in 1945 and the US occupation of Japan from 1945 to 1952 produced a new transformation, creating today's affluent, democratic Japan. Perhaps a third such crisis would do the trick again as the notion says. But it may also be that those historical cases involving respectively a civil war and a devastating wartime defeat finished off with two atom bombs tell us that a thoroughgoing transformation will not happen except in extreme circumstances that nobody should want to repeat.

The collapse of the Japanese government bond market under the weight of public debt has, for the past two decades, been the catastrophe most widely tipped as the next agent of transformation. But it has never happened, and the likelihood of a collapse is diminishing, not rising. Two decades of weak tax revenues thanks to depressed household incomes – Japanese public finances are highly dependent on income-tax receipts, which in times of rapid economic growth were reliable but no longer are – have left Japan with gross government debts worth 248% of GDP, which is far and away the highest level of any developed country. Rapid ageing has driven up health and pension costs. Nevertheless, that gross figure is rather misleading. If you take account of debts owed by one part of government to another, the net debt figure is nearly 130% of GDP, which is still a lot higher than in other advanced countries but not outrageously so, as Figure 7.2 shows.

Moreover, these high net debts have long mainly been owed by the government to Japanese institutional and individual investors, so they have not come with an associated currency risk. Now they are becoming even safer as increasingly the debt is owed by the government to the Bank of Japan, which since the arrival of Haruhiko Kuroda as governor in April 2013 has pursued an ambitious policy of buying government bonds. In extremis, the central bank could just write its bonds off.

By the end of 2016, the Bank of Japan held more than one-third of all Japanese government bonds outstanding, and was buying 70% of all new government debt being issued. So the total amount of government debt in private hands has

FIG 7.2 **Government debt as % of GDP, 2015**

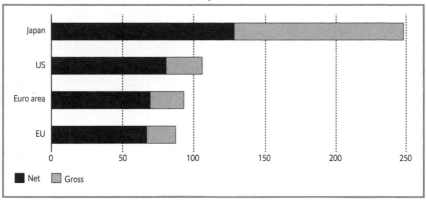

Sources: IMF, WEO

been falling rapidly – by about 15 percentage points each year – even though the Japanese government is still running a large budget deficit of 6% of GDP. What the central bank is therefore in effect doing is printing money to finance public spending directly. This is justifiably controversial with economists and central bankers because it means that any financial discipline exerted by private markets on government borrowing has disappeared and the central bank has become a political tool rather than an independent agency.

In other countries, such money-printing has generated hyperinflation. But today's Japan is not like Zimbabwe. Its most prominent economic characteristics are weak demand and falling or static prices, thanks to depressed wages and thus household incomes, and the effects of a rapidly ageing population. The Bank of Japan's monetary policy has not succeeded in reviving overall demand in the economy. It has merely shifted the economy from a state of mild deflation to one of mild inflation. Only if the inflation rate were to move from mild to wild would the policy become dangerous.

The fundamental problems in the Japanese economy are weak demand, depressed incomes and a shortage of the sort of entrepreneurship or corporate investment that might be capable of producing new wealth and large numbers of well-paid jobs. Plans and programmes have regularly been drawn up for how to turn things around and generate stronger economic growth. Recent examples include those produced by the Rebuild Japan Initiative Foundation, a private think-tank headed by Yoichi Funabashi, a former editor-in-chief of the *Asahi* newspaper, and the "Japan Ahead" proposals promoted by Hiroshi Mikitani, chief executive of Rakuten, the country's leading e-commerce company. New dawns have regularly been announced, most recently by the prime minister, Shinzo Abe, with his "Abenomics" fanfare from 2012 onwards, when he bravely declared that "Japan is back" and promised to fire "three arrows" – monetary, fiscal and liberalising – to revive the country. But so far the revival plans have not really been adopted, whether official or unofficial, and Abenomics has just produced more disappointment.

The central puzzle of Japan is not mainly about debt, demography or disappointment, but about rigidity. In 1983, when I went to live in Tokyo as a foreign correspondent, one of the prevailing wisdoms about the country's success centred on its flexibility and dynamism, especially compared with what was perceived to be the sclerotic old UK. During the 1970s but also in the 1980s, it seemed that Japan was notably good at getting companies, cities and regions to escape their dependency on old industries in which they were no longer competitive and to move into new industries, new products and new ways of doing things, all without causing the sort of social disorder that we were familiar with in rustbelt areas of the UK, western Europe or North America. Japan was an early adopter of new technologies. It was a champion at evolution and adaptation. Moreover, if what you need to be able to manage difficult economic or social change is a deep reservoir of social trust, Japan has a well of such trust that is as deep as the deepest ocean.

How can a country have gone from being super-flexible to super-rigid in such a short time? This is the Japanese puzzle. If we could find the answer, we might be able also to work out what Japan could do if only it could restore its previous flexibility, and how it might go about doing so.

*

When the temple bells tolled in the New Year in towns and villages throughout Japan on January 1st 1990, they brought in more than just the traditional good wishes of *shinnen akemashite omedetou*, or congratulations on the dawning of a new year. They brought in what, at the time, was the most severe crash in financial markets that had been seen in any developed country since the Wall Street crash of 1929. And, albeit more slowly, they brought in a reappraisal, by outsiders and by the Japanese themselves, of what was good and bad, productive or unproductive, about the Japanese way of doing things. Aspects of Japan that on December 31st 1989 had seemed to many to be part of its genius – such as its painstaking processes for seeking consensus, its clannish, closely held companies, interlocked with each other by cross-shareholdings, its development of its own technologies and methods in its own markets first, before trying them out abroad, its suppression of politics in favour of technocratic direction – came, once the new reality had sunk in in 1990 and beyond, to be seen as ingredients in its downfall.

The change of perception was extreme, though it took time to get through in the US in particular. I took part in a number of US television debates in 1990 and 1991, following the publication the previous year of my book, *The Sun Also Sets*, in which the prevailing sentiment was that the Tokyo stockmarket crash was at best irrelevant, at worst an elaborate piece of trickery staged by the Japanese powers-that-be to fool the US into believing that Japan was in trouble when in fact it was still powering ahead and taking over global leadership.

That somewhat paranoid sentiment was fuelled by the ideas presented in a 1989 book by a Dutch journalist, Karel van Wolferen, called *The Enigma of Japanese Power*, which gained a lot of attention in the United States. Van Wolferen argued that there is no real centre of power or direction in Japan, and that everything is guided or promoted by a loose collection of elites in politics, big business and various ministries, which act behind the scenes and are accountable to no one. As a result, he said, superficial impressions often mislead and there is no one person or institution capable of being persuaded to move the country in a new direction.

This idea was not easy for US policymakers to digest, since for the sake of their own political debate at that time many wanted to believe that Japan's success was in fact due to a superbly well-directed industrial policy, which they believed the US should seek to emulate. But the notion that Japan had a sort of equivalent of the fabled "military-industrial complex"[1] calling the shots in a shadowy way nevertheless tempted many to believe that financial chaos couldn't really be happening in Tokyo since the shadowy powers wouldn't have allowed it to.

It took several years of continued financial meltdown, and a rather hapless response to it by the Japanese government, to convince outsiders that something had changed. In one sense, Van Wolferen was proved right:

when things went badly wrong, no leader or centre of power proved capable of getting a grip on things. Japan did not react to its financial turmoil in the rapid way Sweden did to its own collapse in 1991 (see Chapter 8) because it could not find the same sort of decisive leadership, building on a consensus for reform, that emerged in Stockholm. In Japan in the early 1990s there was no consensus for reform because few people in senior positions in ministries, politics, companies, think-tanks, the media or universities had thought before the crash that there was any need for reform. Things had been going well. So Japanese in leadership positions remained in denial for several years to come.

Where those Japanese leaders and Van Wolferen were wrong was in their understanding of the Japan of the 1980s. It was not, as Van Wolferen thought, that the shadowy powers in the Japanese system were driving the country to ever greater dominance and success. It was that the financial bubble from about 1987 onwards was an unplanned response to the country's existing inability or unwillingness to adapt, one that served to cover up Japan's growing deficiencies, its lack of flexibility. There was a smokescreen, as the American conspiracy theorists on my TV debates had wanted to believe. But the smokescreen consisted of the credit boom, not the financial bust.

Japan had entered the 1980s with a highly competitive export sector which was by then specialising in cars, consumer electronics, semiconductors and machine tools. This had emerged during the 1970s, following two externally generated shocks that had forced industry, with some guidance from public officials, to change. The first was the sharp revaluation of the Japanese yen in 1971–73 that resulted from US President Richard Nixon's decision to abandon the fixed exchange-rate system that had prevailed since 1945.[2] The second was an abrupt trebling of dollar-denominated oil prices in 1973 caused by Arab oil producers' decision to restrict their output. These combined to push the country's highly polluting, energy-guzzling heavy industry close to bankruptcy, as its exports became uncompetitive and imported energy became far more expensive. At the same time, public protests against air and water pollution were growing.

Rather as China is attempting to do now, Japan had to clean up its dirty cities, use less energy, and move upmarket into higher-technology, less polluting, higher-value production. From the mid-1970s onwards, the effort was a great success. Domestic industry and services did not change a great deal, but the economy was carried along by exports. Companies such as Toyota, Nissan, Honda, Sony and Panasonic became global brands during that period.

These exports were so successful that the country began to build up a big trade and current-account surplus on its balance of payments. Normally, now that exchange rates were floating on the markets rather than fixed, this would have been expected to bring about a big rise in the value of the yen. It did not because at the same time the anti-inflation policies in the US of the president, Ronald Reagan, and the chairman of the Federal Reserve Board, Paul Volcker, were driving up the value of the US dollar. Many Japanese government officials in the first half of the 1980s thought the country should be deregulating a lot of industries, including financial and other services, to stimulate innovation and create new sources of economic growth. But the weak yen and booming exports helped interest groups that wanted to slow down or block such reform to win the argument. Deregulation felt unnecessary. The impetus for reform and innovation, which had always been weak, faded away.

Then, however, the US dollar changed direction abruptly, helped by co-ordinated policy changes in the US, Europe and Japan that were agreed at the Plaza and Louvre accords of 1985 and 1987.[3] A sharp rise in the value of the yen led to what became known as the *endaka* or high yen recession. Under the Louvre accord, the Bank of Japan was obliged to cut its official interest rates as part of an effort to make the yen less attractive to international investors and so to stabilise the yen–dollar rate. Such low rates also, however, proved helpful to Japanese companies that were otherwise feeling squeezed, in what was never really a recession but was still a sharp slowdown. And, most important, it set off the borrowing and speculating boom that took the stock and property markets to crazy heights and then their crashes after 1990.

The most serious point is that first the cheap-yen export boom and then the cheap-money credit boom enabled hard choices to be delayed. Life was good. Japan seemed to be on top of the world, using ultra-cheap borrowings in its now strong yen to buy assets abroad, most famously the Rockefeller Centre in Manhattan, the Pebble Beach golf course in California and Columbia Pictures in Hollywood. It was a golden age. So why worry about reform? Why deregulate? Why do anything about the country's uncompetitive agriculture? Why modernise corporate governance? Why internationalise universities? Why do anything controversial or costly? The old interest groups that by then had accrued enormous financial and political power – the big business federation, the Keidanren; agricultural co-operatives and banks; the Japan Medical Association, which represents doctors; the most powerful advertising and marketing agencies, led by Dentsu; trade unions and their federations; the big media groups – did not want barriers opened up and more competition stimulated. There was no need, they thought, for new competitors, new entrepreneurs, new ideas. The old ones were working perfectly well.

Until they were not. The shift from boom to bust, from fast growth to slow growth, inflation to deflation, world champion to stumbler, history-maker to has-been, was abrupt. By the end of the 1990s the conventional wisdom had changed completely, thanks to the bursting of the credit bubble in stock and property prices. Japan's banks depended on shareholdings for part of their capital, and were huge lenders for property, so they were hit hard from both sides. Many Japanese firms, with their traditional sources of profit under pressure in the late 1980s from a rising yen, had also tried their hand at gambling in both shares and property, bets which went spectacularly wrong. Then when the crash came, much of the economic system froze. The "creative destruction" that Joseph Schumpeter, an Austrian-American economist, had considered the essence of capitalism appeared to be absent in Japan.[4] The bureaucrats and bankers who had helped direct change and enforce flexibility during the 1960s and 1970s were discredited or else in deep financial trouble themselves.

Instead of being destroyed following the financial crisis, unviable and outdated companies were kept alive as "zombies", as ultra-cheap financing was extended to them by banks that could not bear to kill them off or to disclose that loans to them were duds. To simplify to make the point, all and sundry – banks, borrowers, bureaucrats – decided to wait and hope that things would work themselves out, rather than engaging in much painful adjustment. The main adjustment came by virtue of Japan's deep reservoir of social trust and cohesion: in place of masses of job losses for the least economically viable employees, as would have happened in the US or the UK, the pain was shared by reducing pay, first by cutting the twice-annual bonuses and overtime pay (which in the Japanese employment system were important) and then base pay, across the board. This deflation of costs through pay was also mitigated by massive amounts of public spending, especially on capital projects such as bridges, roads and tunnels, designed to keep employment up, to keep construction companies in business despite the property crash, and to inject money into the economy.

Japan became a case study not in success but in stagnation, conservatism and rigidity. This applies not just in business and economics but in politics too. At the time of the 1990 crash, Japan's government had been run since 1955 by just one party, the Liberal Democratic Party (LDP), which had taken plenty of credit and spoils during the country's long period of economic success. It thus presided over the vast expansion of credit in the late 1980s, later known as the bubble economy, which had resulted in evident absurdities such as tracts of land in central Tokyo (most famously the Imperial Palace grounds and gardens) having a theoretical real-estate value higher than that of the entire state of California. It had exploited the seemingly relentless rise in share prices to raise some of its own campaign finances through insider trading.

You might have expected the LDP to be punished severely and swiftly by the electorate once the financial crash occurred. Such an expulsion of incumbent parties happened frequently in Europe and the US after the 2008 crash. Yet in Japan politics barely changed. The LDP lost a bit of ground in the first few years of the 1990s and had to govern through coalitions with other parties – even allowing the head of the Japanese Socialist Party, Tomiichi Murayama, to act as prime minister in one of those coalitions in 1994–96. Nevertheless, the LDP remained pretty much in charge until 2009 when it finally was kicked out of power completely by the Democratic Party of Japan (DPJ), itself a centre-left concoction of old parties, including many splinter groups from the LDP. Since the DPJ then made a botch of governing, and was criticised especially for its handling of the deadly March 2011 earthquake and tsunami in north-east Japan which led to the disaster at the Fukushima Dai-Ichi nuclear power plant, the LDP was back in power a mere three years later. Which is where it remains.

You can detect rigidity and conservatism elsewhere too. While in Europe and North America the structure and ownership of mass media have changed vastly during the past 20 years, with the internet driving newspaper groups out of business and satellite, cable and now video-on-demand disrupting the old order in television, in Japan there has been far less change. It is not that Japan is backward in the use of the internet: far from it, access to and use of superfast broadband is more extensive there than in much of the developed world. Rather it is that the emergence of new digital services has had far less impact on incumbent businesses than elsewhere.

When old, giant broadsheet newspapers such as the *Yomiuri* (daily print circulation 9.1 million) or the *Asahi* (6.6 million) complain of pressure from digital innovation it is a complaint about a slow and gentle squeeze compared with the sharp pain felt in the US by the *New York Times* (590,000 daily print circulation) or even more so in the UK by the *Guardian* (170,000) as they switch urgently to digital. Meanwhile the principal TV companies, many of them linked to major newspapers, are all the same as they were 20–30 years ago. There has been innovation in cable and especially satellite television, but it has not upended mainstream TV: at least, not yet. Attempts have been made by disruptive investors to buy their way into TV businesses – such as the effort by internet upstart Livedoor to buy Nippon Broadcasting System from Fujisankei Communications Group in 2005, or the stake taken in the same year in Tokyo Broadcasting System by e-commerce company Rakuten – but the disrupters failed to wrest control away from the old owners. With broadcast licences being allocated not even nationally but prefecture by prefecture, it is hard to break into the national market without acquiring one of the existing firms.

Such media conservatism could reflect consumer tastes. But it is more likely to reflect the conservatism of big advertisers and their choice of where to invest their marketing budgets, which in turn determines the cash flow which the TV and newspaper companies have to spend on their programmes, their editorial content and their own marketing. Big advertisers' choices also reflect the power of one giant advertising agency, Dentsu, which as well as holding 25% of the country's advertising market also sells advertising space and holds shareholdings in several big TV broadcasters. Dentsu, founded in 1901 as both a news agency and advertising firm, is no disrupter.[5]

Looking at the leadership of Japan's big business federation, the Keidanren, which is the equivalent of the Confederation of British Industry, it is immediately obvious that traditional companies still dominate. The current chairman, Sadayuki Sakakibara, is from Toray, a synthetic-fibre giant. His predecessor was from Sumitomo Chemical. The man before that, Fujio Mitarai, was from Canon, a camera and optics company, which is certainly high-tech though not in the way today's Silicon Valley thinks of it. The Keidanren is more than just a business federation; it is also an influential think-tank on public policy, which has for more than half a century been working closely with the LDP and with relevant ministries to shape legislation and regulation. So it is not surprising that such legislation and regulation bears the stamp of traditional big business interests so firmly and clearly.

The Keidanren's conservatism has been challenged, but unsuccessfully. Hiroshi Mikitani, founder of the country's biggest e-commerce company, Rakuten, quit the organisation in June 2011 over disagreements with its policies, especially those related to the tsunami and nuclear accident earlier that year. He has since set up the Japan Association of New Economy as a rival organisation, so far (December 2016) with 521 member firms – which compares with 1,340 firms in the Keidanren. This shows the difficulty of changing a powerful, deeply entrenched organisation. But it also shows that clamourers for change can at least find other places in which to get their voices heard. The Keidanren's influence is declining, but slowly.

Another, more negative indicator of Japan's appetite for change, however, has been the decline in the number of Japanese university students choosing to go abroad for part of their studies. In 2004 the number of young Japanese going abroad to study peaked at nearly 83,000. By 2012 the total had dropped by a third to 54,000, since when the number has begun to rise again. You might have imagined that a perception that Japan was falling behind other countries or not providing adequate opportunities for young people would lead to an increase in those studying abroad, as a stepping stone perhaps to getting a job abroad after graduation – as it has in Italy and France. Yet the trend went the other way, at least for men. It is female students, whose ambitions feel blocked in Japan's male-dominated organisations, that have remained keener on going abroad.

Nor has university education in Japan internationalised to anything like the degree seen in some other countries, if tuition in English is taken as a proxy for internationalisation. At Korea University in Seoul, 70% of classes are given in English, according to a presentation by Naoto Onzo, a professor at Tokyo's Waseda University, in April 2016.[6] Waseda is one of Japan's top private universities, yet Onzo observed ruefully that even there fewer than a fifth of classes are in English. At Japan's top public institution, Tokyo University, such international courses are dominated by non-Japanese students; few Japanese students want to take part.

*

Some Japanese companies have certainly tried to internationalise themselves, promoting foreign executives to senior management positions, even to the very top. There are many famous examples, the most famous of all being a

Lebanese-Brazilian, Carlos Ghosn, who became chief operating officer of Nissan in 1999 when his French employer, Renault, took a 36.8% stake in the then troubled Japanese carmaker, and then chief executive in 2001. He still holds this role, but having made a great success of reviving the firm's fortunes now combines it with being chairman and chief executive of Renault, too. A more recent example came in 2015 at Takeda Pharmaceutical, the country's biggest drugs firm: following a worldwide search, the firm appointed a Frenchman who previously worked at GlaxoSmithKline in Europe, Christophe Weber, as chief executive after only a year working at the firm.

Not all such international appointments have been as clear a sign of change as those at Nissan or Takeda. A revealing illustration of how Japanese conservatism can coincide with an apparent embrace of modernisation-through-globalisation can be found in the sad, scandalous story of Olympus. This camera to medical optics firm, famous worldwide for the quality of its products, appeared in the spring of 2011 to be placing itself alongside Nissan as a pioneer of new global thinking when it appointed a Briton, Michael Woodford, first as its company president and then as chief executive officer. Woodford had been working for the company for 30 years, having in 1981 joined KeyMed, a British firm that became a wholly owned subsidiary of Olympus in 1986. Unlike Nissan when Ghosn took its helm, Olympus appeared to be healthy. By October 2011, however, after barely six months in the job, Woodford had been dismissed by the Olympus board.

The reason for his dismissal was that he had ordered an independent inquiry into accusations, published that summer in a small Japanese magazine called *FACTA* and based on information from a whistleblower inside the company, of a multibillion-dollar scheme of false accounting designed to cover up investment losses at Olympus that dated back about 25 years to the late 1980s. Once the independent report by PricewaterhouseCoopers, an accounting firm, had been completed, Woodford circulated it to the board of directors, demanded answers as to what had happened and called for the resignations of the chairman and the vice-president responsible for the fraud. Rather than provide answers or instigate resignations, the board fired him. The result was that the whole story – which had previously been ignored by mainstream Japanese and international media – appeared in the *Financial Times*, as Woodford contacted the British newspaper's Tokyo office just before he left the country, evidently in some fear for his own safety.

Like other companies, Olympus had tried to make up for the squeeze on its conventional profits arising from the strong Japanese yen in the late 1980s by speculating in securities of various kinds, including derivatives, and had got badly burnt when the market crash happened in 1990. It had never owned up publicly to those losses, presumably preferring to hope that one day the markets might recover sufficiently to eliminate them. When that did not happen, it eventually bought some small companies in fields wholly unrelated to its own in order to transfer the losses to them and then write them off, and paid large fees to the somewhat mysterious intermediaries that had supposedly arranged the deals.

No one has yet got to the bottom of exactly where the money went. One natural speculation was that entities connected with Japanese organised-crime clans, or *yakuza*, could have been involved. Such groups have been heavily involved in shady financial dealings ever since the stockmarket bubble of the 1980s. As in Italy, Japanese organised-crime groups often operate through seemingly legitimate businesses. Their involvement would also help explain why the company acted in such a defensive and ultimately self-destructive way when the *FACTA* revelations first appeared and then when Woodford sought to address the issue. But no evidence has emerged of *yakuza* involvement.

There is another explanation for the defensive response. It is rooted in what could be called the social anthropology of big Japanese companies. Peter Drucker, an Austrian-American economist and management writer, identified the modern corporation as the central social organisation of modern times in his 1946 book about General Motors, *The Concept of the Corporation*. Japanese corporations have gone a considerable step further, making themselves the central social entity for the whole lives of their full-time employees, from joining the firm until retirement. For many managerial employees, the company is even more central to their lives than their family. As such, many companies have come to see their principal purposes as being to serve their employees rather than customers or shareholders, which as in any power structure chiefly means serving and protecting the interests of their senior employees, past and present. This was displayed in the way that Olympus closed ranks once the scandal broke, tried everything it could to deny any wrongdoing or even financial problems, and sought to avoid penalties for its present and former executives. In doing so, it rewarded loyalty over any duty of morality, transparency or even legality.

Another difficult question prompted by the Olympus affair concerns why Woodford was appointed as president and then CEO in the first place by what we now know to be such a conservative, inward-looking company, whose top executives knew they were concealing big losses and using false accounting to do so. Was this just a superficial gesture to make the firm look modern and Western? He had been a successful head of KeyMed and then of other Olympus operations, but even so his appointment was quite a gamble. It was presumably made in the expectation that Woodford would never discover the truth of the concealed losses. Certainly, had it not been for a whistleblower[7] passing the information to *FACTA* he might never have discovered the losses, though as time went on he might still have begun to ask questions about the strange acquisitions Olympus had been making in earlier years. One of the problems with appointing foreigners to top executive positions is their tendency to have ideas of their own and their willingness to rock the boat if they think it necessary. The likeliest theory is that Olympus's board knew that the company's boat needed to be rocked in some respects, by engaging in restructuring to make it more profitable so as to help get the firm past those old losses, and thought it useful to have a highly competent foreigner do the dirty work.

The main conclusion to draw from the Olympus scandal is that many, perhaps most, big Japanese companies are defensive and conservative, dedicated to protecting themselves and their senior managers as much as possible. They innovate, by developing new technologies to improve their products, but they do not innovate much, if at all, in the way in which they operate and do business. Moreover, although Woodford drew a huge amount of popular support in Japan for the public stand he took against Olympus's wrongdoing, there was also a surprising (to outside eyes) amount of sympathy for the senior Olympus executives who had done all the wrong. In truth, they were protecting their own well-paid jobs and future pensions, along with the pensions of their predecessors who had created and covered up the losses. Yet in much of the media and in public commentary, there was still less outrage than there would have been in Europe or the US over similar scandals.

Alongside that, however, must be placed two more optimistic points. One is that there was a whistleblower in Olympus who was brave enough and morally conscious enough to believe that exposing the scandal through *FACTA* was the right thing to do. The corporate clan was not entirely closed or loyal.

The second is that *FACTA* existed to publish investigative journalism of this sort. The monthly magazine had been founded in 2005 by Shigeo Abe, a journalist who had worked at the *Nikkei*, Japan's also conservative equivalent to the *Wall Street Journal*, and who with colleagues in 1994 had uncovered information indicating that a big securities firm, Yamaichi, was about to collapse, only to have the story spiked by his bosses (Yamaichi eventually did collapse in 1997). After a spell working in the *Nikkei*'s London office Abe left because he had seen investigative reporting being done in the UK and wanted to do some himself. After a short time working for another Japanese magazine, he raised money to launch *FACTA* from six investors, whose names he has kept secret. By late 2016 the monthly publication had 20,000 subscribers. With a staff of just nine writers, specialising in examination of corporate accounts and in following up tips from company insiders, it is now making a small profit.

*

The big Japanese companies that prospered in the 1960s, 1970s and 1980s are showing little sign of changing their ways. They lobby for their interests through the Keidanren. They pay lip service to the new codes of corporate governance that governments promote from time to time, appointing some independent directors and being somewhat more transparent, but if it makes any difference at all the progress is slow and hard to detect. Every so often an accounting scandal breaks out – Olympus in 2011, Toshiba in 2015 – which produces a wave of expectations or predictions that finally things will change. But they don't, not really. Pressure for change from Japanese shareholders or banks is gentle, at best. Now and then a well-known company brings in something that sounds radical, such as paying executives according to performance rather than seniority, or hiring senior managers from other companies. But it remains an interesting exception, not a sparkling new rule.

Japan is not seeing the sort of change in the corporate establishment that has been seen even in France, which is also a conservative and quite rigid country. Big French companies are highly internationalised in their methods and management, and many use English as their official corporate language. But while big French companies have no choice but to see their home market as being Europe rather than just France, big Japanese companies can still see their home as being quite separate from whatever it is they do in the rest of the world. So the prevailing philosophy of internationalisation is much the same as during the 1970s or 1980s: to treat overseas operations as distinct, probably run by a specialised cadre of managers, rather than intrinsically tied into their domestic or headquarters operations. A few companies have gone further than this in becoming global. But the reality is that most big Japanese companies have not internationalised in terms of management structure, nationality of staff or ways of doing business, because they haven't had to.

Although the Japanese domestic market is scarcely booming, it remains large enough to allow companies to stick to their old ways. It also remains large enough to allow separate technologies and standards to become established there, just for Japan, which are not easily saleable elsewhere. This "Galapagos effect", named for the separate evolution of species evident in Ecuador's Galapagos Islands, can be seen in many different industries, but has been especially notable in mobile phones. In mobiles, Japanese companies have been pioneers in providing all sorts of new functions and services – in Japan but not in the rest of the world.

The real source of hope for change, and for breaking out of this conservatism, rigidity and the Galapagos effect, lies not in old companies changing their ways but in new companies rising to take over leadership. New companies not only may develop new technologies but also are likelier to feel able to run themselves in new ways, avoiding the structures of seniority pay and lifelong commitment that characterise older generations of firms. This is not merely a comment about business and economics. As Drucker said, companies are the principal social organisations of the modern era, and that is especially true of Japan.

This brings us back to Hiroshi Mikitani, founder of Rakuten and president of the Japan Association of New Economy. Mikitani is an evangelist for a new type of Japanese company as well as the most visible role model for such a thing. In his 2014 book, *The Power to Compete*, based on a series of conversations with his father, Ryoichi, who was a noted economist at Kobe University and had also spent time at Harvard, Stanford and Yale, the younger Mikitani painted a portrait of the sort of companies he would like to see in Japan: ones that are open to hiring the best talents, at all stages of their career; ones that hire talented people from around the world; ones in which English is their common language; ones which bring the best ideas and people from all over the world and then put them in a very Japanese context of collaboration, solidarity and social sensitivity.

Clearly, this is how he sees his own company, Rakuten. Other large, new-style companies also exist. One is Softbank, a telephone and software company, led by Masayoshi Son, a Japanese of Korean origin, which has not only built its own business domestically but has also invested successfully in non-Japanese internet firms, such as China's Alibaba, and in 2016 bought a British chip designer, ARM, for £24.3 billion. In a different field, Fast Retailing, the parent company of the Uniqlo clothing stores, is also a more American-style company than were previous generations of Japanese retailers. A video-game company, Nintendo, has just reminded us that Japanese firms still have what it takes to set off crazes all over the world with the "Pokemon Go" game designed for it by Niantic, a Californian developer.

The biggest challenge for Japan is to agree on what is preventing more new companies from starting up and expanding, and then on what to do about it. During the 1990s there was a spate of start-ups, often begun by people who had started their careers in banks that ran into trouble, such as Industrial Bank of Japan – like Mikitani. There have been plenty since the turn of the millennium too, in finance, retailing, software, video games, mobile telecoms, even in agriculture. I recall a presentation by a perennial optimist about Japan's ability to renew itself that featured as a prime example of innovation a company that makes cube-shaped watermelons. Japan is full of innovation, and indeed of highly competitive companies even at a local level, especially in manufacturing. But this new generation of companies has not become big and powerful enough to challenge the old. It has not created a truly new paradigm in business, which would also mean in society.

Could that happen, any time soon? It is not easy – or else it would have happened already. New companies and new ways of doing things inevitably threaten old ones. They threaten not just the power, prestige and livelihood of old-style companies but also of those who set the rules that help determine whether and how new companies or entities can enter the field: bureaucrats, both at national and at local level. Politicians, too, have a greater incentive to protect old companies than to foster new ones, for their campaign-finance contributions and support networks overwhelmingly come from old-established firms. And yet it would not take a revolution to bring about change.

Often in Japan change happens in a stealthier, more gradual way. Jeff Kingston, a professor at Temple University in Tokyo, documented in his 2004 book, *Japan's Quiet Transformation*, how changes in the laws governing non-profit organisations led to a flourishing, nationwide, of such social enterprises, offering public services, pressuring governments, demanding and obtaining justice, demanding and providing information, organising citizens' groups into more effective lobbies. There need be no "big bang" for a corporate revolution either, which could come step by step. Already, special economic zones have been allowed to make selective, local deregulations. A similar recent story can be told about a stealthy rise in immigration and relaxing of the rules governing it, albeit from a low base:[8] the number of foreign permanent residents in 2015 was more than 70% higher than in 1995, but was still small at 2.23 million, or 2% of the population, a figure which includes about 500,000 long-time residents of Korean origin. A determined period of legal changes and deregulation, whether in corporate or social life, could lead to another "quiet transformation".

It hasn't happened, yet, because those in power have not felt sufficiently that it has needed to happen. There have been other ways out of economic traps or cul-de-sacs. There has been deregulation of the low-skilled labour market, described in detail in Chapter 2, which has created a huge army – 40% of the labour force – of cheap if fairly unproductive workers for companies that are otherwise losing their competitiveness and profitability. With Japan now at full employment, that reservoir of cheap labour, chiefly women, the retired and the young, is running short. There has also been monetary policy, the flooding of the Japanese financial system with liquidity provided by the Bank of Japan. But this too is running out of effectiveness. With the central bank already buying 70% of the government bonds being issued each year, there are limits to how far it can go.

Winston Churchill once said of Americans that "they can always be relied upon to do the right thing. Once they have exhausted the alternatives". This may be cynical, but it is beginning to feel as if it might now be true of Japan too. Japan is running out of options. Dealing with interest groups, introducing genuine, economy-wide deregulation, liberalising immigration, introducing full competition in cartelised sectors such as energy, the media, advertising, marketing, wholesale distribution and many others would produce a quiet, but dramatic transformation, even if done only in part. It would represent a real move towards openness. If it could be combined with a reform of labour laws to unify employment contracts and place all workers on the same basis, such openness would also be balanced by greater equality of rights. And labour equality would begin to boost consumer demand if reform to employment laws could also be supplemented by increases in the country's statutory minimum wages, which are set at prefectural rather than national level. In 2016 the average minimum wage was ¥823 an hour, or about $7, which places Japan below even US levels.

This is what Abe described in 2012 as the "third arrow" of Abenomics. But it has never been fired. Mikitani has, in his "Japan Ahead" proposals, plenty of ideas that Abe could adopt to release the pent-up energies of Japan, especially of the young and of the provinces. The only question is whether Abe and his LDP colleagues will ever gather enough political will to implement them and to override anyone in big business who tries to stand in the way. The opportunity is there, dangling in front of the government. What it needs to do is to grab it.

8

Swedish and Swiss Houdinis

Yesterday I was clever, so I wanted to change the world.
Today I am wise, so I am changing myself.

Jalāl ad-Dīn Muhammad Rūmi, 1207–73

My chief task has been to conquer fear.

Harry Houdini, 1874–1926

GIVEN THE THREATS AND PRESSURES that are now felt by the countries of the West, the temptation is great to hand the keys of government, nay even the nuclear codes, to a "strongman" willing to trade off some of those equal rights for other assumed benefits such as security against terrorist attacks or protection against competition from cheaper producers. Yet the rich world has yet to see any case of a country successfully revived and re-energised from an economic or political torpor by a reversion to authoritarian rule. Those that have achieved revival in modern times have all done so through some new combination of openness and of restored or reactivated equality.

There is plenty of torpor about. And the odds do look stacked against Europe, Japan and the United States, in wearying ways. They are increasingly countries of old people in a world full of vigorous young upstarts. They have become accustomed to rising living standards and high wages that are difficult to sustain in the face of competition from billions of Chinese and Indian workers, workforces that are becoming better educated every year, eroding one of the West's main advantages. And those Chinese and Indians are being hotly followed along the road of economic and technological change by a vast army of robots, predicted to take over the jobs of hundreds of millions of people.

Here, however, is an alternative hypothesis: that this accumulation of problems, of traps, straitjackets and chains, is as much an illusion as were the tricks performed by Harry Houdini, a Hungarian-American escape artist, a century ago. Our restraints and encumbrances are as self-imposed as Houdini's were, even if the difference is that we do not always realise it and have no intention of tricking ourselves.

This chapter examines two such recent Houdini acts, from Sweden and Switzerland, so as to draw lessons for other advanced, open, liberal and currently stuck societies. These are relatively small countries, just as some other turnaround stories of the past quarter of a century, such as Canada, New Zealand and Finland, have also been places with fairly small populations. It is not obvious why being small should be a great advantage in achieving revival – look at Greece, for example – but it could be argued that smaller populations have a greater chance of having the sort of homogeneity and community feeling that make it easier to achieve agreement to changes that can be painful to some parts of the population in the short term.

Nevertheless, revivals have occurred in larger countries too. The UK, as was described in Chapter 5, achieved a remarkable transformation during the 1980s and 1990s, even though that transformation has been followed by renewed troubles during the past decade. California, an American state that would if independent be one of the world's biggest economies, is also in the early stages of a turnaround, especially in its public finances and its political institutions, as Chapter 4 showed. All these revival stories are about throwing off rigidities, whether cultural, social, political or economic, and thereby regaining the ability to adapt and evolve. They are about defeating interest groups that stand in the way of change and renovation, and diminishing the power of those groups. They are not, and can never be, stories of permanent success or of immunity from external shocks. None of these Houdinis has been entirely insulated from the effects of the 2008 financial crisis, since all are open, trading countries, though Sweden and Switzerland have come close.

In Sweden, Switzerland and the UK, the power of evolution was successfully restored during the 1980s and 1990s, through a new period of openness. All three have prospered economically and culturally, and have raised their status and reputation internationally, but all three have recently encountered domestic political limits to how much of one sort of openness is acceptable: immigration. As was outlined in Chapter 1, immigration challenges the principle of equality of rights in any political entity. There are limits, evidently, to how far a population is willing to go in sharing its rights with outsiders.

*

In the international media, the main appeal of "the Swedish model" has long been that writing about it gave papers an excuse to run pictures of beautiful blondes. In today's context Sweden's appeal is rather different: it is that a rich, highly regulated, highly taxed, rigid society that had for a decade or more looked doomed to decline, managed during the 1990s and thereafter to become a much more flexible, more moderately taxed place, with more freedom of choice and creativity.

This is more than just an economic story, but measures of living standards relative to other countries offer a good summary of the plot. In the 1960s Sweden had been the world's second-richest country in terms of GDP per head; by 1990, after more than two decades during which its economy grew far more slowly than those of its EU neighbours or the West as a whole, it had slid to 14th richest among the OECD member countries (see Figure 8.1).[1] But then it began to catch up, and by 2012 its self-transformation had brought it back up to sixth

FIG 8.1 **Growth in real GDP per head, 1970–2014** 1970 = 100

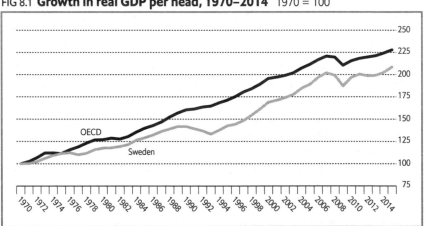

Source: OECD

place if measured at current exchange rates, or ninth if adjustments are made according to purchasing power.

Sweden has succeeded in changing itself in economic but also in social terms. A place that many ambitious, creative young people had in the 1970s and 1980s been drifting away from has turned itself into one of Europe's capitals of cool, a centre not just of innovation and wealth but also fun. The old Swedish model, blondes aside, was a dull and dependable Volvo. The new Swedish models are the Spotify music-streaming business or Mojang's video games. The Volvo Car Corporation is now owned by a Chinese company, Geely.

The turning point was, by common consent, a financial crisis. In 1991 the country suffered a big banking and currency crash, an event which helped bring to power what was then only the country's third centre-right government since 1932. For more than half a century, Sweden had seemed like a one-party state, dominated by the Social Democrats. As well as performing what has since been considered an exemplary and rapid clean-up of its collapsed banking sector, the new centre-right government, led by Carl Bildt as prime minister, embarked upon a programme of reducing taxation and deregulating all manner of industries that continued, step by step, for more than two decades. That is what produced the economic turnaround indicated earlier.

Clearly, Sweden used its crisis constructively. In that, it can be compared with the two other wealthy Western countries that also had financial collapses at the same time: Japan and Italy. Japan's 1990–92 crash was, like Sweden's, a crash in property and stockmarkets that followed a 1980s boom in credit. The property slump in particular brought both countries' banks to their knees. Italy's financial crisis in 1992 was one of public debt, which coincided with a political meltdown following a huge corruption scandal that brought down much of the post-war governing establishment and led to a big devaluation of the Italian lira. As in Sweden, new political brooms swept into power in both countries. But, as Chapters 6 and 7 showed, in both Italy and Japan the crises essentially went to waste. Italy has endured nearly 25 further years of decline, and the country is losing many of its best-educated young people to emigration. Japan's fate has been better, but it has still not restored the sort of dynamism for which it had once been feted.

So why did Sweden do better? One tempting answer is trust. Once the financial calamity hit, Swedish citizens, as individuals and in interest groups such as trade unions, professions, farmers, civil servants or others, proved willing to sacrifice old protections or privileges because they held enough trust in the political and business establishment, and in each other, to believe the eventual outcome would be fair and in the interests of all.

There is probably a lot of truth in this explanation: Sweden has long been, after all, a consensus society, famed for its egalitarian approach. In that respect, it is utterly different from Italy, which is known to be a low-trust society, one in which all levels of government and all forms of power are viewed with suspicion, and have been for centuries. But the limits to this explanation are revealed by two further points. Japan is a similarly high-trust and consensual society, one famous for its social cohesion: so if trust is the key, why did Japan fail and Sweden succeed? Second, if Sweden is so trusting and consensual, why did it need a crisis to jolt it into life?

The second of those questions is also a good rebuttal to a standard excuse given for waving Sweden aside as an inspiration, namely the idea that this Scandinavian country, with a population of just 9.96 million, is simply an exceptional, close-knit, small community which for as long as can be remembered has been able to come together and sort out its problems, so that it cannot be used as an example for more disputatious mortals elsewhere, in larger, less homogeneous countries. Michael Booth, a British journalist resident in Denmark, described all Scandinavians as *The Almost Nearly Perfect People* in the title of his entertaining 2014 book about the region, and speculated, not entirely kindly, that one reason Swedes can be so taciturn with one another is that they all know each other so well that they already think they know what each other would say.

For sure, during the heyday of Swedish social democracy, during which the party bearing that name was in government without interruption from 1932 until 1976, the country was run by a consensual triangle of the Social Democratic Party, the Swedish Trade Union Confederation and the Employers Federation. Yet it still went into a long decline, stuck with taxes and public spending at 60% of GDP (Japan's figure has fluctuated at 30–35%, the UK's at 40–50%), with high annual rates of price inflation, no real policy option to keep its economy going beyond blasts of public subsidy for troubled firms, and periodic sharp devaluations of the Swedish kronor to restore export competitiveness for the country's industry for a short time until further inflation eroded that advantage.

In that respect, the Sweden of the 1970s and 1980s bore a close resemblance to Italy, a country which also lurched from devaluation to devaluation, whose economy too was dominated by big, often state-controlled industries that were failing to keep up with their competitors, and which was rife with monopolies and cartels, despite being a founder member of the EU. In the 1970s Sweden was also a country of cartels and restricted competition, one in which a few big companies, often state-owned but always privileged and protected, ruled the roost.

There is one important difference, however, between the Swedish story and the Italian one. This is that Swedish governments had started, albeit tentatively, to open things up and provide more economic freedom much earlier than 1991, beginning at least as long ago as 1980. It had been dawning on many Swedes, in the establishment and out of it, that things were no longer working, and that it did no good just to nationalise or subsidise companies when they got into a mess, or to devalue the currency. That early realisation did not occur in Italy, at least not to the same extent.

So, for example, even as the UK was gearing up for the 1984 privatisation of its state-owned telecommunications monopoly, and preparing to allow more competition in that field, Sweden too was starting to open up telecoms.[2] In allowing private competition in radio and television, Sweden was a laggard (permission finally came in 1992), but in railways and postal services the country was a pioneer. Income-tax reform, beginning the process of cutting back draconian top tax rates for high earners, was agreed upon in 1981. The top marginal income-tax rate, which had peaked at nearly 90% in the late 1970s, was brought down below 80% by 1986 and to 70% by 1990, before being cut to 50% in 1991. A start was made to the reform of the pension system in 1984.

Deregulation of bank credit was begun in 1982, controls on interest rates and bank lending were removed in 1985, and exchange controls, under which only the central bank had been allowed to trade in foreign currencies, were lifted in 1989. Moreover in 1990, a year before the financial crisis hit, the taxi industry and domestic aviation were both deregulated, a start was made on introducing competition into the railways, a comprehensive tax reform was implemented that widened the tax base and sharply reduced tax rates both for individuals and companies, and, last but far from least, Sweden applied for membership of the European Union (then known as the European Community).

The list of reforms during the 1980s shows that awareness of the need for change was already growing well before the financial crisis hit. But it also offers a clue to what happened next: it was the deregulation of bank lending and of interest rates from 1982 onwards that produced the credit bubble that then burst so disastrously in 1991. In that respect the supposedly cathartic crisis of 1991 was the result of deregulation, not the cause of it. Put more fairly, it was the result of a partial deregulation that produced unintended consequences and was not sufficiently matched in other parts of the economy. Moreover, the change to a liberalised financial system was not accompanied by adequately strong regulation of the banks and other lenders. Sweden is hardly alone in failing to anticipate the effects of financial deregulation. It is difficult to get deregulation and reregulation right at the same time.

What the 1991 financial crisis did, though, was to act as an accelerator for the reform trends that were already under way, for the ideas about shaking the country up that had already been circulating. And, arguably, 1991 showed that there was no real option of reverting to the old ways.

In the end, the chief lesson from Sweden's Houdini act concerns the value of achieving cross-party, cross-society consensus and, in relation to this, of persistence in carrying on with persuasion and with reforms for a sustained period of time. The process in Sweden took at least 15 years, perhaps more, depending on when you date its initiation and completion. The 1991 crisis was helpful but would have been unlikely to have caused Sweden's transformation on its own had there not already been awareness of the existence of problems and of the need for change.

The seminal 2012 study by economists at the World Bank of Europe's economic challenges, *Golden Growth*, summed up Sweden's new formula well:

But it is not easy being like Sweden. What does it take? Make it so easy to register property, trade across borders and pay taxes that the World Bank ranks the country as one of the top 15 for doing business. Create the conditions that get four out of every five people of working age into jobs, and get almost everybody who works to pay taxes. Have an efficient government that provides high-quality social services, so that taxpayers get their money's worth. Institute the pension rules that make it difficult to retire before 65 and impossible until you reach your 60s. Cultivate the social trust that allows both a generous social safety net and a transparency in government so that abuse is minimal. The list is long. If a country can do all this, big government will not hurt growth.

Many of these themes can be found in other contexts in this book, especially the benefit both for economic activity and for the public finances of encouraging more people to take up jobs and to retire much later. Japan and Italy, for example, have had problems getting women into the labour force. France and Italy have a problem with early retirement and too few people working even part-time over the age of 60. Many European countries, along with Japan, make it surprisingly difficult to start new companies, register property, trade, enforce contracts and accomplish other aspects of doing business. The US has a problem of people giving up looking for work altogether, even when they are of prime working age.

The real difference between consensual, trusting Sweden and consensual, trusting Japan is that in Japan's case there had been little real awareness ahead of its 1990–92 financial collapse that change was necessary. In fact, the feeling in Japan in the 1980s was mostly the opposite: that the country was in a kind of golden age. The great trust in Japan's society that pre-dated the 1990–92 crash was a trust that all was going well and that the institutions of the state knew what they were doing. The crash severely damaged this by showing citizens that they had been wrong, previously, to believe in bureaucrats, politicians and big business. Trust was weakened exactly when the country needed it most.

Sweden's case ought, though, to be inspiring and reassuring to the many embattled and often despairing reformers in France and Italy. In both countries tentative reforms have occurred, amid some consensus about what needs to be done. But what has not yet occurred is a big breakthrough. Sweden's experience implies that that consensus and those tentative reforms are helpful, perhaps essential preparation for the transformation to come.

A reasonable but simplified narrative of the Swedish transformation is that the country moved within 20 years from being one of the world's most regulated rich economies, one in which state intervention and spending was one of the world's highest outside the communist bloc, to being one of the most deregulated, with much lower levels of state intervention, taxes and spending. But, crucially, it emerged still with a broad and generous welfare system.

Public spending peaked in 1993 at the extraordinary level of 72% of GDP, though that figure was inflated somewhat by the aftermath of the financial crisis. By 2007 it was down to 49.7% of GDP. Even during the world financial crisis it rose only to 53.1% of GDP in 2009, and was back down to 50.4% by 2015. So it is a story that detractors might call neoliberal, since the state has

FIG 8.2 **Taxation and welfare spending as % of GDP, 1990–2014**

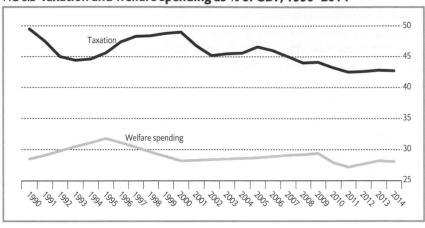

Source: OECD

been trimmed back. Yet despite that pretty drastic cut of (depending on the choice of year) 10–20 percentage points of GDP in public spending, it would be just as true today as in 1990 to say that Sweden has one of the world's most well-developed welfare systems. Public spending has been cut, but not at the expense of the welfare system, or at least of perceptions of it. Inequality of income and wealth has risen, but not very much. Sweden remains one of the most equal societies in Europe.

This is, in large part, because Sweden has successfully achieved higher levels of annual economic growth, over a long period, than its EU neighbours have. While in 1976–95 it always underperformed those neighbours, from 1995–2016 it always outperformed them. Liberalisation, extra competition, the spawning of new creative industries have all meant that there has been more tax revenue available to maintain spending on welfare (see Figure 8.2). But also money has been reallocated away from subsidies and supporting state-owned companies, and has been saved in public services by introducing more freedom of choice.

The result is that Swedes have not experienced the sort of painful trade-off between liberalisation and a smaller state on the one hand, and public services and their feeling of security on the other, that many others have since 2008. Reforms have been necessary, including to the welfare system, but a sense of trust and fairness has been maintained. Crucially, Sweden spends about half as much a share of GDP on public pensions (7.4%) as does Italy (15.8%).

The biggest anxieties that most Swedes have today are about education and immigration. On education, the worry is about falling standards in state-run schools, which have pulled Sweden lower on the OECD's PISA tests of literacy and numeracy.[3] This cannot, however, be attributed to the main educational innovation introduced during the era of reform, namely the permission given to privately run but state-funded "free schools", the owners of which are permitted to make a profit, as only 13% of pupils attend them and their average standards are higher than in conventional state schools. The deterioration has come in conventional state schools.

On immigration, the anxieties are not solely about the number of immigrants, but more about the nature of the immigration and its potential impact on public services. The overall share of the Swedish population that is foreign-born is about 16%, according to 2013 data from the OECD, which is a little higher than in the UK, France and Germany, but lower than in Ireland, Austria or Switzerland. The most politically controversial form of immigration has been that of refugees from Syria, Afghanistan, Eritrea and elsewhere in North Africa: Sweden has been accepting 80,000–100,000 such refugees each year, the highest per-head level in Europe. During the country's general elections in 2014 an anti-immigrant party, the Sweden Democrats, ran a campaign advertisement showing a race between Muslim women wearing burqas and headscarves and an elderly Swedish pensioner, portraying them as competing for public money. The Sweden Democrats shocked the political establishment by winning 12.9% of the vote. As the flow of refugees across and around the Mediterranean increased during 2015 and 2016, so the Sweden Democrats rose still higher in opinion polls, at times even topping the polls with more than 25%.

That worry about money and refugees shades into one that welfare systems might be strained by the cost of the inflow. As in many countries, the perception is that refugees have often been sent to poorer cities and regions where rental costs are lower and vacant property can be found. So while landlords profit from the refugees it is local citizens who bear the principal burden, culturally and financially. Hence the popularity, especially in such areas, of the Sweden Democrats, and the reluctant reintroduction by the Social Democrat-led government in 2015 of border controls on the long, beautiful and famous bridge connecting the Swedish city of Malmo and the Danish capital of Copenhagen. This will not shut off the country from immigration altogether, or even reduce the inflow greatly, but it will calm some of the fears of being flooded by refugees. Sweden may have been transformed and re-energised, but that has not insulated it from the problems of the world.

*

No one can insulate themselves from the problems of the world, except possibly North Korea. Within Europe, however, the country that for centuries has seemed most insulated, despite being culturally, ethnically and commercially closely linked to its neighbours, has been Switzerland. Nowadays, the Swiss feel like a remarkable hold-out from the prevailing Western mood of decline. But that was not true 20 years ago.

In the early 1990s, if Western declinists had held a box-ticking exercise to predict future candidates for failure, Switzerland would have scored highly. Conservative, rigid society? Yes. Property boom that has just gone bust? Yes. Large financial sector heavily dependent on unsustainable secrecy laws? Yes. Manufacturing vulnerable to competition from China? Yes. High wage rates and a highly valued currency liable to make exports uncompetitive? Yes. Not a member of major international collaborative institutions, such as the EU and NATO? Yes. Society with a tradition of craft and professional guilds prone to pursuing their own interests? Yes.

Well, you get the point. In the early 1990s the virtues that had made Switzerland rich, safe and stable, such as its neutrality, its tradition of banking secrecy, its decision to stay out of the big trading and security blocs, all looked liable to turn into vices. The Soviet Union was collapsing and the rest of Europe was converging on the EU, whose single-market programme, launched in the mid-1980s by the UK's prime minister, Margaret Thatcher, and the European Commission president, Jacques Delors, was looking attractive. Liberalisation, especially of trade but also through privatisations and measures to increase competition, was all the rage. Switzerland, hit by the aftermath of a property boom and bust from the 1980s and chastened by the damage done to its big watch industry over the previous two decades by cheap Japanese competition and technology, felt vulnerable.

This is not the way things look now. After a sub-par 1990s, Switzerland has flouted all the box-tickers' concerns. It even navigated the 2008 financial crisis without serious damage, despite having two giant global banks – Union Bank of Switzerland and Credit Suisse – that were heavily involved in the investment banking and derivatives trading businesses that got others into deep trouble, and even despite a series of scandals about foreigners' tax-avoiding accounts in Swiss private banks. Against the Western trend of steady decline, manufacturing still makes up 19% of its annual GDP,[4] concentrated in three successful and resilient sectors: pharmaceuticals and chemicals; precision instruments, including watches; and the machinery industry. Measured per head of population, Switzerland's manufacturing output tops the world rankings. Wage levels have remained among the world's highest, defying pressure from a steadily rising exchange rate for the Swiss franc, competition from both China and Germany, and a surge in immigration. Switzerland is feeling the squeeze of a sharp appreciation in early 2015 of the Swiss franc, of negative interest rates which annoy savers and financial institutions alike, and a backlash against immigration. But compared with other European countries, its cheeks are positively glowing.

The process that restored this rosy glow began with the response to the EU's post-cold-war appeal. In 1991–92 the Swiss government took part in negotiating an agreement between the four countries seeking designation as the European Economic Area (EEA) – which were then Norway, Iceland, Liechtenstein and Switzerland – and the EU to provide them with full access to the EU's newly deepening internal market, and then applied for full membership of the EU itself. The country – or, rather its government – felt it could not thrive in the post-cold-war world while being relatively closed and isolated. But in December of that same year the Swiss voted in a national referendum to reject membership of the EEA by a wafer-thin margin of 50.3% against 49.7%, as a result of which the government withdrew its application for full EU membership. Isolation was preferred, even if narrowly. Yet the debate may have been salutary. For it ended up playing a central role in developing what might be seen with hindsight as a policy of isolated openness. Or perhaps it might better be called loosely connected openness.

Switzerland has long been noted for its openness, give or take a few mountains standing in the way and the difficulty for outsiders of becoming fully Swiss in what is a socially conservative place – though exceptions to that openness include its farmers, who are highly protected, and still a few industrial sectors, including textiles. Through the centuries, it has both exported and imported talent and ideas, often being a refuge for émigrés and dissidents, most famously Lenin, who left by train from Zurich to launch what became the Bolshevik revolution in Russia. But following the 1992 vote and their argument over the EU, the Swiss opened their doors still further and shook up some of their internal rules and structures too. Membership of the EEA was substituted for by a set of painstakingly – and painfully – negotiated bilateral treaties with the EU that gave Switzerland a lot of the benefits of access to the EU/EEA single market in return for allowing EU citizens to come to live and work freely in Switzerland.

This right did not come fully into place until 2007 when a system of annual quotas for EU immigration was lifted. The consequences have been striking: rates of net immigration that had been running at 30,000–50,000 people per year during the 1990s more than doubled to 80,000 a year, with the result that by 2014 nearly 24% of the Swiss population of 8.1 million was made up of foreigners.[5] That is nearly twice as high a proportion as in most EU countries, including the UK and Germany,[6] or in the US. The inflow represents population growth through immigration by about 1% a year, which is twice as fast as the recent net immigration into the UK. Such openness to new people coincided with greater internal openness to competition and innovation.

Two crucial Swiss characteristics need to be mentioned at this point, for both contribute to its current success and the sense of fluency or dynamism that goes with it – and contrast especially with the accurate perception that Switzerland is a relatively conservative society. One is the flexibility of its labour market, both in higher-skilled jobs and in lower-skilled ones. Unlike Italy, Germany, Japan or France, Switzerland does not have a dual labour market with one set of contracts for temporary, short-term workers and another for permanent ones. Jan-Egbert Sturm, a Dutchman who is director of the KOF Swiss Economic Institute at the Swiss Federal Institute of Technology in Zurich, says that he could be fired at any point, whereas in a German university he would have a permanent contract.

The second is the strong emphasis on research and development collaboration between universities and private companies which, in combination with the influx of highly educated employees from EU countries, has enabled productivity growth and technological improvements to outpace wage levels and the appreciation of the Swiss franc. Such innovation is very much a bottom-up affair, but it has been pushed along over the past 20 years by more public investment in universities and by an increased number of commercial spin-offs from those research institutions.

Nevertheless, immigration has provoked tensions in Switzerland just as it has elsewhere, which is not surprising in a country of tight-knit communities in which the largest city, Zurich, has a population of just 380,000 people. A net inflow of 80,000 immigrants per year is equivalent to adding another Zurich every four to five years. What is more surprising is that it took so long for such tensions to come fully to the surface.

The main explanation for that delay may be that the surge in immigration coincided with, and contributed to, high rates of economic growth, even after the 2008 financial crisis. There is also the fact that unlike in the 1960s (when immigrants to Switzerland were often low-skilled "guest workers" from Turkey and the Balkans) much of the EU immigration during the past 15 years has been of well-educated professionals, particularly from neighbouring Germany and Austria. Rather than a brain drain Switzerland benefited from a "brain gain", importing skilled people who other countries had spent their taxpayers' money educating and training. If there was a democratic problem with this influx, it seemed likelier to be the fact that foreigners do not have the right to vote – which is significant in a country in which so many decisions, both national and local, are made by referendums – than that Swiss citizens might object to there being so many foreigners taking their jobs and perhaps snaffling promotions. But that is what did happen, eventually.

A referendum in 2009 sought a ban on the construction of one of the symbols of non-Christian immigration, namely mosque minarets, and was passed by a clear majority (57.5%) even though the country at that time had only four minarets. The rumbling of anti-immigrant sentiment, led by the right-wing Swiss People's Party, grew sufficiently noisy that in February 2014 a further national referendum was held to challenge mass immigration itself. To the shock both of the EU and of the Swiss establishment, the referendum against mass immigration was won by a majority just as narrow as in the 1992 vote against EU membership: 50.3% against 49.7%. The vote was almost as shocking at the time to Switzerland's EU neighbours as the UK's Brexit vote two years later. So the Swiss government has had to go back to the negotiating table with the EU. The referendum's demand for a return to controls, perhaps based on quotas, contravenes the agreement struck with the EU in the bilateral treaties.

Open Switzerland has thus opted to close its doors, at least to some extent. How much it closes them remains to be negotiated – and the EU has made clear that for it free movement of people is an all-or-nothing affair. If Switzerland cannot find a formula that continues to permit EU citizens to live and work there freely (and vice versa), it is likely to find its commercial access to the EU single market hindered and its institutions' participation in EU-funded programmes such as joint university research curtailed.

The only potential scope for compromise lies either in a vaguely worded "emergency brake" agreement under which immigration could be slowed or suspended only at times when it is unusually rapid, or in the setting of a maximum annual quota that limits immigration in theory but in practice is higher than the numbers actually expected to arrive. Neither type of loose control is likely to be enough to satisfy the political forces that were behind the 2014 referendum – the Swiss People's Party has doubled its share of the vote in federal elections, from 14.9% in 1995 to 29.4% in 2015.

Does an insistence on limiting immigration mean that a country such as Sweden or Switzerland is turning from being open to closed? It could do, but it doesn't have to. It means that Sweden and Switzerland are becoming a bit less welcoming, but this needs to be placed against the fact that both, in their different ways, were already a great deal more welcoming than most other Western countries.

For small countries like all the Scandinavian nations and Switzerland, being closed is not an option: trade and the exchange of technology and ideas are too important for such countries and for their citizens. The same is not necessarily true of bigger countries, such as the UK, France or the US. For them, closing the doors is a more viable choice – though that does not make it a wise one. The bracing winds of new opportunities, new freedoms, new competition and new ideas that have been necessary for all the revival stories seen so far among modern, advanced democracies, do not flow as freely through closed doors as they do through open ones. Although size can make you more self-sufficient, it does not make you more dynamic, innovative or adaptable. Openness is needed too, aided always by equality.

9

Silver hair and smart drones

"You are old, Father William," the young man said,
"And your hair has become very white;
And yet you incessantly stand on your head –
Do you think, at your age, it is right?"

Lewis Carroll, Alice's Adventures in Wonderland, 1865

WHAT MIGHT OSWALD SPENGLER SAY TODAY if he were putting forward civilisational arguments for why the West is doomed to decline? Transported to 2017, he might begin by lingering over the traps our democracies have set for themselves, a form of government of which he was always sceptical as being merely a tool of money. He might argue that we had gone much too far over human rights, privacy and other such sentimental nonsense, all in his view a disguise for class war. He would surely take an interest in how we mess up in our military adventures by being still so arrogant that we cannot resist the urge to intervene abroad but too lily-livered to carry through our interventions to the full-blown conquest, occupation and colonisation in which we once specialised – just as countries had felt able to start the Great War but not to finish it decisively.

Finally, though, Spengler would find his eye drawn to two of the most common current arguments for why Western civilisation could be heading for trouble: demography and technology. He would note that because of our unwillingness to have enough children to replace ourselves the balance of our populations was swinging towards the elderly and would wonder how we could possibly as an ageing society come up with new vigour and new ideas. Our populations are shrinking and growing wrinklier, which has never before been the sign of a dominant civilisation. The West, he would say, will eventually be overtaken by those that do have children, that create peoples that have a strong sense of identity, and that, to use a modern term, are able to reap a "demographic dividend" from an abundant supply of educated young adults. And he would look at the latest trends in technology and shudder in disbelief at the fact that we have set many of our brainiest scientists the task of making ourselves obsolete by producing artificial brains for robots and other automated machines – final proof of our self-destructiveness as a civilisation.

A sprinkling of statistics can reinforce this Spenglerian gloom.[1] By 2030, nearly one-quarter of the population of today's 28 EU countries will be aged 65 or over, and by 2050 the elderly's share will be about one-third. These elderly fractions compare with an already substantial 18.5% in 2014, compared with 14% in 1994. Even in the immigrant magnet of the United States, the share will rise from 15% today to nearly 25% by 2050.

Japan is already at that point: by 2014 more than 26% of the population were 65 or over. Moreover, Japan is home to more than 60,000 people aged 100 or more; when it first started compiling statistics of that age group, in 1963, there were just 153 centenarians.[2] In April 2016 I visited a Japanese abstract artist, Toko Shinoda, who had her first public exhibition in 1940 and is still producing art every day at the age of 103. In 2015 she had a book published jointly with a journalist who interviewed her which sold more than 500,000 copies, an indication that the Japanese public is now fascinated by such centenarianism. She lives alone at her apartment and studio in central Tokyo, and is looked after by a maid who commutes one hour each way, six days a week, for the task. The maid is 78.

Meanwhile the population of Africa, which totalled 477 million in 1980, has nearly tripled to 1.2 billion and is projected by the UN Population Division on the basis of current trends in birth and death rates to double again to 2.4 billion by 2050. Where Westerners are having fewer births each year than at any time in the past two centuries and in almost every country have fertility at or often well below the replacement rate of an average of 2.1 children per woman, Africans are multiplying, often with fertility rates still of 5 children per woman, and are being kept alive by better health care. Perhaps, a contemporary Spengler might speculate, a future dominant civilisation could emanate from the very continent that gave birth to *Homo sapiens* in the first place.

It might, of course. Today most commentary on Africa's population growth takes a more pessimistic tone, concerned about the pressure of population amid climate change, stress on water resources, interstate conflict and civil war. But then so it once did about Asia, where population "explosions" in South Asia and China were causes célèbres in the 1950s and 1960s, leading the Swedish Nobel prize-winning economist Gunnar Myrdal to write his book *Asian Drama: An Inquiry into the Poverty of Nations*. Someone today might be planning a book called *African Drama* and, like Myrdal, could find their predictions confounded by events – though, to be fair, Myrdal was less wrong about India, Bangladesh and the rest of South Asia than he would have been had he devoted more of his attention to China and East Asia. Be that as it may, the more telling point against a Spenglerian perspective is that if a large number of African countries really did succeed during the next half century or more in emulating East Asia's economic development model, educating their growing populations as they did, then two things would almost certainly happen. The first is that with development and education their birth rates would plummet, for this is what happened in China, South Korea and other East Asian successes. The second is that many or even all of them would adopt the idea of the West, as their growing middle classes demanded the openness and equality of political rights that South Koreans, Taiwanese and others have demanded before them. Civilisations would not clash, but would converge.

Our demographic destiny is not a matter of being overrun or superseded by more demographically vigorous peoples. It will be a matter of adapting to and trying to overcome the economic, social and political consequences of ageing, which is itself a consequence of success. Given the past record of Western ideas in overcoming previous challenges, it would be unwise to bet against the West adapting to ageing too – especially since, as this chapter's analysis will show, ageing is a phenomenon that is shared with much of the world, most notably the West's biggest current rival, China. The proper bet will concern which of China (and other authoritarian regimes) or the West will adapt more successfully to ageing.

So here is a question to start to educate that bet. If you had laid the aforementioned scenario of one-third of Europeans being over 65, or of Japan's population of centenarians climbing rapidly towards 100,000, in front of the science-fiction writers of the past, what technological solutions or consequences would they have dreamt up? The answer would surely be intelligent robots and other applications of artificial brainpower, to supplement or make up for the declining physical and mental faculties of the elderly. Indeed, the very idea of a humanoid machine has come from fiction, not just recently but through the ages. Like so much else, drawings of robots can be found in Leonardo da Vinci's works. Far from the development of artificial intelligence for machines being an insane act of self-obsolescence, it is exactly what is needed as part of the process of adaptation to ageing.

It is the idea that brainy robots will in future make humans obsolete and bring about unemployment that is truly far-fetched. Yet, remarkably, that notion has become more or less conventional wisdom. A book forecasting just that, Martin Ford's *The Rise of the Robots*, won the 2015 Business Book of the Year prize awarded jointly by the *Financial Times* and McKinsey & Company.

*

The idea that mass unemployment might be caused by technological innovation, especially an army of brainy robots, is evidently tempting, intriguing and worrying, even to economic and business experts such as those at the *Financial Times* and McKinsey. If people can lose their jobs because of the arrival of millions of cheap Chinese, Vietnamese and Indian workers on the world market during the 1990s and 2000s, which is what is meant by the damaging consequences of globalisation, why shouldn't the same kind of thing happen as a result of automation? It could in theory, just as many forms of economic, social or political apocalypse could happen in theory. But that does not make it likely. For the idea runs up against three major objections: one empirical, one practical and one based on economics.

The empirical objection is today's equivalent to what economists came in the 1980s to call the Solow productivity paradox. At a time when the arrival of personal computers and all the rest of the information technology revolution were hot topics and that era's source of breathless optimism, Robert Solow, an American economist who won the Nobel prize for his work on economic growth, quipped in 1987 that "you can see the computer age everywhere but in the productivity statistics". A lot seemed to be happening, but it did not appear to be having the expected economic impact.

However, we did start to see some impact from the computer age in the mid-1990s, an impact that lasted for roughly a decade (depending on the country), during which the annual rate of growth in labour productivity perked up. But since then, even as the digital age has brought new wonders of connectivity and of processing power carried in the palm of every hand, productivity growth has slowed or at best been disappointing, on all measures. If digital innovation – all those labour-bypassing novelties such as airline boarding passes issued to your mobile phone or income-tax returns filed online – has not brought noticeable gains in productivity by displacing costly, inefficient workers, why should we expect such gains to become spectacular as software adds intelligence to more and more machines, now or in the future? If automation were to bring mass unemployment, it would have to do so by eliminating millions of workers and making the remaining ones more productive. It would be seen in the productivity statistics.

It is possible, as with computers and IT, that there will be a time lag before ways of doing business are reorganised to exploit intelligent machines. There was a time lag before the invention of electricity led to factories being reorganised to exploit it.[3] It is also possible that some of the gains may be being missed in productivity measurements, especially in the service industries that now dominate all Western economies. But still, what the facts so far indicate is that the impact of automation on overall levels of employment remains somewhere between small and undetectable, relative to other macroeconomic factors. There has of course been high unemployment in Western economies during the past decade, but we need look no further than the biggest financial crash and recession since the 1930s to find an explanation. Automation may, like IT and Chinese competition in manufacturing, be influencing the types of jobs that are being filled, and as such could be contributing to inequality by further undermining the bargaining power and employability of people with relatively few skills. This is important but is a very different matter from mass unemployment.

It is not as if robots and drones are rare. According to the International Federation of Robotics more than 229,000 industrial robots were sold worldwide in 2014, which compares with the 97,000 sold in 2004. Japan alone already uses more than 250,000 industrial robots, and caught media attention in 2015 when a new hotel at a theme park near Nagasaki, on the south-west island of Kyushu, proudly boasted of using androids as multilingual receptionists and cleaning staff.[4] As the theme park where the hotel is located is itself a pretend Dutch town, Huis ten Bosch, the artificiality of android staff is somehow fitting. Meanwhile, at least 1 million drones (that is, miniature, pilotless aircraft) were sold in 2015; according to *The Economist*,[5] as recently as 2010 the US Federal Aviation Authority had predicted that there would only be around 15,000 drones in use in the United States by 2020, a forecast which will join the pantheon of dud predictions alongside that attributed to Thomas J. Watson, creator of IBM, in 1943 to the effect that there would only ever be a world market for about five computers.

It may be too early to draw clear conclusions, but the age of the smart drone and brainy robot is not yet detectable in the productivity statistics. Indeed, the second, practical, objection is that the age of true robotic braininess may be even further away than today's enthusiasts think. Artificial intelligence has achieved some impressive feats, thanks to growth in processing power. The victory of IBM's "Watson" computer in the TV quiz show *Jeopardy* in 2011 was one landmark; the victory of Google's "AlphaGo" computer in a three-match series of the Chinese board game Go in 2016 over a South Korean Go champion, Lee Se-dol, was another. But as the head of the Stanford University Artificial Intelligence Lab, Li Fei-Fei,[6] told a group including me at a small conference in Palo Alto a few months later, there is still a vast gap between such achievements and scientists' ability to master the task of matching even simple functions of the human brain, especially vision. Sensors can do extraordinary things. But the human brain, through its ability to recognise and interpret images in subtle, associative ways, can do things that are even more extraordinary.

The Stanford AI Lab is ranked as the best in the world. In Li's judgment, there is an enormous amount to be done before the prediction by Ray Kurzweil, in his 2005 book *The Singularity is Near*, can come true, namely that by 2045 the brain power of all machines will surpass that of all human brains. This is not to belittle the prediction, but rather to say that "singularity", as Kurzweil terms it, is half a century away even on his own estimation, and perhaps even more. As with previous waves of innovation, we cannot know in advance how rapid the progress will be or how quickly it will find its most widespread applications. It could surprise us in either its rapidity or its slowness. But whichever surprise occurs, it is surely likelier that the impact of artificial intelligence will come not as a sudden shock but as a series of events – just as has occurred with the broader IT revolution. Mass unemployment is what comes from sudden shocks, to which people, companies and wider economies cannot readily adapt. When technology develops incrementally, even if rapidly, the effect is not a shock but an adjustment – which can be painful or otherwise for many people, but it is an adjustment nevertheless.

Many of the great advances of the digital age have surprised us. But many of these advances have changed what we do as much by creating new opportunities, not all of them productive in a directly economic sense, as by replacing old activities. None of us is quite clear whether our smartphones have, on balance, added to our productivity or just enabled us to do, and get information about, new things and to communicate with each other more often. The impact of smartphones may be more a matter of improvements in the quality of information or of entertaining experiences, including social ones, rather than of increasing the quantity of what we can do, at least for those of us in the West who already had telephones, televisions and mass literacy, and thus had already made the greatest leaps of the information age. It may be like owning a smarter, fancier car: it cannot transport us more quickly or frequently from A to B, but it makes getting there more comfortable and pleasurable. The same could prove to be true of some applications of AI.

That said, just as computing power and better communications have displaced some human labour, or else enabled cheaper humans far across the world to do work previously done in affluent Western countries, so brainy robots, smart drones and other forms of more intelligent automation are bound to have some effect on work and who does it. It would be surprising if it didn't. If Amazon really does carry out its rumoured plans to use an air force of drones to deliver some of its goods, this will have some effect on its employment of other delivery methods. The same would be true if it were to deploy autonomous, driverless vans to make deliveries. Yet it is hard to foresee what such automation would displace – conventional Amazon deliveries or driving yourself to a shop – just as with driverless cars it is not obvious whether their biggest effect will be to put taxi drivers and chauffeurs out of work or to enable car owners to be more productive while they are travelling, just as they are thanks to WiFi on trains. There could also be a more positive sort of displacement effect: if more basic services such as delivery became automated, companies could compete more on the basis of the human element, of judgment, empathy, personalisation and more, to win customers and justify their pricing.

In the end, the real questions about intelligent machines concern the balance between displacing people and liberating them to do more or better things, and at what scale and speed either of these effects will occur. Which brings in the third objection, which arises from economics.

For there to be a massive and rapid move to replace human labour with machines there would need to be a massive wave of capital investment in such machines. Today's low interest rates on borrowing could make such investment more readily financeable than before. But what companies also need before they embark on capital investment is demand, or an expectation of it. Admittedly, some might invest in these smart machines in the hope of stealing demand from existing firms and ways of doing things – "disruptive" investment in the manner that the Uber ride-hailing company has been competing with taxi and other transport firms for transport demand. But diversion of demand is unlikely to be enough to produce the massive effect that the rise-of-the-robots view envisages.

In the aftermath of the financial crash and long post-crash recessions, private investment has been weak, not strong, regardless of the technological progress going on at the same time. Investment has been declining in all the main Western economies. This is not what you would expect if technology were sweeping all before it.

There is a fundamental logical problem: the more that automation causes unemployment or drives workers into lower-paid jobs, the more it will undermine overall demand in the economy, and so weaken the incentive to make further labour-replacing investment. Someone needs to be able to buy the goods and services that the brainy robots produce, since unlike Henry Ford's new factory workers 100 years ago when he pioneered mass production, the robots are not themselves going to be consumers. Those who profit from the investments – entrepreneurs, shareholders, senior managers – might spend some or all of their gains on goods and services. But whether such consumption would be enough to drive demand for automation has to be doubtful.

For that reason, the spectre of labour-displacing automation should not be understood as being a matter of mass unemployment, a sort of neo-Marxist crisis of capitalism. More likely by far is that it will continue, perhaps even exacerbate, the phenomenon that is already being seen in Western economies, namely some rise in inequality and a spread of low wages as previously well-paid employees find that their skills are less valued in the labour market than before. This is what Japan has lived through for the past decade or more, and it is what the US and the UK have seen during their long recoveries from 2008.

How much of that weakness in demand and wage levels arises from technology and how much from broader macroeconomic factors consequent upon the financial crash is hard to determine. Some economies, including the US, can date their current weakness in earnings to well before 2008, but not all can do so. Technology is the most transferable of factors: not instantly or identically, but it does tend to flow across borders. If the effect was really powerful, you would expect to see its manifestations in all the advanced economies, even if at differing levels. So why isn't it happening in Switzerland? No one would think of that country as being technologically backward, or being one where there is a supply of cheap labour, yet despite its highly flexible labour market it has so far seen none of the adverse effects of automation that are widely mooted. Nor are such effects obvious in Sweden, our other revival story from Chapter 8. The impact of technology on inequality may not be as automatic or inevitable as is commonly thought.

In the context of ageing societies, moreover, another aspect should be borne in mind. It is that the use of intelligent machines may prove constructive as much as destructive. What if it is not to be a matter of humans versus brainy machines but of humans enhanced by brainy machines?

*

One way in which a continuing, probably growing, demand for brainy robots or other machines is likely to be generated is among the rising numbers of elderly Westerners. Their demand for health care, which is highly labour-intensive, is already huge. The need for nurses and doctors forms one of the least controversial cases for permitting immigration in all countries – even Japan – since everyone knows they will need nurses and doctors at some point, and are happy the cheaper they are. Robots are currently too primitive to replace either nurses or doctors, and health-care work is clearly personal and requires both sensitivity and judgment. But in time that will change. Nurses will be supplemented by androids, and it is a safe bet that this will happen first in Japan, which is already leading the world in the development of technology to serve its ageing population.

A basic conundrum, or sometimes contradiction, in forecasts of Western societies over the coming decades concerns whether or not those countries should expect to have a surplus of workers or a shortage of them. If the fears about brainy robots creating mass unemployment were to come true, the answer would be a surplus. Or, in a more moderate version, these intelligent

FIG 9.1 **Working age (15–64) population, 1950–2050** million

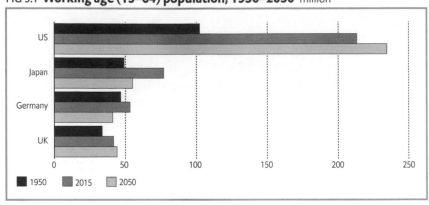

Source: UN Population Division

machines would drive more and more people into lowly paid jobs, such as nursing. Yet if you look at demographic forecasts, the supply of people of working age, which statisticians traditionally define as being those between 15 and 64, is set to decline in some Western countries, most notably Japan and Germany (see Figure 9.1).

This suggests that the future should bring a shortage of labour. But what, really, is meant by "working age"? If we are healthier than our parents and grandparents' generation as we enter our 60s and 70s, and are enjoying a longer life expectancy, shouldn't we rethink our working lives, too? This is increasingly what is happening, whether by financial necessity or by a desire to keep active and fit. Yet the extent of such adjustment varies hugely among Western countries, showing that it is a consequence of public policy choices, even if some are disguised as cultural ones. As Figure 9.2 shows, South Korea and Japan are the pioneers in extending working lives.

Although Japan has seen its old-style working-age population decline quite rapidly (and its total population has also begun to shrink, rather more slowly), the size of its population actively engaged in the labour force has remained fairly stable. A large increase in participation by adult women of all ages has contributed a lot to this. But so has participation by the over-65s. As with women, much of the work for the over-65s has been part-time and fairly low-paid. With official Japanese unemployment rates at only 3% of the labour

FIG 9.2 **Employment rate of over-65s, 2015** %

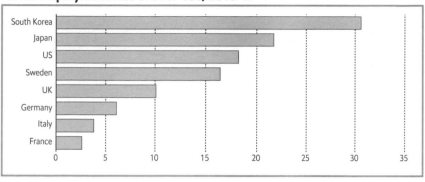

Source: OECD

force, this could well change as and when a labour shortage starts to bite, sending wage rates higher and increasing demand for the skills and experience accumulated by older workers. To stay part-time might be a popular choice among the over-65s. But to be poorly paid is not.

Japan has done much more to adapt its practices and its people to its new demographic condition than has France. That country still has persistently high unemployment (it has ranged between 9 and 11% of the labour force during the past five years), though there is little evidence that this has much to do with automation. What France has as a consequence is a big financial burden on the public purse that arises from the interaction of retirement ages, pensions and increasing life expectancy. Figure 9.3, compiled by Nicholas Eberstadt of the American Enterprise Institute in Washington, DC, shows the issue rather starkly.

If the lines for life expectancy and retirement age look like the jaws of a crocodile, this is because if nothing is done about it this is how the West's solvency, economic vigour and even political viability will be gobbled up. It is not simply that the French are living longer. Despite a considerable reduction in the physical stress of a typical working life over the past three decades, as the hard manual occupations of agriculture, mining and factory work have declined massively as a share of employment, the average age at which men have retired from the labour market dropped from 67 in 1970 to a low point of 58.5 in 2006, since when it has risen to just below 60. And although France,

FIG 9.3 **France: male life expectancy and retirement age, 1970–2014**

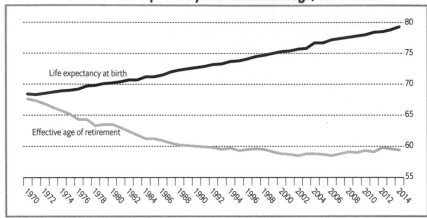

Sources: OECD; Human Mortality Database

along with Italy, is a particularly clear case of this trend towards earlier retirement even as lifespans lengthen, it is not alone. In 2014, on the OECD's definition of the average effective retirement age, 19 of the organisation's 35 member countries had a male retirement age of less than 65.[7]

Adaptation to ageing societies will require a rethinking of what is meant by working age, which also means a rethinking of the whole cycle of our working lives, as well as a rethinking of public-pension entitlements, in terms of both their affordability and the incentives they create. None of this will be easy, especially at a time when the West feels less than economically and politically robust. There is, however, one important silver lining to this cloud. It is that the West is not alone in having to adapt and rethink in this way. Ageing is a global phenomenon.

Over the past three decades, we have grown used to the idea that Western industries and workers face stiff competition from the huge supply of cheap and increasingly well-educated and well-trained workers elsewhere in the world, most notably in China. Over the next three decades there will still be truth to that – India has a large, young population, as does Africa, though neither population is yet well educated – but one large part of the story is going to change. It is that China's population is now ageing too, just as rapidly as in the West.

FIG 9.4 **Median age of population, 1990–2050**

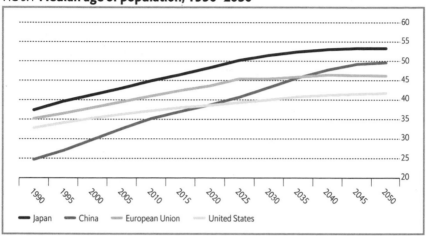

Sources: Eurostat; UN Population Division

At some point in the 2030s the median age (the age at which half the population is younger and half older) in China is due to overtake that in the United States. It is due to catch up with the median age in the EU in the late 2040s. China will remain younger on that measure than Japan, but the gap between these East Asian rivals will have narrowed considerably. China's working-age population began to fall in 2014, nearly 20 years after the same turning point had been reached in Japan.

China has, however, already caught up with Europe on another aspect of ageing. We do not think of China as being like France, with a generous welfare state and pension entitlements. Nor do we think of the Chinese as living lives of leisure. Yet perhaps we should begin to do so. For the average effective age of retirement in China in 2016 was an extraordinary 54, about six years younger than in France.[8] The official retirement age in China is 60 for men and 50–55 for women, ages which have not been adjusted to account for rising life expectancy (which at birth in 2015 was 76). But the effective age is a lot younger for reasons that would be familiar in France or Italy: state-owned enterprises have been forced to lay off millions of workers since the late 1990s, and retirement on state pensions has been a convenient way to cushion the blow, avert protests and pass the cost on to the government. Such state pensions are not exactly generous, but retirees' incomes are often supplemented by their (generally one-child) families. Not coincidentally, the national pension scheme fell into deficit in 2014 and 2015.

The result is that the Chinese government is engaged in a tug of war between those who want to push back retirement ages to make pension schemes affordable and those who want to restructure loss-making industries such as coal and steel with the help of early retirement. The French government, like those in several other European countries, is engaged in a tug of war between pensioners and soon-to-be pensioners who want to keep their right to retire in their late 50s and enjoy perhaps three or four decades of retirement while collecting a taxpayer-financed pension – often as long a retirement as their working life – and those taxpayers, politicians and economists who think some of that public money would be better spent on education, science or infrastructure, or returned to the taxpayer through lower taxes.

Over the next decade or so we will thus witness what is almost a laboratory-quality experiment in whether an authoritarian government is better equipped to deal with such tensions and trade-offs between conflicting priorities and interest groups, or whether advanced democracies prove better at doing so. If demography has an impact on national competitiveness, the decisive factor will not be your country's particular demographic profile. It will concern how well you are able to adjust to it.

*

The answer may often depend on the smartness and political will of politicians and policymakers. But it will also depend on the attitude of electorates. The main danger for Western countries is that their ageing electorates could become increasingly conservative and selfish. A new form of the old scourge of democracy, the tyranny of the majority, could emerge along with silver hairs.

Older voters are more numerous than before, but they are also, as always, more engaged politically than are the young. In the British general election of 2015, turnout among those aged 18–24 was just 43% of eligible voters, and for those aged 25–34 it was 54%, compared with an overall electoral turnout of 66.1%. Among those 65 and over, however, it was 78%, and among the 55–64 age group it was 77%. The American presidential election of 2012 showed a similar pattern: a 40% turnout for those aged 18–29, 70% for those aged 60 or older. And registration rates for 2016 reflected that disparity. In Japan the gap between the young and the old is also wide: in the 2012 general election just 38% of those in their 20s voted while 75% of those in their 60s did so, and 63% of those in their 70s.[9]

With the over-65s now forming 20–25% of the population in most Western countries and soon to be 30% in some, these differences in voting behaviour will become more and more important, politically. No wonder that even as the UK's Conservative–Liberal Democrat coalition government of 2010–15 was cutting public spending, including many welfare benefits, to try to get the budget deficit and public debt back under control, the prime minister, David Cameron, made a special point of pampering the elderly by guaranteeing a "triple lock" for state pensions by which they would rise every year by the higher of the consumer price index, average earnings or 2.5%, and by protecting perks such as a "winter fuel allowance" that is not means-tested and so is sent to millionaires and paupers alike. Older voters may then have played a crucial role in securing Cameron his surprise absolute majority in the 2015 election, making that pampering of pensioners look like money well spent. One year later, however, older voters repaid Cameron by voting strongly in favour of leaving the EU in the Brexit referendum, leading to his resignation. (Polls suggest that 60% of those 65 and over voted to leave, while younger voters voted to remain by similar margins.)

The tug of war to make ageing societies affordable is likely, given this political background, to become a war of attrition in many Western countries. The financial issues are more complicated than they look, especially in societies where family ties remain close and important. Italy is a prime example: its young are suffering from low pay, precarious jobs on temporary contracts and a consequent inability to do family-building things such as taking out a mortgage to buy a house; meanwhile the cost of public pensions for their parents and grandparents eats up nearly 16% of GDP. Yet in many families the parents and grandparents share both their capital – that is houses – and their pension income with their children and grandchildren. Such dependency would look unhealthy and undesirable to a Swede, a Briton or an American, but to an Italian it is normal, even admirable. So attempts to cut back that flow at one end will also face objections from younger voters, partly out of filial loyalty but also self-interest. If there was confidence that alongside cuts there would also be new economic growth, new jobs, new opportunities, it might be different. But for the time being, there isn't.

The result is that adapting to ageing feels similar to the task of adapting to climate change. It is hard to persuade people to make sacrifices or adjustments today in the cause of gains in the distant future for the sake of later generations, so a more incremental, ratcheting approach is required. Small steps need to be made that are then entrenched in law, in institutions and in cultural assumptions, in so far as it is possible. This has already been the approach used in many countries to push back the retirement age and thus the beginning of eligibility for public pensions. Personal awareness that savings and entitlements are inadequate will also steadily gain hold, increasing the incentive to continue to work rather than retire.

A bolder, but potentially costly, option could be to implement a legal right, or perhaps employment-related entitlement analogous to maternity leave, to a period or periods of education and training later in life, so as to make a longer working life more palatable and manageable. If people are to expect working lives lasting 50 years or more, the education they received when young is never going to be enough to prepare them for it. Employers and outsourced training provide most of the continuing education that workers need or want, but in a fluid and insecure labour market they cannot be relied upon to provide all of it. Forms of institutional supplement to that education are necessary but also can helpfully add to people's confidence.

Human capital – education, experience, training, social skills – is becoming more important in our digital, information age than ever before. It is hardly a novel observation to say that we live in a knowledge society. That comment has been made ever since the Enlightenment drove forward scientific and technological progress, but probably also before then and certainly many times since. Peter Drucker was perhaps the most insistent writer in recent decades on this point that knowledge is now the basic resource of all economic and indeed social development, as well as the basic determinant of personal, corporate and national success and failure. Drucker continued to publish books and articles into his early 90s. Writing a special report for *The Economist* in 2001, at the age of 92 (he died in 2005 aged 95), he was remarkably prescient both on demography and on the impact of the knowledge society:

> *Politicians everywhere still promise to save the existing pensions system, but they – and their constituents – know perfectly well that in another 25 years people will have to keep working until their mid-70s, health permitting.*

What has not yet sunk in is that a growing number of older people – say those over 50 – will not keep on working as traditional full-time nine-to-five employees, but will participate in the labour force in many new and different ways: as temporaries, as part-timers, as consultants, on special assignments and so on. What used to be personnel and are now known as human-resources departments still assume that those who work for an organisation are full-time employees. Employment laws and regulations are based on the same assumption. Within 20 or 25 years, however, perhaps as many as half the people who work for an organisation will not be employed by it, certainly not on a full-time basis. This will be especially true for older people.

Today, the rise of the self-employed in the labour force – often caricatured as the Uber generation – is looked at with shock and awe. Yet Drucker already saw clearly, 15 years ago, the way things were likely to develop, simply as a logical consequence of the interaction of longer working lives and digital technologies.

This rise of the self-employed is in reality a return to a previous era: at the opening of the 20th century, most people either ran their own businesses as farmers or supplied their services to farmers, industrial companies or construction firms as external contractors and casual labourers. In his book *The Sharing Economy*, Arun Sundararajan, a professor at Stern School of Business at New York University, says that in 1900 the proportion of workers in the US who were self-employed was three times as high as it is today. They didn't necessarily like it, since they were insecure, and in the absence of widespread public education they were far from being the "knowledge workers" of today. But they lived with it. Our era will be shaped by similar trade-offs between insecurity and freedom, between the power of knowledge and a sense of powerlessness.

In his *Economist* special report in 2001, Drucker predicted that two big trends were likely to become politically controversial, even toxic, in the West: the decline in manufacturing, which would lead to a new protectionism; and immigration, deemed necessary to fill demographic gaps but deemed undesirable or uncomfortable by many ordinary people. Both of these trends have been seen in the rise of populist anti-globalist, anti-immigrant parties in Europe over the past decade. But see also what Drucker wrote about the politics of immigration in the US, the country most culturally attuned to it:

A future Democratic candidate for the American presidency may have to choose between getting the union vote by opposing immigration, or getting the vote of Latinos and other newcomers by supporting it. Equally, a future Republican candidate may have to choose between the support of business, which is clamouring for workers, and the vote of a white middle class that increasingly opposes immigration.

Chip in some references to trade, whether the Trans-Pacific Partnership that the US under President Barack Obama was negotiating with 12 countries around the Pacific but that both Hillary Clinton and Donald Trump chose to disown, or the US's relationships with countries such as China and Japan with which it runs large trade deficits which Trump pledged to bring to an end, and this could have been a description of the 2016 presidential race. What needs further to be considered, however, is the impact of those predicted tendencies towards protectionism and hostility to immigration on international relations. It is always tempting, during troubled times, to pick on foreigners so as to have someone else to blame. The problem is that some foreigners have a habit of picking on you, too. And to deal with such enemies, the West's greatest asset in the past has been its friendships. The quickest way to lose those friendships would be to pick fights with each other over trade and migration.

10

Barbarians at the gate

And I will show you something different from either
Your shadow at morning striding behind you
Or your shadow at evening rising to meet you;
I will show you fear in a handful of dust

T. S. Eliot, *The Waste Land*, 1922, I: "The Burial of the Dead"

Old pond
A frog jumps into
The sound of water

Matsuo Basho, 1644–94

You're not going to like what comes after America.

Leonard Cohen, 1934–2016

RUTHLESS, VIOLENT PEOPLE have many advantages. No scruples stand in their way. They can use fear to impose their will and to serve their interests. Max Weber, a German sociologist, gave us a standard definition of statehood as being an entity in possession of a monopoly of the legitimate use of physical force within a given territory. The vital word there is legitimate, but its synonyms are not "benevolent", "nice", "popular" or even "constitutional". These words would, give or take a dose of democratic debate, be applicable in the West. But they are not applicable in Russia or China, and they are not the words that would be used by Abu Bakr al-Baghdadi and the organisation he wishes to call Islamic State in the territories in which he is seeking to monopolise the use of force. For such states or would-be states, the meaning of legitimate is instead "accepted", or perhaps "unchallenged", showing merely that the monopoly has been successfully established. Which is where the fear comes in, laced with forms of ideological, nationalistic or religious inducements.

Today, we have a lot of fear all around us. There is a lot of use of physical force or threats of it, near our borders, in our cities, in seas that previously were thought to be calm. We always did have fear around us during the post-1945 decades, and there always has been violence near at hand. On many measures, the raw quantity of violence has actually been diminishing.[1] What is different today is that Europe, Japan, the United States and the rest of the West feel weak and impotent in the face of it, potential victims rather than having any real sense of control or ability to contain it. Moreover, recent events in Ukraine and the South China Sea have led the West to fear that its attempt to place that Weberian notion of "legitimate use of physical force" within an accepted framework of international law might have run its course. Now, a new American president has arrived in the White House bringing rather different ideas of his own about how to operate in international affairs and about whether rules really matter. When the UN Charter and other treaties were being set up after 1945, the US secretary of state, Dean Acheson, wrote subsequently about having been "present at the creation". The fear now is of being present at the destruction.

How different things feel compared with that brief, more confident time in the 1990s, after the cold war and its fear of nuclear conflagration had ended, when those lucky enough to live in affluent, peaceful, open societies were able to tell themselves that fear and violence were in decline, perhaps permanently. Russia was no longer able or wishing to stir up violence in proxy wars around the world, and seemed to be on a path to becoming a collaborator in establishing peace and the rule of law. China still killed its own people, but seemed to be focusing on economic development and on settling border disputes with its neighbours rather than on exporting revolution or otherwise causing trouble overseas. The two serial troublemakers in the Middle East and North Africa, Saddam Hussein of Iraq and Muammar Gadhafi of Libya, both seemed contained, weakened and quiescent. That left the pariah would-be nuclear states of North Korea and Iran, but in both cases there seemed to be some chance of international collaboration to contain or even – in our dreams – disarm them.

This prettier, more peaceful picture depended on a large measure of wilful blindness. Life did not look less violent to the residents of swathes of sub-Saharan Africa, where millions died during the 1990s in wars in Somalia, in what is now the Democratic Republic of Congo, in Sierra Leone, Liberia and most notoriously Rwanda – to name just the worst conflicts of that period. Nor, closer to Western homes, did life feel less fearful to the residents of the former Yugoslavia, where the series of wars from 1991 onwards led to a death toll variously estimated as between 150,000 and 250,000 people, right on the borders of the European Union. Nor to those who died in Indonesia's separatist wars over the provinces of Aceh and East Timor, the latter since 2002 independent under the new name of Timor-Leste. Nor to those in Chechnya who fought unsuccessfully for independence from Russia, and saw their capital, Grozny, reduced to rubble, nor indeed to Afghans, the strife in whose country disappeared from Western TV screens and newspaper headlines once neither the Soviet Union nor the United States was involved.

It was not a peaceful decade, despite all the hopes with which it began. The main feature was that more of the violence took place in internal conflicts or civil wars than in battles between states, civil wars which technological progress brought more quickly and clearly to television screens than had been the case before. Indeed, although the violence of the 1990s was especially eye-catching and heart-rending, in global terms it represented a decline compared with previous decades and was followed by a sharp increase in such violence during the first decades of the 21st century.

The notion, emanating not from US governments but from some commentators in Washington, DC, that from 1990 on the world had become "unipolar",[2] led by a country whose dominance could be compared to that of the Roman Empire at its height, was grossly misleading, even though that hegemon had just successfully led a wide military coalition to victory over Saddam Hussein in 1990–91 in the first Gulf war, driving him out of Kuwait and defending the post-1945 principle that international borders should not be redrawn by force. This was much too sharp a swing in thinking and analysis to be credible. After all, much of the talk among journalists and historians during the previous five years had been of American decline, of the country being surpassed economically by Japan and of it suffering from "imperial overstretch"[3] in military affairs. The US had supposedly been the superpower heading for the scrapheap, not the Soviet Union. Those ideas of American decline and of American supremacy could not both be right within a decade of one another. But they could both be wrong.

In fact the US, after its Gulf war success was followed by embarrassing failure in Somalia in 1993, became noticeably less willing to intervene militarily abroad for several years. Under President Bill Clinton, the emphasis became one of building collaborative networks and of seeking ways to bring in and bind in former foes to those networks. This was a sign of reluctance and of gentle withdrawal from the role as "global policeman" often allocated to the US by its allies, but it was also an attempt to build a set of international rules of the game, policed by multilateral institutions. In the eyes of President George H. W. Bush, who was in the White House when the Soviet Union fell, and even more in the eyes of his successor President Clinton, the most significant change was not American hegemony but the fact that the world no longer contained an entity – the Soviet Union – dedicated to undermining multilateral institutions and the rule of law. Hence President Bush's call for a "new world order".

The new buzz-phrases, following the genocide in Rwanda in 1994 and various massacres in Bosnia, most notably that in Srebrenica in 1995, became "humanitarian intervention", "failed states" and "war crimes", with the great innovations of the decade being the International Criminal Tribunal for the Former Yugoslavia (set up in 1993) and the International Criminal Court (which opened in 2002). Intervention, whether by law, by "soft power"[4] influence or by force, in support of universal principles and even moral purposes, came into vogue, if fitfully and reluctantly. Those who stood back from such intervention, unwilling to put their forces or reputations at risk, became nagged and criticised for their lack of spine and of moral responsibility. The US, as it had throughout the post-1945 decades, supported and sometimes promoted these initiatives while standing well back from the notion that any new legal procedures might also apply to itself – at least, that was the approach in Congress, even if the government generally was warmer to the idea.

And so ideals, illusions and reality collided on September 11th 2001 and in the two wars – Afghanistan and Iraq – that followed. The eventual failure of those wars also flipped on its head the prevailing spirit in the West about military intervention overseas: from being a growing moral duty, in many eyes in the late 1990s and early 2000s, it reverted to being seen as an outgrowth of colonial heavy-handedness, arrogance and even brutality. "Responsibility to protect" turned into "responsibility to steer clear".

When those four civilian aircraft were hijacked by al-Qaeda members on that bright, sunny September morning in 2001, two to be flown into the World Trade Centre towers in New York, one to crash into the Pentagon building in Washington, DC, and the other to fail its mission and crash into the Pennsylvania countryside, the headline we at *The Economist* put on our cover on September 13th was "The day the world changed". But what really had?

*

Karl Marx was wrong about many things as an economist, but as a historian he was surely right when he observed that:

Men make their own history, but they do not make it as they please; they do not make it under self-selected circumstances, but under circumstances existing already, given and transmitted from the past.

Those circumstances include the shock of the moment, amplified today through democratic politics and a global media, but also pre-existing forces received from the more distant past.

Al-Qaeda had attacked targets on the US mainland and in Europe and Western assets elsewhere before: it had first attacked the World Trade Centre as long ago as 1993 with a truck bomb that killed six people but failed to bring the towers down and to kill thousands as had been intended. And it had mounted truck bombings at the US embassies in Kenya and Tanzania in 1998 that killed 224 people. What was new about the 9/11 attacks was not the intent but the scale of their success, in the heart of Western capitalism.

By the same token, the other aspects of international affairs that preoccupy us now were also already emerging at the turn of the 21st century. Russia, through its conduct in Kosovo in 1999, racing to take control of Pristina airport ahead of its supposed partners from NATO, had shown that it still saw itself as being as much a competitor of the West as a collaborator. Ideas of a deeper partnership and even of some sort of NATO membership were by then fading as Russia switched leaders following its 1998 debt default from Boris Yeltsin, who had established democracy and a free media, to Vladimir Putin, who was a former KGB officer. As Putin himself said much later, "there is no such thing as a former KGB man".

A rising China was already making plain its desire to control what it sees as its own strategic space around its coastlines and in the South China Sea, through its conduct, for example, in the case of a mid-air collision between a Chinese air force jet and a US reconnaissance plane near the Chinese coast in

April 2001. China's interception of the US plane was intended to make the point that US military planes should not in future operate in what China considered its own strategic space.

Meanwhile, states were failing, especially in North Africa, and thereby creating vacuums into which violent extremist groups such as al-Qaeda could move. And the number of countries in possession of nuclear weapons was on the increase, with India and Pakistan having both revealed their nuclear capabilities in 1998, and with North Korea and Iran both known to be working on the uranium-enrichment and missile-development programmes that are the precursors to nuclear status.

So 2001 was the culmination of a long series of developments, just as have been subsequent events in Georgia, Ukraine and the South China Sea. Since the terrorist success of that year, three main things have changed. The first is that the West has become economically much weaker, which has made it more politically divided, both between countries and within them. The second is that the military and political responses to 9/11 have made the situation in the Middle East and North Africa worse. The third is that Western, and especially American, intervention overseas has gone through a similar cycle to that which accompanied failure in Vietnam in the 1970s, of retreat and withdrawal from other international entanglements followed by remorse over the weakness that such withdrawal appears to imply.

To the second point should be added the caveat that it is not possible to know what would have happened had the US not invaded Iraq in 2003,[5] or had kept its focus on Afghanistan, or had not dismantled the Iraqi army, or any number of other "what-if" scenarios. The status quo in the Middle East before the 2003 invasion was already dangerous and might have developed in other deadly and unstable ways, whether or not you believe it was reasonable to think that Saddam Hussein still possessed weapons of mass destruction that he was willing to use or trade.

Western economic weakness and Middle Eastern instability are also related to one another, with causation running both ways. The principal reason for the economic weakness of both the US and the EU has uncontestably been the occurrence in 2008 of the biggest financial collapse since the 1930s. This collapse discredited the US and Europe as role models; weakened the economic leverage over others that they held by virtue of their trade, foreign investment and overseas aid; and weakened the will and ability of the US and Europe to exert themselves in foreign affairs. The main responsibility for the collapse lies in the hands of Western policymakers and Western financial institutions. But Osama bin Laden should also be given some indirect credit (or debit).

The 9/11 atrocity and the wars in Afghanistan and Iraq created a high state of alert and a patriotically sensitised political and psychological atmosphere to which policymakers, especially at the Federal Reserve but also the Bank of England and the European Central Bank, cannot have been immune. This state of alert discouraged them from doing in 2001–07 what they are supposed to do – in an old saying, to "take away the punch-bowl just as the party gets going".[6] They might have anyway made the mistake of letting the credit bubble stay inflated, such was the complacency that a long period of steady growth and mild inflation had created, but it is equally plausible that the wartime atmosphere contributed to their urge to avoid raising interest rates or clamping down on credit, and thereby keep Western economies growing and unemployment low. It would be a stretch too far to suggest that al-Qaeda included this among its objectives, but the fact is that the group did want to provoke the US, put it on a war footing and make it feel under threat.

It is not surprising that this had consequences in economic policy as well as military retaliation. The Vietnam war, after all, contributed to the inflationary excesses that confronted the US in the early 1970s, which in turn led to the abandonment by President Richard Nixon of the dollar's fixed exchange rate against gold, with consequences that were felt around the world. It makes no sense to separate analysis of domestic economic policy from events in foreign affairs, at times when those international events are as costly and traumatic as were the Vietnam and post-9/11 wars.

The other ways in which 9/11 and its aftermath contributed to the West's economic weakness were through the direct costs of the wars in Afghanistan and Iraq and through the huge rise in oil prices that occurred roughly from 2003 until 2013, with a brief interruption in 2008–09. The two wars' direct costs were chiefly borne by the United States, though allies also contributed. There is no definitive estimate of their total since the costs go well beyond purely military budgets, but Linda Bilmes of Harvard University and Joseph Stiglitz of Columbia University described it in the title of their book in 2008 as the *Three Trillion Dollar War*, which Stiglitz updated in a 2015 interview as a total cost of $5 trillion–$7 trillion – which can be compared with the US's annual GDP which is now more than $18 trillion. Such figures do not all represent new costs

– the US military would still have existed, with or without war – and nor can all be defined as waste, at least in economic terms. But much of the money will have been spent in Afghanistan and Iraq rather than the US, and much would count as a diversion of spending away from more productive uses.

The rise in oil prices had several causes, not least the growing demand for energy, as for other commodities, in China. But interruptions, actual or feared, to the supply of oil played a big part too, interruptions that were exacerbated by a war in a country with large oil reserves – Iraq – that is in the neighbourhood of many other oil producers. The popular uprisings from 2011 onwards in the so-called "Arab spring" then added to the concerns about oil supply.

High oil prices act like a tax on the oil-consuming countries, which include Europe, the US and Japan, sapping households' ability to spend on other things and raising costs for business. In 1998, the price of a barrel of crude oil fell to $10, which is also why one of the world's biggest oil exporters, Russia, went bankrupt in that same year. At its peak in 2008 the price hit $145 a barrel, before plunging in 2009 but then rising again to more than $100 a barrel by early 2011, where it stayed until late 2013. During the West's already long and deep recession, the tax squeeze represented by costly oil made matters even worse and more long-lasting than they would otherwise have been. And high oil prices not only repaired Russia's finances but gave it the wherewithal and the confidence to ramp up its military spending and improve the training and morale of its forces, which it deployed in Georgia in 2008, then Ukraine in 2014 in support of pro-Russian rebels there and subsequently in Syria. High-priced oil also provided some of the financial fuel for *jihadi* groups and ultimately Islamic State, through donations by the oil-rich in the Gulf and, more particularly, through giving Islamic State a large income once it succeeded in gaining control of oil-producing territory in Iraq.

The legacy of the past decade and a half is painful and largely negative. It is clear that the weakened West now faces some pretty tough international-relations and security problems, all of which have been building for a long time. These problems fall into three separate categories, with a fourth as a general, contributory addendum. The one thing that unites them is the weak state of the West in responding, largely because of its economic troubles, along with the political divisions and stop-the-world-I-want-to-get-off feelings that those economic troubles have created.

The three categories are, first, the pressures and demands of a rising great power (China) that is seeking to define its own space in world affairs and thereby to reinterpret or recreate international rules in its own interest. Second, the difficulty of dealing with a declining, somewhat paranoid former superpower (Russia) that is throwing its weight around in order to create (or preserve) its sense of national identity, and is seeking to prove that rules of the game do not apply to it. Third, what might best be termed the civilisational challenge posed by Islamic State, its precursors and no doubt its successors, violent groups all using an extreme interpretation of a mass religion to create a movement and an identity defined largely by its opposition to what the rest of the world – including China and Russia – considers as modernity and taking that battle to anywhere and everywhere they can. The contributory addendum is the problem of failed or failing states, especially in North Africa, the Middle East and Central Asia, that provide the room and some of the recruits for this civilisational challenge and make it hard for outside powers to bring enduring stability to those failing states or to help settle their civil wars.

*

The arrival of a new "leader of the free world" in the White House, one proclaiming "America First" as the basis of his foreign policy, will cast these three issues in a harsh new light. Contrary to Trump's starting assumptions, of the three barbarian issues that are thumping on the gates of the open societies, the most fundamental and long-term one is not the violent brutality of Islamic State and its sort, even if that is the one that most often forces its way through the gates and into our cities. Nor is it the bully-boy behaviour of Putin's Russia, a Russia President Trump seems inclined to do deals with, if it helps resolve other sources of instability. These are both difficult pressures but they can be managed, or eventually dealt with, by traditional means. Much more problematic is the rise of China and, more particularly, of the demands for special treatment and respect that that rise is bringing. This is an epochal event and challenge, not a case of firefighting or even traditional deterrence. China will prove President Trump's most awkward foe.

China, like Russia and Islamic State, may face its own difficulties in coming years of an economic sort that then feed into politics. But unlike with Russia and Islamic State, such internal difficulties or weaknesses will not make the challenge of China's demands and expectations go away. Indeed, they may intensify them. In any case, while the harshest pressures of Russia and Islamic State promise to be temporary – even if temporary is measured in terms of quite a few years – the pressure posed by China promises to be permanent.

This pressure has been building for several decades and is leading towards a largely unknowable destination. Things would be so much easier if there existed somewhere in Beijing a plan, a blueprint for how China wants the world to change in order to accommodate its needs and its desires. At least other countries' intelligence services could then get to work stealing a copy of that plan, or finding agents who would tell them what it contained. But if there ever were such a plan, it would keep on needing to be superseded by a newer version. This is inevitable in a country whose economy has been doubling in size every seven years or so for the past three decades, and whose engagement with the world, through trade, capital flows, overseas investments, environmental issues and much more keeps on not just increasing but evolving too. Hence China's needs and desires keep changing, and will carry on doing so.

The closest thing to a plan that can be detected is the pattern that is revealed by China's recent actions and attitude. China sees itself as what international-relations scholars call "a status quo power", a power that has a conservative view of the world. But China's definition of the status quo differs from the normal, Western one. Its attitude reveals that its political and military policymakers have an older status quo in mind.

This has been shown most clearly by its approach to its neighbours and to territorial issues. Ever since its brief war with Vietnam in 1979, China has shown no sign of wanting to fight any of its neighbours, even (give or take some sabre-rattling) its "renegade province" of Taiwan. Nor, since its seizure of Tibet in 1950, has it actively sought further expansion. Even its victorious border war with India in 1962 left India with a bloody nose but its frontiers unchanged. With the notable exception of the long border with India, China has over the past 20 years settled all the territorial disputes on its land borders. But it has not settled disputes out at sea. These are becoming more important as China's navy becomes more important and as trade and overseas investments become larger and larger. Moreover, modern weaponry and geopolitics suggest that if China were ever to be threatened militarily in the future, it would probably be from the sea or the air, not the land.

In the light of this, what China has done is to try to increase its maritime control and its strategic freedom of manoeuvre in the regions around its long coastline and the sea lanes that serve it – in other words, in the South China Sea and the East China Sea. Such control and freedom of manoeuvre are, in its view, simply the conditions that are fitting and necessary for a great power of its size and history, and its military vulnerability.

That is the logic of the now notorious "nine-dashed line", an official Chinese map that in effect lays claim to the entire South China Sea, brushing aside claims to islands and rocks in that sea that are made by the other littoral states. Geographically, the map is akin to the United States laying claim to the whole of the Caribbean Sea and the Gulf of Mexico, or a European power laying claim to the whole of the Mediterranean. First used officially in 1947 by Chiang Kai-Shek's Kuomintang government, this official map and its nine-dashed line has remained since then a stock part of Chinese foreign policy, although not one that was stressed until recently – which made neighbours hope it had been superseded. Recent events have proved that it has not.

In principle, the nine-dashed line violates the international status quo, which is also true of China's long-standing claim to the Japanese islands in the East China Sea north of Taiwan, known in Japan as the Senkakus and in China as the Diaoyu. The various post-second-world-war treaties, along with the UN Charter and the later UN Convention on the Law of the Sea, have, on the face of it, established at least the rules governing maritime territorial sovereignty but also in the case of the Senkakus the specifics of which country holds sovereignty. This is what the West, and with it much of the rest of the world, thinks is the status quo, as laid down in international law and convention. But China believes in a status quo that dates back far longer, to before the country's decline and semi-collapse.

In May 2014 at the Shangri-La Dialogue of defence and security officials that the International Institute for Strategic Studies[7] organises every year in Singapore, with support from the Singaporean government, a senior Chinese military official was challenged publicly about the basis for the nine-dashed line. Jaws dropped when he justified this claim not with any reference to international law or modern conventions, or even to the sort of historical documentation of 18th- or 19th-century trading and settlement activity that is the standard fare in territorial disputes, but rather to the history of China's Han dynasty, more than 2,000 years ago. It was as if a modern Italian were to lay claim to control of the Mediterranean based on the history of the Roman Empire.

Such a claim sounds preposterous. But China is not Italy. The military man's claim needs to be understood not as a statement of scholarship or law, but of realpolitik. The attitude he was demonstrating was the view that the Han dynasty was the sort of great power of its time that felt a need and an ability – and so a right – to control the South China Sea. And so is modern China. Thus it must do so, as part of the logic of being China and of being a great power.

Chinese actions in support of these claims in the South China and East China Seas have become more assertive. Those actions have represented a desire to put "facts on the ground", or rather on the sea, to borrow an Israeli phrase, often to prevent others from doing so. Control may not be needed today, but it must not be lost. Hence the sending of an oilrig to waters disputed with Vietnam, and the dispatch of flotillas of ships, both military and merchant, and of aircraft, to sail and fly through Japanese waters around the Senkakus. Hence, most notoriously, China's construction of artificial islands on reefs, including some claimed by the Philippines, creating runways suitable for military aircraft and setting up missile batteries. When challenged about the artificial islands, China's official response is that it is establishing public goods: in other words, it is setting up military and security facilities that will protect the area in the interests of all peaceful nations. Many scoff at this explanation, but even if it is taken literally it confirms the attitude being described here: China, like the US, sees itself as a superpower with a right and an ability to decide of its own accord what "public goods" it wishes to provide. It has no need to ask the public first.

China has for much of the post-Mao era positioned itself as a strong adherent to international law and the role of multilateral institutions in settling disputes. But in 2016 when the Philippines challenged China's island-building and its historical claims through a case lodged at the Permanent Court of Arbitration in The Hague, China responded simply by rejecting the court's jurisdiction. The Permanent Court of Arbitration has no fixed role in adjudicating disputes under the UN Convention on the Law of the Sea, but UNCLOS has designated it as a recognised arbitrator and so its view ought to have weight. China, unlike the US, has ratified UNCLOS.

In its ruling, the court dismissed China's historical, Han dynasty-based claims to the area within the nine-dashed line as invalid and inapplicable. But China just ignored it, to the anger of many of the South-East Asian littoral states around the South China Sea, including the Philippines. It then used its leverage over Cambodia and Laos, which are heavily dependent on Chinese aid and investment, to thwart an effort in the Association of South-East Asian Nations (ASEAN) to criticise its stance. And then it achieved its greatest triumph by simply being China: President Rodrigo Duterte of the Philippines, who had been elected to office in May 2016, as the case was nearing its end, suddenly fell out noisily with the United States over American criticism of his brutal battle against drug cartels, declaring he was going to kick out all US military personnel in his country. "For as long as I am there, do not treat us as a doormat because you'll be sorry for it," he said. "I will not speak with you. I can always go to China."

The implication of all this is that there is little or no scope for negotiation with China, and China sees little need for it. It will not yield in its claims or seek compromises. It sees them as strategic necessities as well as, in effect, entitlements, now that it is in the course of restoring its historical status as the dominant regional power of Asia. Indeed, on the basis of this attitude, the true disrupter of the status quo is the United States of America, for it is a parvenu power. Its history of size and scope, and even existence, is short by Chinese standards. Although US global power and interests are a reality that must be lived with, this does not mean that China wishes to accept US interference locally in Asia, and specifically in the South China Sea. Moreover, and most crucially, while China accepts the US's presence and power globally, it wants to be treated as an equal, not an inferior.

Most probably, and in line with its attitude in the South China Sea, this means that China will claim the right to take the same attitude to international law and institutions that the US does, namely that such laws are to be respected and supported but not necessarily obeyed. After all, runs the logic, both are exceptional great powers. They are not like other countries. Both expect to be one of that small group of powers that set rules for others but keep the right to decide whether to abide by those rules themselves.

One might interject that Russia, or at least Putin, has the same sort of expectation. The US invades countries and changes regimes: so why shouldn't Russia also do so when it sees fit? China, judging by its recent attitudes, would not agree. In its view Russia is a declining power, and it is not in China's interests to have lesser, declining powers taking on such rights and causing chaos. But it is more or less inevitable that China and the US will both exercise such rights. Perhaps at some point in the future India might be able to do so too, though that remains a long way off. For the moment, the world's two great powers, equally deserving of respect in the Chinese view, are the US and China.

A further proof of this belief in Chinese exceptionalism was the country's initiative in 2015 to launch a new development bank, the Asia Infrastructure Investment Bank (AIIB), essentially as a China-led multilateral financial institution in competition with, or alongside if you prefer, the existing UN-sponsored banks such as the IMF, the World Bank and the Asian Development Bank. By launching and guiding the AIIB, China must also hope that other Asian countries will come to see it as a benevolent regional leader rather than as a threat.

If this interpretation holds true, the big questions are, first, to what extent this attitude will be compatible with the hope that China will become, in the words of Robert Zoellick in 2005 when he was US deputy secretary of state, a "responsible stakeholder" in the international order; and, second, whether China's desire for US-like status will be accepted willingly by others.

On the first question, the answer is likely to be yes, but the Chinese will themselves wish to define "responsible", just as they did with the launch of the AIIB. On the second, it is trickier. Over time, China's legitimacy may come to be accepted, partly as others become more dependent on it – like Cambodia and Laos – but also as and when its actions come to be seen as on balance more well-intentioned than ill-intentioned.

For the moment one thing is clear, and it gives the West a huge advantage: many more countries currently accept the legitimacy of the US and indeed the rest of the West than accept China's legitimacy. The use of that legitimacy has to be far more careful and consensual than was the case 20, 30 or 40 years ago, and certainly more so than its use has often been since 2001. But it is still there. And it is part of a broader point that the open societies forget, neglect or even take for granted at their peril: they have far more friends and allies than do those who challenge them.

*

China can count only North Korea as a full ally, and it is a painfully unreliable and unpredictable one. Pakistan occasionally plays the role of Chinese ally, though mainly with the purpose of unnerving India and of balancing its power, or of showing the US that it cannot be taken for granted. Access to military bases abroad is one reasonable proxy for trust, friendship or dependence, and China has currently just one, a shared anti-piracy facility in Djibouti in East Africa, which it is busy expanding to become its first true overseas base. It is building or financing new ports in both Pakistan and Sri Lanka, but there is as yet no evidence that either will be used as a permanent Chinese base.

Around its borders, China's closest relationship apart from North Korea is with Cambodia, but although the Cambodians often feel dependent on China and offer it support within ASEAN, they would not yet describe themselves as formal allies of China, any more than would the many countries in Africa that have benefited from Chinese investment, trade and aid, since they fear a kind of colonial dominance if they allow dependency to go too far. China is also building closer connections with other neighbours and near-neighbours through its investment and trade facilitation projects known as "One Belt One Road" (OBOR), aiming to create a new "silk road" through Central Asia to match the historic trading route, and a similar maritime trading belt. It will take time, but OBOR is bound to add to China's tally of friends and dependants, especially in Central Asia – which will put it in competition with Russia.

Russia's firm allies number six countries, namely Syria (where it has air and naval bases) and the five states with which it has a collective security treaty: Armenia, Kazakhstan, Kyrgyzstan, Tajikistan and Belarus. To these can be added the military bases it holds in areas that have broken away, sometimes with its encouragement, from its neighbours: Abkhazia and South Ossetia next to Georgia, a peacekeeping force in the Transnistrian[8] province of Moldova and of course Crimea. Russia for many years had a naval base at Cam Ranh Bay in Vietnam, dating back to the cold war, which it gave up in 2002, but it has recently signed a new agreement to begin using the base again, alongside other foreign navies including that of the US. It has also had a close relationship with India, but that reflected India's desire during the cold war to remain always independent of the West. In military matters India in those days interpreted "non-aligned" as meaning "be a democracy but also buy military hardware from the USSR". Since the 1990s the relationship has cooled.

By contrast, the list of the US's alliances and overseas military bases is long. In Asia it starts with Japan and South Korea, with which the US has long had formal security treaties and military bases galore, Singapore, where its naval vessels have basing rights, Thailand, New Zealand, Australia and the Philippines, and it has a surprisingly close (though informal) relationship with Vietnam, given the recent history of war. Since the late 1990s, the US has drawn closer to India too, giving support to its civil nuclear energy programme despite that country's nuclear weapons tests in 1998, and it is a big supplier of aid to Pakistan, despite – or because of – that country's dubious relationship with Osama bin Laden and the Afghan Taliban. One of the US's closest allies, the UK, also is part of the Five Power Defence Arrangements that since 1971 have made the UK, Australia, New Zealand, Malaysia and Singapore collectively interested – though not quite formally committed – in the defence of Malaysia and Singapore.

There are now 27 countries connected to the US through NATO, in this case with an explicit treaty commitment to defend each other against attack. Then there are 28 European countries, most of them NATO members, closely connected to each other through the EU, even if the UK is about to make its own connections somewhat more distant. US relationships in the Arab world have weakened considerably in the past decade, especially as the popular uprisings that began in 2011 were perceived as having occurred with American support or interference. But you can still spot US naval ships in Bahrain, Kuwait and Qatar, British military advisers in Oman, and all sorts of covert presences in Saudi Arabia. Lastly, Latin America has long been prickly about dependency on the *Yanquis*, but even so the US has close military ties in particular with Colombia and Panama, as well as with Puerto Rico. It also has military presences in Brazil, Honduras, Ecuador, El Salvador, Aruba and Curacao, and one cannot omit Guantanamo Bay on Cuba, land that the US holds on an indefinite lease.

All this, you might say, is but a legacy of the second world war and the cold war, the trail left by a hegemon whose power is nevertheless fading, just as the UK retained bases and ties far afield long after its empire had begun to unravel. A more demanding, selfish or unreliable United States could push some of those ties to breaking point, just as the late-imperial UK occasionally did. There would be some truth in this view, but at best such a judgment would be premature. US power has indeed been weakening. But that does not mean it is disappearing. It is still extraordinary in its scale and scope. More pertinently, however, the range of US and other Western alliances and more informal support no longer depend on any sort of "hegemony", if they ever really did. They are essentially voluntary.

Today countries rich or poor, big or small, have many more choices and more freedom of action than they did in the 1960s, 1970s or 1980s, say. They do not want to be bossed about by the West, or to be dependent on it for anything. They are perfectly able to play one great power off against another. They want respect and autonomy. They do not want to feel let down by it, as Japan and other Asia-Pacific countries have in the case of the demise of President Obama's "Trans-Pacific Partnership" effort to set trade and investment rules in the region. They fear, understandably, that such American inconstancy will hand the initiative to China to set its own rules for the region – but they will likely continue to resist Chinese rule-setting rather than actively embrace it. For if polled under some duress to give an honest answer, far and away the vast majority of countries around the world would say that if they had to choose sides, they would choose the Western one against virtually whoever was on the other side, unless to do so would put them in mortal danger.

Why? Not because they love the West. Many have plenty of reasons, especially historical ones, to hate it or at least be suspicious of it. The decision of the military regime running Myanmar to wriggle away during the past five years from what it saw as overweening Chinese influence is a small but significant example. The country has introduced democracy even if with still a strong influence for its old military rulers, is presided over by the West's great heroine, Aung San Suu Kyi, despite her formal exclusion by the constitution,[9] and has thereby made its peace with the Western world. Myanmar is not now and perhaps never will be explicitly a Western ally. It had been subject to economic sanctions by the EU, which could have made it resentful and caused it to fall into China's arms. But evidently its military rulers did not want to be a tributary state of China or of its other big neighbour, India, even though both of those countries brought aid, trade and investment rather than sanctions. Perhaps its military leaders also felt that political reform was desirable or unavoidable for its own sake. No matter: the country as a result has positioned itself as being autonomous and more open than before. To be viewed relatively favourably in North America, Europe and Japan has given Myanmar a greater sense of freedom.

This shows the gravity of what is at stake from President Trump's disdainful, or perhaps transactional, attitude to alliances. The reason the West's network of alliances, friends and sympathisers is so powerful is that the principles the West has established since 1945 and normally stands for – justice, the rule of international law, openness, the market economy – are principles that benefit and protect other countries rather than harming them. The West is more an agent of freedom and autonomy for smaller, weaker countries than a threat to them. As long as it stays that way, and looks plausibly ready to defend those principles when they are challenged, support for the West will remain strong, even if often silent, giving it a huge advantage over China or any other rising power. It is when the West itself undermines those principles or shows itself to be unreliable that it puts its support and legitimacy into question.

*

Russia and its actions need to be examined in the light of this narrative of the West's alliances and continued legitimacy. Most notably, of course, in 2013–14 Russia reacted to a popular, if undemocratic overthrow of the president of Ukraine by providing support to pro-Russian rebels in the east of the country, and by colluding with the takeover of the Ukrainian province of Crimea by local separatists and the holding of an unconstitutional referendum through which the province detached itself from Ukraine and joined the Russian Federation. But why did it do that?

The reason is that Ukraine, formerly an integral part of the Soviet Union and historically closely linked to Russia, was becoming uncomfortably friendly with the EU. It was doing so simply through signing a trade agreement, but there was also loose talk of it being allowed, at some point in the future, to apply to become a member of NATO. Perhaps, in the far distant future, it might have followed the Baltic states and other former communist bloc countries in joining the EU itself. There was no technical or legal reason why this friendlier relationship with Europe should have precluded Ukraine from also making trade deals with Russia, or even entering some kind of security agreement with its giant eastern neighbour. Russia's famous Black Sea naval base at Sevastopol in Crimea could have been protected, its presence guaranteed. But allegiances matter just as, to an insecure Russian regime, do national pride and a strong sense of identity rooted in Russian history, both Soviet and pre-Soviet.[10]

It is not a question of who is right or wrong about Ukraine in historical terms. A fair analogy for Ukraine's relationship with Russia could be Ireland's with the UK: they are countries that share many centuries of history and a huge amount of cultural interaction, but which nevertheless have now gone their separate ways, apart from one region, Northern Ireland, that has stayed British. Russia sees Crimea and eastern Ukraine in a similar way that the UK sees Northern Ireland, with the added desire to retain influence over the rest of Ukraine. Most of all, Russia did not want its old ally – one of its very few allies – to fall into the European or American camp.

Russia's military bullying of Georgia and then Ukraine, its annexation of Crimea as a fait accompli, its cyber-attacks on the Baltic states, its cyber-based efforts to interfere in the US presidential election to weaken Hillary Clinton and boost Donald Trump, have all focused attention on the country and made President Putin look strong and aggressive. Russia is keen to challenge international norms and laws, and to show that it remains a superpower that needs to be listened to. But its aims go beyond just looking good. It has also been trying to undermine the very Western solidarity and alliances that otherwise make Russia look alone and weak.

It has been doing this by classic cold-war means: financing political parties that oppose their country's membership of the EU; pushing propaganda through its overseas broadcaster, Russia Today (now renamed RT), to sow doubt in the West about the versions of events conveyed by Western governments and media; and using cyber-attacks to intimidate vulnerable countries. Praise for Putin from Hungary's prime minister, Viktor Orban, will have sounded especially sweet to Russian ears. The British decision to leave the EU will also have brought pleasure to Moscow, though more for its potential to further the disintegration of the whole EU than for any likelihood that the UK, one of the US's closest allies, would ever be detachable from the Western camp.

Russia's military intervention in Syria, in support of President Bashar al-Assad, has sought thereby to preserve the country's military bases on the Mediterranean, to turn Assad into (or keep him) a Russian client more than an Iranian one, and to prove that Russia counts. Russia's impact has been particularly great on Syria's neighbour, Turkey, a NATO member but not always a happy one. The fact that Syria's civil war has sent millions of refugees heading across and around the Mediterranean to the EU, causing division within it, has no doubt counted for Russia as a bonus. It confirms how much Russia stands to gain from Western disunity and how diminished it feels now that, unlike in the days of the Soviet Union, it has many fewer friends and allies than do Western countries.

*

So far, the Western response to these Russian tactics has been nervy and sporadic. Western unity – meaning all of the EU, the US and Japan – was achieved over the imposition of sanctions on Russia following its intervention in Ukraine, against considerable difficulty. But responses to Russian efforts to intervene in the domestic politics of European countries, or its corruption of Western political systems, or its propaganda and its cyber-attacks, have been muted. Plenty of people, companies and countries want to do business with Russia and so prefer to take a brighter, rather sanitised view of what Russia has been doing. Japan has a realpolitik-based desire to strengthen its commercial and political relationship with Russia to help counterbalance China, despite also having a seven-decades-old territorial dispute with Russia over the four Kuril islands north of Japan. And all Western powers, especially the United States, have to face up to the fact that Russia has shown in Syria that it remains a key player in determining the future of that country and therefore of the whole of the Middle East. That the journey towards any solution has to pass through both Russia and the US counts as a definite Russian success, even if a costly one.

There is no comparable mood of either sympathy or realpolitik towards Islamic State or its *jihadi* competitors. No other countries have any illusions about Islamic State's nature and the dangers it poses, both directly and by example. Neighbouring countries to Islamic State territories in Syria and Iraq have traded with it, but that is as far as it goes. None of the Sunni Muslim majority countries will admit to providing finance or weapons to the brutal Sunni *jihadis* of Islamic State, even though the organisation's religious ideology is similar to the Wahhabi sect of Islam that is an integral part of the richest Sunni state of all, Saudi Arabia. Even the Wahhabis do not preach the sort of violence used by Islamic State, and the Saudis and other Sunni countries in the Gulf and Middle East see Islamic State as a mortal threat to them, not an asset or even a tool. So, naturally, does Iran, the principal Shia Muslim country.

The issue with Islamic State is simpler than that with Russia, even if it is devilishly hard to resolve. Confronting the *jihadi* state-builders is a matter of containing or defeating them to a sufficient extent that they no longer look viable in the Weberian sense that this chapter opened with, so that they will then no longer be sustained by a flow of recruits from Africa, the Middle East or Europe.

For as long as Islamic State looks like a winner, one that might even establish a functioning, sustainable state with control over territory, it will have appeal. Young men will go to fight for it for both money and status. Women, even with their children, will go to support it, care for its sick and wounded, act as brides, help set up its imagined community. But this will end as soon as Islamic State ceases to look viable. By the end of 2016, it was in retreat and looking considerably less successful than it had a year earlier.

Defeats, cheaper oil, the ganging up against it by other Sunni Arab countries and groups, all will eventually cause the demise of this particular group and its leaders. With the end of Islamic State will not come stability in the Middle East, for it is as much a parasite upon instability and conflict as it is a cause of it, nor will it bring the end of *jihadi* terrorism: others will try to take its place, and both the knowledge and the wherewithal for terrorist violence are too widespread simply for it to disappear.

Individuals and even cells inside countries in Europe, North America, Asia and Africa will still be able to cause fear and havoc. Boko Haram in Nigeria is the most successful such group, which like Islamic State has succeeded in tapping oil money as well as kidnappings as a source of finance while it holds swathes of territory in the north of the country. Such violence, whether as attacks on the West, on Muslim countries, or indeed on others who intervene economically (and thus politically) in those countries, such as China, must be considered a permanent feature.

A greater threat is division and indecision inside the West itself. Other people's civil wars are always hard to deal with, perhaps impossible to deal with well. The legacy of the badly botched US invasion of Iraq is a dark and enfeebling one, one which has also damaged long-standing alliances within the Middle East, unsavoury though many of these may have been. But the enfeeblement, like the divisions, has fed on itself.

In the case of Syria, the understandable (though regrettable) reluctance to get involved militarily has fed into a now much more damaging failure to get involved properly and fully with the consequences of the war in the form of refugees, displaced people and migrants, a problem coming also from and through Libya. A more united and confident West would have thrown large amounts of money and effort into helping the countries neighbouring Syria – Jordan, Lebanon and Turkey chiefly – to look after the millions of refugees that are in camps there and to enable those refugees to stay and lead autonomous lives, which means working. Instead, the West, especially European countries, has responded with half-measures at best, making it not surprising that after more than five years of civil war and displacement, millions have tried to move from those camps to Europe.

Yes, the barbarians are at the West's gates. Certainly, China's pressure to dominate its neighbourhood and be treated as an equal partner to the US is hard to deal with. By any stretch of the imagination, President Putin is an enormous thorn in Western sides. Iran, though not currently a direct opponent of the West, retains always the potential in both its power and its interests to become one. North Korea can always be relied upon to rock boats. Yet while the tactics of dealing with these challenges will always remain imperfect, awkward and hazardous, the strategy to deal with them is clear.

It begins with allies, friendships and legitimacy: building them, nurturing them, not letting them disappear in a divisive morass, for they are the greatest assets the West has. Such assets are aided by hard military power but also depend crucially on the defence of clear principles and international institutions: the rules, laws, norms and bodies at whose creation Dean Acheson was present, and which matter so much to the many weaker countries in the world that are keen on Western leadership. The US, and its deeply entrenched habit of exemptionism from many of the rules and institutions it has championed, poses a particular problem, one that is bound to grow under a president who considers rule-breaking a virtue. The EU's recent trajectory towards a mixture of disintegration or paralysis is certainly not helpful, nor is the UK's decision to leave the EU. To preserve and reinforce the strength and influence of the West and all its values, the US is going to have to preserve its faith in international law, even if through gritted teeth, and the EU its faith in itself.

Ultimately, the be-all and end-all of Western strategy in facing these challenges has to be a stark and simple one, the same as at many fragile and nerve-racking moments of the cold war: to rebuild economic and hence political strength. The two go together. The West's economic and political weakness in recent years has essentially been self-inflicted. It can therefore be self-cured.

11

The fate of the West

Liberty is not a means to a higher political end.
It is itself the highest political end.

Lord Acton, lecture to Bridgnorth Institute, 1877

Remember, democracy never lasts long.
It soon wastes, exhausts, and murders itself.

John Adams, letter to John Taylor, 1814

DEMORALISED, DECADENT, DEFLATING, demographically challenged, divided, disintegrating, dysfunctional, declining. That is the state of the West today, as seen through many Western eyes as well as those of its detractors. But this is not the fate of the West, or at least there is no need for it to be. For the idea of the West, the world's most successful political formula ever, remains powerful, valuable and eminently revivable.

The combination of openness and of equality of civic or political rights pioneered and developed in a variety of forms across Europe, the United States, Japan and other like-minded countries will always bring prosperity and social progress to whichever nations take it up and stick with it. The reason is that it allows and encourages a society to evolve, to roll with history's punches, in a way that is organic rather than unnatural and imposed, one that soothes social tensions even as it causes them.

The real issue is whether the nations that have for the past half a century or more made up the West are still confident enough in the idea and its main values to stick with it, and to revive it by reinventing what it means and requires for their particular circumstances today. Or will they undermine their own creation, cripple the sources of their own dynamism, and then stand by and watch others eventually emerge to exploit an idea that they will by then have abandoned, rather as the Republic of Venice did once it had passed its medieval heyday?

There are plenty of good reasons for the West to feel dispirited and to think that a change of course is needed. It is not easy to pick oneself up and regain confidence after hammer blows such as the 2008 financial crisis, the worst in more than 80 years; or after the extraordinary terrorist attacks in the US on September 11th 2001; or after the near-collapse and heavy costs from Europe's greatest experiment in continental unity, the launch of the euro; or after the enduring effect for Japan of being transformed since the early 1990s from global champion to has-been. The West has been taking quite a pummelling, much of it self-inflicted.

Nor will it ever be easy to adjust to and find a way of living peaceably with a rising, hugely populous superpower like China, one seeking a leading role in the 21st century but run by a political system drawn from the 20th-century ideas of Lenin and Mao Zedong. As long as this condition holds, it will be hard to dodge the so-called "Thucydides Trap", the notion based on the history of the Peloponnesian war between a rising Athens and a fearful Sparta that a fear of conflict and tension can become self-fulfilling. To that ancient trap can be added a very modern dilemma, that to intervene in other people's civil wars in support of interests or humanitarian goals often brings costly disaster, as it has in Libya and repeatedly in Afghanistan, but to fail to intervene can also bring costly disaster, especially when the wars are in your own neighbourhood as the one in Syria is for Europe. There has been no good choice for the West in Libya, Syria or Ukraine, just as there wasn't in many previous such conflicts.

Yet the West can still stand tall. Neither the authoritarian, officially communist China nor the illiberal, bully-boy, propagandist semi-democracy of Russia poses a true systemic alternative to the open, liberal societies that is attractive to others, except to other budding dictators, and the caliphate desired by Islamic State is hated by all but its own devotees. For all the talk of a "Beijing consensus" emerging to replace the supposed Washington free-market version, the Chinese system has no emulators. Francis Fukuyama has in that sense so far been proved right in his famous 1989 essay, "The End of History": the long historical and ideological battle over what is the best and most sustainable political and social model has been won by liberalism and democracy. Nothing new has come along to rival it. What has not happened, however, in the ensuing quarter century is the full demise of the old alternatives, especially the non-ideological one of brute dictatorship. They, in all their forms, caused trouble for liberal societies before 1989 and still cause trouble today.

What is special about this second decade of the 21st century is not the international weakness of Western countries, or systemic rivalries. Certainly, the distribution of economic and political power is more equal than ever before, so that more countries have to be taken into account when governments gather together to discuss new policies or rules or respond to new calamities: what Fareed Zakaria in his 2008 book, *The Post-American World*, accurately called "the rise of the rest". But that welcome product of the spread of economic development has been arriving now for more than a quarter of a century. A richer and more equal world is a more complicated one, but that price is well worth paying. Europe gave up its aspirations for empire during the decades immediately after 1945, and Japan had abandoned such aspirations in the rubble of defeat. What is special, rather, about this decade is the internal weakness of Western countries, which is leading to divisions within and between those countries, and fostering as on previous occasions the rise of purveyors of simpler solutions, based on identity, nationalism and strong leadership – top-down solutions that involve making open societies more closed, supposedly for their own good.

Revival for the West depends on dealing with the internal weaknesses, policy mistakes and self-entrapping habits of democracy that have made life so difficult over the past decade. Such a revival always requires leadership, as it did in the UK of Margaret Thatcher in the 1980s, or the more consensual revivals of Sweden in the 1990s under Carl Bildt, or Canada in the 1990s and 2000s under Jean Chrétien and Paul Martin. But the leadership that has succeeded in such cases has been a leadership that opens doors rather than closes them, that removes obstacles so as to release energies and new ideas, that takes privileges away from groups that have been exploiting and protecting them at the expense of the rest of society. And as such, it is a leadership that needs to build a broad base of public support if it is to succeed and be sustained. Populists are good at winning public support today by offering simple solutions. But to retain support tomorrow and for the longer term requires a different approach.

This can be achieved only if both aspects of the formula are attended to: openness and equality. These are the lodestars of the Western idea. Without openness, the West cannot thrive, for countries need the ideas, the competition, the new elites, the wide opportunities that openness brings if they are to keep on evolving. But without equality, the West cannot last, for it is in the inclusive nature of citizenship and a sense of the broad public interest that the secret of Western sustainability has lain, by offering hope of mobility and improvement to all social groups, and means to resolve divisions and conflict fairly peaceably.

If, as seems likely, China struggles during the next decade or two to maintain its development and make the transition from a poor developing country to a rich, complex developed one, that nation's struggle will come because it has been unable to provide the equality of rights that openness demands if a society is to be kept stable. China's society is politically and socially far more unequal than are any in the West. The emerging Chinese middle class is already demanding that its voice be heard, that its civic rights be extended and protected. The incumbent political class – the Communist Party – is already gagging at the consequences of permitting greater openness and the equality it requires. Western countries are far better placed to balance the two.

Values and principles often conflict with each other and require reconciliation. The French revolutionaries' cry of *liberté, égalité, fraternité* made stirring sense as a rebellion against monarchy and aristocracy, but like most populist slogans it contains inherent contradictions. If fraternity imposes obligations, it infringes liberty. If liberty is genuine, the competition it sets forth will produce inequality and erode fraternity. It is the same with openness and equality. In most circumstances, one assists the other, by providing the social trust and wide participation that permit change to occur and be absorbed, by generating the resources and scope through which aspirations for mobility and advancement can remain alive. But at times they come into conflict.

This is one of those times. Openness, an openness enhanced by globalisation and by the liberal reforms pioneered and promoted by Thatcher, Ronald Reagan and others, has had huge success, all over the world. But it has also eroded and undermined equality of political rights and thus social trust in many countries by producing concentrations of wealth and power that have proved capable of subverting democracy and manipulating public policy, as well as making free markets less free by establishing new monopolies to replace old ones. The loss of the resources and scope for mobility is being felt especially sharply in the glum environment that has followed the 2008 crash, on both sides of the Atlantic. Now, fuelled by that glum environment, equality of political rights is finding itself in particularly fierce conflict with openness on the issue of immigration, for citizens are demanding a right to limit the access of non-citizens to come and live in their societies.

One option in response is to ditch openness. This is the course argued for by Donald Trump and many of his acolytes in the US, by Marine Le Pen in France, by Viktor Orban in Hungary and by some in the pro-Brexit UK Independence Party. Yet to do so would be to throw away the greatest source of Western prosperity, progress and strength, just at a time when Western countries' ageing populations are adding to their burdens and sapping their natural vitality. We muddled our way through periods of substantial closure in the past, but to do so now would be harder. A far smarter approach, which advocates of the Western idea need now to argue for with all their might, is to think much harder about how to restore and nurture equality, in ways that support openness rather than undermine it.

What is needed is new thinking about how openness and equality can be made to live happily together, a "neo-neoliberalism" that restores a more classical understanding of what is meant by, and required from, equality. This is the sort of understanding that was held two centuries ago by Adam Smith and John Stuart Mill, both thinkers who were sensitive to the moral requirements for societies to function well and the need to deal with the trade-offs and other consequences of untrammelled liberty.

Such new thinking about equality needs above all to unshackle itself from the corpse of socialism. In the second half of the 20th century socialism distorted discussion of equality by focusing attention onto redistributive and material equality, on the slogan of "from each according to his abilities, to each according to his needs".[1] When implemented, this principle has offended natural sentiments of fairness, under which except in extreme circumstances people should get what they deserve not what they need, and has often proved counterproductive, dividing societies rather than uniting them. Their abhorrence of this somewhat amoral form of equality has led liberalisers – neoliberals, if you must – too often to neglect the effect of their reforms on equality of political rights and on the sense of fairness and shared circumstances that bind a society together.

To achieve revival, liberalising policies and movements are always necessary. Obstacles to innovation, enterprise and ideas have to be removed; barriers and privileges that reward and enrich some groups at the expense of the wider public interest have to be dismantled. There is no other way to treat the scleroses and rigidities that are sapping the energies of Western societies, that are fulfilling the predictions of Mancur Olson in his book *The Rise and Decline of Nations*. For they are the natural yet also debilitating consequences of democracy and liberty themselves. But liberalisation alone is not sufficient. It needs to be done in harmony with equality, in ways that preserve a sense of fairness, a belief in the equality of voice and rights that makes citizens feel they belong, that they are indeed citizens and not subjects or victims. Liberalisation must be aimed at equalisation of rights and opportunities, not at shifting privileges from one set of hands to another in the belief that the new unfairness will be more productive than the old.

There is no single formula for how such a revival can be achieved. Western societies vary too widely in their histories, cultures, institutions and even social mores and expectations. However, the two lodestars against which every country and every policy can be measured are openness and equality of rights. And from these lodestars can be derived eight principles to be followed in all Western societies in order to reverse or prevent decline and ensure that they will remain envied and admired by other less fortunate countries.

1 Openness is all, but not everything has to be open, all the time

It has been by opening the doors and windows to bracing draughts of fresh air that democracies have prospered, exchanging people, culture, ideas, goods, services and capital, letting "ideas have sex", as Matt Ridley memorably put it in his paean to the Western formula for progress, *The Rational Optimist*.[2] Enforced chastity for ideas has never been a recipe for scientific, cultural, economic, political or social progress and reproduction. Openness to trade has at times been grating and unsettling, as any sudden change in the terms of business and the competitive climate would be, but it has brought huge benefits. The same cannot be said with such equanimity of total openness to capital movements. And plainly openness to the movement of people – immigration, as the recipients call it, migration to be more neutral – is now the focal issue for all those afraid or resentful of openness.

Openness to capital movements brings many benefits, of allowing investors to seek opportunities all over the world, to diversify their portfolios so as to spread their risk, to permit prices to adjust smoothly rather than in great lurches one way or another. But the last benefit does not always apply, as has been shown in the succession of financial collapses that have occurred during the era of free capital movements that began in the 1970s. Some of those collapses – such as Japan's in 1990–92 – have been chiefly domestic in nature, but most have been international. The biggest examples have been the East Asian financial crisis of 1997–98, which led to Russian debt default and a wider emerging-markets crash the following year; the Lehman shock of 2008, which set a financial tidal wave surging around the world; and the euro sovereign-debt crisis of 2010 onwards, which followed on from the US-led collapse.

These calamitous events do not automatically support a case for controls on capital movements, for the costs of calamity have to be placed against the benefits of freely flowing investment, and we can note that after the East Asian financial crisis, for example, the returning flow of capital, often hunting bargains, helped accelerate the recovery. On the 20th anniversary of this crisis, what will be highlighted is that virtually all the countries of East and South-East Asia have done well in the ensuing years, and that the main casualty of the crisis was the dictatorship of Suharto in Indonesia.

Yet there are two big problems posed by totally free movement of capital, problems which feed on one another. The first is that free, and potentially volatile, flows of capital are well beyond the ability of any national regulator, supervisor or central bank either to understand or to influence in any substantial way. Efforts to agree upon pan-national forms of regulation have had a partial success at best. As Chapter 3 explained, vast parts of international finance remain uncharted territory for regulators. The second is that, in a business which depends entirely upon confidence held by financial counterparties in each other, global flows of capital entail inevitable asymmetries of information which, again, pan-national regulation has failed so far to deal with. Given these two problems, the case for more controls, through taxes, regulatory requirements about the risks particular institutions are allowed to take, steep capital requirements or limits on permitted leverage, or even bans on some of the most complex and volatile activities, has become strong.

Migration is a more subjective issue, though no easier to deal with. The case for permitting, even embracing migration can be readily made by pointing to the great businesses and scientific discoveries that have been launched or made by those with the will and the wit to migrate. Most "British" merchant banks of the City of London's heyday had their origins in German, Huguenot and Jewish immigration, just as many American technology companies have been founded by immigrants. The ability to migrate is also an aspect of liberty and openness that should be welcomed by all those who value their own liberty, even before addressing the strong humanitarian and political cases for helping refugees from conflict and persecution. But it cannot be denied that immigration can also have consequences for feelings of citizenship and the equality of political rights. If citizens are to value the rights that they hold and exercise, they must also, by logic, be entitled to a say on who else is permitted to come and hold those rights.

By ignoring this issue and its impact on the sense of equality and fairness, successive British governments have landed the country with the most perverse of outcomes: a vote to leave the EU so as to "take back control" of precisely the sort of immigration that is most helpful to the British economy and most easily integrated in cultural terms, namely that of generally well-educated people from western and central European countries. The variety of immigration about which people most commonly voice concern, rightly or wrongly, is that of low-skilled, poorly educated people from other continents and cultures who take more money and time to integrate.

Migrants are a welcome and necessary injection of youth and fresh ideas and energies to any society. But the case for some controls on the speed and volume with which they can arrive in a particular society is also strong. With hindsight, the transitional periods during which new, poorer members of the EU in 2004 had to wait before their citizens could enjoy freedom of movement to other EU countries should have been longer than the seven years that was then agreed. A longer, perhaps phased introduction of free movement would be wiser for future EU members. At the same time, more public resources need to be devoted to facilitating integration of all kinds of immigrants and to supporting areas that may feel especially sensitive about the economic and cultural impact of migration.

2 Equality is all, but it isn't all about money

We live in an age of inequality of income and wealth. What has been seen in both Europe and the US over the past decade, however, has been less the cry of envy or resentment that class-based politics yielded in the past and more the cry of victimhood and unfairness. The ability to become rich is generally accepted as a part of our liberty and an advantage of openness. But when wealth comes to harm our sense of shared citizenship, when it erects barriers rather than defining opportunities, and when it becomes expressed in differential rights in such matters as access to work or to education, then the glue that holds our societies together starts to fail. This is what we have been seeing in many Western societies.

The right response, and what is likely to be the most productive target for popular pressure and protest, is to set to work on tackling as many of the sources of unfairness and differential rights as possible. It is not, in other words, a matter of the state acting as Robin Hood, redistributing money from the rich to the poor, though some countries may opt for that. Direct state intervention in labour markets through higher statutory minimum wages is another method likely to be helpful in current conditions. Mostly, however, it should be a matter of the state acting as the flag-bearer for equal citizenship and as the guardian against the unfair entrenchment of advantage or hindrance of choice and mobility.

A prime target in Japan, Italy, France and any other country in which employment rights are divided by law between different varieties of worker can and should be the restoration of unified labour rights: one contract and one set of rights for all employees, whether part-time or full-time. Any country in which corporate or individual concentrations of wealth are yielding a disproportionate influence over politics and public policy can respond to this principle by tackling and exposing such inequities, some of which may anyway be iniquities. In the US, pressure on the Supreme Court to revise its definition of money as a form of free speech will be one way in which this battle can be fought. Others will include reinforcement of antitrust laws and practices, the breaking up of mega-banks and the public privileges they hold, and international co-operation to deter tax evasion.

Inheritance and wealth taxes are an important means by which to discourage wealth from becoming entrenched, generation after generation, but they have fallen from favour in recent years. They need to be revived, especially in places – such as the south of the UK – where rising property prices have provided huge windfall gains for lucky owners and are acting as a high barrier against younger people, and those – such as the US – where concentrations of wealth are becoming especially problematic, politically. Most of all, any country in which wealth or the lack of it is creating a rising barrier to access to good school or university education should follow this principle by making a bigger public investment in equality of access and in the quality of education available to poorer citizens.

3 Education, at all levels and ages, is the single most vital support for equality as well as being a country's most vital economic and social resource

The greatest contributions to equality and a spreading sense of citizenship in Western countries in the post-1945 era have come from two sources: the restoration of full employment or something close it, following the poverty of the interwar years; and the spread of access to public education, first in schools and then in colleges and universities. The first is not wholly in the control of public policy. But the second is a direct consequence of public policy, even if the exact requirements to be placed on education have varied over time.

The mantra that we live in a knowledge society and that brainpower and its economic expression, productivity, are our most important assets is heard virtually daily. Every successful aspirant to modernisation and economic development, from Japan to South Korea, China to Chile, has got there with a big emphasis on education. And yet in the West public funding for higher education is frequently allowed to decline, student debts pile up, and educational institutions of all levels are sacrificed at times of budgetary stringency.

There is an important debate to be had about how to make tertiary education cost-effective and productive for the 40–80% of young people (depending on the country) who pass through it. Increasingly, however, there are also debates to be had about how best to provide education and retraining to people later in life, and at whose expense, so that they can adapt to changing technologies, think in new ways and adapt to extended working lives. Apprenticeships, on the German and Swiss model, are much admired in other countries, but to work well they need to be designed and cherished by the companies and industries that provide them, rather than simply being required by government. But in all of these arguments the principle must not be lost sight of: public investment in and oversight of education is the main way in which societies as a whole have created the equality and sense of fairness from which they have flourished and which they need constantly to nurture.

4 Equality between the young and the old is as important as between social classes or ethnic groups

For the past decade and certainly for the decades to come, one of the biggest sources of inequality and social tension has been the ageing of Western populations, even if it was not always apparent that this was the cause. Welfare states are under severe financial pressure, whether in Europe, the US or Japan, in part because of recession or slow growth but largely because of the rising costs of public pensions and health care for the elderly. The young are generally too polite to blame the cuts in their education or the inequity in their labour rights on their grandparents, but it is true nevertheless.

In the 20th century, it would have been correct to say that liberal democracies would thrive or collapse depending on whether they were able to provide a political voice and economic opportunities to the rising and restive working classes. In the 21st century, the equivalent decisive issue stands to be the management of ageing and the inequities it threatens to cause between generations. The idea that citizens of Western democracies can remain entitled to live for 30-plus years after retirement on incomes transferred to them by government from taxes levied on younger people, with health care financed in the same way, is for the birds. It simply cannot be sustained. Any country – Italy, France – that seeks to do so will be throttled by public debt and, eventually, convulsed by social disorder.

Working lives, and the distinction between work and retirement, have to be wholly rethought. Retirement ages – or, more importantly, ages of eligibility for public pensions – need to be raised to 70 as soon as possible. Only those countries that do so will be able to afford generous welfare provision for the rest of their populations, for pension and health-care systems will otherwise bankrupt them. But this also represents an opportunity, for individuals, companies and other institutions alike, to think of and plan life cycles, their approach to employees and the services they provide in new and creative ways. The one thing that is definitely known about the world in 2050 is that many more people alive then, in both the West and the rest, will be well over the age of 65. This is the era of the 100-year life, at least from the point of view of those being born today, and our sense of equality and the rights it brings will have to adjust accordingly.

5 The rule of law is a non-negotiable guarantor of equality and source of confidence among citizens and between nations

Adjustment to demography will be the biggest test of all in social and economic terms. One of the biggest political tests, however, will be whether Western countries succeed in maintaining a strict adherence to the rule of law as a fundamental governing principle of their societies. It is often forgotten or overlooked that the rule of law is the fount of equality: the right to equal treatment before the law for everyone whether high or low, government or citizen, is what guarantees our freedoms, protects our property and underwrites our citizenship.

The rule of law is challenged by inequalities of income and wealth because of the unequal access to costly justice that wealth can provide, and by the ability of huge corporations to bully and manipulate the law in their own interests. It is challenged on each and every occasion by corruption at any level, and by shoulder-shrugging tolerance of corruption by judicial, police, media or political systems. Corruption seeps further into our societies than we often realise, since it is not only a case of bribes but also of the favouritism that arises when public officials and private interests become entangled. The rule of law is challenged, above all, by populists like President Trump who demand the right to stand above it.

The rule of law is also eroded by the surveillance society, by permissions given to or taken surreptitiously by government agencies or large corporations to invade privacy and hedge in or entirely remove civil liberties. A Magna Carta that said that any baron could be imprisoned or spied freely upon should King John suspect him of contemplating terrorist acts or radicalising others would not have been a document still revered nearly a millennium later. As the great charter said, "To no one will we sell, to no one deny or delay right or justice." These are fine promises, if only we would stick to them.

6 Freedom of speech is a vital bridge between openness and equality, not a trade-off between them

The free exchange of ideas, the cross-fertilisation between people, cultures, nations and companies, depends on freedom of speech and information, and in many ways such freedoms are greater now than ever before. Each of us can hold a smartphone or tablet in our hand and seek information about almost anything, anywhere, instantly, and can share whatever we think, find or feel through social media, our own websites or old-fashioned e-mail. It is part of what we mean by openness, part of the essential distinction between an open society and a closed one. But free speech is also crucial to what we mean by equality, the ability like an ancient Greek to have our voice heard in the arena of debate, whether serious or trivial.

The fact that free speech is more available than ever before does not make it universally welcomed or valued, however, nor does it put it out of danger. Some of the danger to free speech is self-imposed: for fear of making groups feel unequal or beleaguered we often place limits on our own openness such as so-called "safe spaces" in universities or "no-platforming" campaigns. Much of the danger to free speech comes from holders of power, whether governmental or corporate, who seek to exploit the fact that while everything can be said or known in principle, in practice attention spans are limited and credibility is scarce, making control of the most attended-to or most credible channels of communication potentially even more powerful than in the past.

Silvio Berlusconi used to say when he was prime minister that in Italy anyone and everyone could say anything about him that they wanted to, which was true, but his near-monopoly of commercial television and his political influence over the most-watched state broadcasting channel made his voice a great deal louder than anyone else's. Japan's prime minister, Shinzo Abe, has been interfering with that country's state-owned broadcaster, NHK, while also intimidating commercial broadcasters to be less critical of government policy. Above all, Donald Trump has proved a master of the freedoms provided by the information age, as well as of the fact that in such a cacophonous free-for-all the line between truth and fiction has become harder to define. Now that he is the US tweeter-in-chief he will continue to exploit those freedoms, either to communicate or to distract, and it is vital that other communicators – media, academics, civil society – do so too to maintain accountability. We are not in a "post-truth" age, contrary to popular assumptions, but we are in an age when truth is again – as it was during the cold war – vulnerable to distortion and manipulation. We must fight to protect it.

Marshall McLuhan, a Canadian writer, opined half a century ago that "the medium is the message" to show how television was itself shaping society, and it remains true that to control the medium offers the chance to control the message and to shape society and what it thinks. The fight to keep speech free by also keeping control of the media as free and pluralistic as possible is as important as ever – but arguably more difficult as belief in the quality and credibility of what is said and seen is itself eroding.

7 A boring consistency is a fine goal for economic growth

Economics is not the only goal of revival but it is the means by which living standards rise, opportunities are created and people gain the resources and projects through which to live fulfilling lives. Medieval monasteries were among the richest institutions of their time. As well as not being an end in itself, economics is also not the stuff of miracles. Often, the worst damage to economies has been done by the pursuit of miraculously rapid spurts of growth, which then end in inflation, collapse, unemployment and division. The better goal, and really the only feasible one for Western countries that dwell already on the technological frontier and have well-educated populations, could be characterised as a kind of magical mediocrity.

Mediocrity is rather magnificent when it is achieved and sustained. The reason is that the steady accumulation of economic growth leads, over time, to rises in living standards that can be shared by all and to public finances capable of sustaining whatever are the politically desired levels of welfare support and public investment over the long term, in a predictable way that allows people and institutions to make plans and stick to them. The UK in the 1980s went through a social and economic transformation under Thatcher but it was a bumpy ride, from bust to boom and back again, a ride which added to the social tensions that Thatcherism caused. From 1992, when the UK pound was humiliatingly ejected from the EU's Exchange Rate Mechanism, until 2007–08, however, the country enjoyed steady, beautifully boring growth of 1.5–2.5% a year. It was the loss of control, amid a credit boom and a malign neglect of financial regulation on both sides of the Atlantic, that produced the sharp slump of 2008–09 and undid much of the mediocre, steady gains that had been made before.

It is steady, sustained growth that allows living standards to keep on rising, and shocks and policy blunders that make them fall. Countries such as Japan in the 1950s and 1960s or China in the 1990s and 2000s that are adopting more advanced technologies, educating their previously unskilled workforces, and moving millions from farming into factories and offices, can have lengthy periods of rapid economic growth during which living standards can double in less than a decade. Developed countries that are already using the best ideas cannot do that, but nor should they want to do so. Rather than going for broke in ways likely to make them literally broke, their policy aspiration should be the economic equivalent of what Barack Obama said of US foreign policy: "Don't do stupid shit."

8 Fostering the international rule of law and international collaboration is essential

As a foreign-policy principle President Obama's makes some sense, given the legacies of Iraq and Afghanistan, but it would be more useful for the future if it were adapted to read: "Don't be so stupid as to do things on your own." Nor, indeed, so stupid as to act to undermine the rules of the international game that you successfully set up yourself.

The greatest strength the West has is strength in numbers, a strength built as much by a shared set of interests as by history, culture or obligations. Its second-greatest asset is the array of international laws, or rules of the game, that it has built up chiefly since 1945 through the wide variety of international institutions that it established, from the United Nations to the World Trade Organisation, from the European Union to the UN Convention on the Law of the Sea.

The threats posed by Russia's territorial seizures in Georgia and Crimea, by China's rejection of rulings by the UN Convention on the Law of the Sea concerning its territorial claims in the South China Sea, by Islamic State's rejection of Western-led laws or borders are all assaults on this system of law. They come associated with efforts to undermine the institutions and alliances that have, formally and sometimes informally, buttressed the move from utter disorder to some semblance of order.

Faced with these assaults, Western countries have essentially three choices: to give in, throw their hands up and declare the international order to be defunct; to make deals with those assaulting that order so as to seek new compromises, to placate the challengers and salvage what they can; or to stick together, strengthen their alliances when possible, and take whatever steps are needed to make international rules more credible and legitimate in the eyes of the bulk of the 196 countries of the world.

To choose the first of these options would be tantamount to suicide. To choose the second, while clearly a tempting option for those populists seeking a quieter, more inward-looking life for their countries, would be to repeat the mistake of the 1930s of appeasing aggressors and thereby trading away and harming both the interests of other countries and the long-term interests of the West. In a truly connected world, to concede 19th-century-style spheres of influence is to allow such influence, by Russia, China or others, to reach into your own countries and pockets too. That, above all, is what President Trump needs to realise. The third represents the only real, and principled, choice. It is also far and away the best choice from the point of view of Western revival.

Choosing it is not straightforward. It would require a change of heart in the United States, with the country moving away from the exemptionism – laws are great, but they apply to other people, not us – that has characterised its politics for decades. This would be a difficult move to make at a time of domestic anger, international pressures and an instinct for more exemptionism, not less. But it will have to be made in due course, perhaps alongside or subsequent to a return to a tougher, more resolute US foreign policy after the war-weary, rather hesitant Obama years. For a grave weakness of US efforts in Asia to prevent China from annexing the South China Sea is that Congress has long refused to ratify the UN Convention on the Law of the Sea on which those efforts, and the complaints of American allies in the region, are based.

Such a move towards stronger international rules and international collaboration will also, however, require greater humility from Western leaders of all kinds, breaking from the years of George W. Bush and Tony Blair during which presidents and prime ministers arrogantly assumed they knew what was best for other countries. Writers may be entitled to take such a view but not political leaders, for arrogance implemented in public policy is invariably counterproductive.

There is humility aplenty in the EU now, but it needs to be backed by a stiffening of spines over defence spending and dealing with threats from Europe's neighbours, as well as a new effort to avoid disintegration and nationalist divisions, a tendency reinforced by the UK's vote to leave. And to boost international collaboration will require a fresh spirit of confidence and realism about history in the case of Japan, a country which has hampered its own search for friends and allies through its constant domestic debate about its imperial and wartime history.

Throughout the West, the temptation to shun collaboration and instead fight each other over trade, defence spending or environmental rules will be strong. Yet it would also be futile and would represent a renunciation of all the lessons of the post-1945 decades, during which collaboration and internationally agreed rules brought huge benefits, not least in eliminating mutually destructive competition in both war and peace. A keen awareness of that history and of national interest ought to push the West to follow this eighth and final principle rather more dutifully than it has since the end of the cold war.

The end of the cold war is also a good place to end this book. It is the most recent reminder of how wrong pessimistic forecasts about the West can be, and how quickly the picture can change. As the eponymous lead character in David Lean's great film, *Lawrence of Arabia*, said in a riposte to his fatalistic Arab colleague, "nothing is written".[3] The fate of the West is in our hands, as Westerners. Revival, with the next spin of the evolutionary cycle that has made us strong, stable and prosperous before, is possible, even probable. But it is not inevitable. A great battle of ideas is under way within the West, the conclusion of which will determine our ability to revive and to continue to evolve. It is up to us to win it.

Notes and references

Introduction

1 Spengler, Oswald, *Decline of the West*. In German this was *Der Untergang des Abendlandes* or, more strictly, *The Downfall of the Occident*. It was published in two volumes, in 1918 and 1923.

1 Let battle commence

Notes

1 Islamic State is also known as Daesh, an Arabic acronym for the Iraq-based forerunner of the group. American officials like to use that name, as do French and British ones, but the group itself prefers Islamic State as that term captures its essential aspiration. Since that aspiration, and its success in commanding territory in Syria and Iraq, is also the main reason the group poses a special threat to today's world order, Islamic State is the name used in this book.

2 The speech was in London, to advertisers, in October 1993, three months after Murdoch's News Corporation acquired Star TV, a Hong Kong-based satellite television company. *Guardian*, "Murdoch and China", August 24th 2003.

3 For an example, see www.margaretthatcher.org/document/107821

4 Peter Drucker emigrated from Austria first to the UK and then to the US, making his name there with a seminal management work, *The Concept of the Corporation* (1945), a study of General Motors.

5 As is outlined in Ian Morris's book *Why the West Rules – For Now: the Patterns of History and what they Reveal about the Future*, Profile Books, 2010.

6 For example, in John King Fairbank, *China: A New History*, Harvard University Press, 1992.

7 For example, by Fareed Zakaria in *The Future of Freedom*, W. W. Norton & Company, 2003.

8 When I put the words "Let Them Wed" on the cover of *The Economist* (January 4th 1996) as its then editor, the weekly was the first mainstream publication in the UK

or the US to advocate equal marriage rights. Progress since then in the enactment of such rights in Western countries all over the world has been much faster than we could possibly have expected.

9   *Anni di piombo* or years of lead, referring to the lead in bullets that flew as terrorist groups of the extreme right and left fought each other and the state.

10 I was a member of the Trilateral Commission for 11 years until 2009.

11 See, for example, Rauch, Jonathan, *Government's End: Why Washington Stopped Working*, Public Affairs, 1999, a revised version of a book first published in 1994 under the title *Demosclerosis*.

References

Crozier, Michel, Huntington, Samuel P. and Watanuki, Joji, *The Crisis of Democracy: A Report on the Governability of Democracies*, The Trilateral Commission and New York University Press, 1975.

Freedom House, "Freedom in the World 2015": https://freedomhouse.org/article/freedom-world-2015-freedom-declines-ninth-year

Friedman, Thomas L., *The Lexus and the Olive Tree: Understanding Globalisation*, Farrar, Straus & Giroux, 1999.

Popper, Karl, *The Open Society and its Enemies*, Routledge, 1945.

Runciman, David, *The Confidence Trap: A History of Democracy in Crisis from World War 1 to the Present*, Princeton University Press, 2013.

Soros, George, *Open Society: Reforming Global Capitalism*, Little, Brown and Public Affairs, 2000.

UN Department of Economic and Social Affairs, Population Division, *International Migration Report 2015*.

2 Inequality and fairness

Notes

1   Trump began to raise external funds for the general election once he became the Republican nominee in June 2016.

2   www.supremecourt.gov/opinions/09pdf/08-205.pdf; www.nytimes.com/2014/04/03/us/politics/supreme-court-ruling-on-campaign-contributions.html?_r=0

3   Lord Ashcroft's donate-and-tell attack on David Cameron, *Call Me Dave*, was published in 2015 by his own aptly named publishing firm, Biteback; www.bitebackpublishing.com/books/call-me-dave

4   www.telegraph.co.uk/news/politics/labour/3179770/Revealed-the-truth-about-Tony-Blairs-role-in-the-Ecclestone-Affair.html; www.theguardian.com/politics/2008/oct/12/tonyblair-labour

5 www.investopedia.com/articles/investing/102515/carried-interest-loophole-americas-tax-code.asp

6 See also "Admissions preferences given to alumni children draws fire", *Wall Street Journal*, January 15th 2003: www.wsj.com/articles/SB10425804417935211864

7 The initial enabling law was the Temporary Help Business Act of 1985, but this restricted the use of non-regular contracts to a limited list of jobs and sectors. It was the expansion of that list in the 1990s and 2000s that led to rapid growth in part-time and temporary employment.

8 Peet, John, "So much to do, so little time", *The Economist* Special Report on France, November 17th 2012: www.economist.com/news/special-report/21566238-how-regain-competitiveness-doing-so-so

9 "Decay of the permanent job as France balks at labour reform", *Financial Times*, August 11, 2015.

10 Machnig, Matthias and Schmolke, Oliver, "Distributing the Future: Why More Equal Prospects Matter", Policy Network, August 2016.

11 www.voxeu.org/article/flexicurity-danish-labour-market-model-great-recession. Note that Denmark is not a member of the euro currency union, but pegs the Danish kroner tightly to the euro. So unlike the UK and Sweden, which are also outside the euro, it suffered no currency devaluation against the euro during the financial crisis.

References

"America's new aristocracy", *The Economist*, January 24th 2015.

Keeley, Brian, "Income Inequality: The Gap between Rich and Poor", *OECD Insights*, OECD Publishing, 2015.

Piketty, Thomas, *Capital in the Twenty-First Century*, Harvard University Press, 2014; first published as *Le capital au XXI siècle*, Editions du Seuil, 2013.

3 Democracy and the art of self-entrapment

Notes

1 Having made an estimated $400 million when Goldman Sachs changed from a partnership to a public company in 1999, after his departure as co-CEO in that year Jon Corzine entered politics, being elected as a senator for New Jersey (2001–06) and governor of New Jersey (2006–10). He then became chairman of MF Global, a bond dealer, in 2010, which went bankrupt in October 2011, resulting in civil charges against Corzine by the Commodities Futures Trading Commission alleging misuse of customer funds. The case is under appeal.

2 http://nypost.com/2009/12/13/the-only-thing-useful-banks-have-invented-in-20-years-is-the-atm/

3 http://blogs.abcnews.com/politicalpunch/2010/04/clinton-rubin-and-summers-gave-me-wrong-advice-on-derivatives-and-i-was-wrong-to-take-it.html
4 The best account of why this has happened and why it matters can be found in *The Bankers' New Clothes* by Anat Admati of Stanford University and Martin Hellwig of the Max Planck Institute in Bonn, Princeton University Press, 2013.
5 Vickers, Sir John, "The Bank of England must think again on systemic risk": www.ft.com/cms/s/0/674b16b8-d184-11e5-831d-09f7778e7377.html#axzz40EImfRN0
6 "On microscopes and telescopes", March 27th 2015, at the Lorentz centre workshop on socio-economic complexity, Leiden, the Netherlands: www.bankofengland.co.uk/publications/Documents/speeches/2015/speech812.pdf
7 See, for example, "Bring our elites closer to the people", *Financial Times*, February 2nd 2016: www.ft.com/cms/s/0/94176826-c8fc-11e5-beob-b7ece4e953a0.html#axzz3z1yo9kLz
8 Kay, John, *Other People's Money*, Profile Books, 2015; *The Kay Review of UK Equity Markets and Long-Term Decision-Making*, July 2012, commissioned by the Department for Business, Innovation and Skills.
9 Cecchetti, Stephen G. and Kharoubi, Enisse, "Reassessing the Impact of Finance on Growth", BIS Working Paper 318, Bank for International Settlements, July 2012: www.bis.org/publ/work381.pdf

References

Admati, Anat and Hellwig, Martin, *The Bankers' New Clothes: What's Wrong with Banking and What to Do about It*, Princeton University Press, 2013.
Centre for Responsive Politics, Open Secrets.org: www.opensecrets.org/pacs/pacgot.php?cmte=C00428623&cycle=2016
Olson, Mancur, *Power and Prosperity: Outgrowing Communist and Capitalist Dictatorships*, Basic Books, 2000.
Olson, Mancur, *The Logic of Collective Action: Public Goods and the Theory of Groups*, Harvard University Press, 1965.
Olson, Mancur, *The Rise and Decline of Nations: Economic Growth, Stagflation and Social Rigidities*, Yale University Press, 1982.
Public Citizen: www.citizen.org/google-political-spending-report
Smith, Adam, *An Inquiry into the Nature and Causes of the Wealth of Nations*, 1776.
Turner, Adair, "How to tame global finance", *Prospect*, September 2009: www.prospectmagazine.co.uk/features/how-to-tame-global-finance
Turner, Adair, The City Banquet, Mansion House, September 22nd 2009: www.fsa.gov.uk/pages/Library/Communication/Speeches/2009/0922_at.shtml

4 Setting America straight again

Notes

1 See "To Paris, US Looks Like a Hyperpower", *International Herald Tribune*, February 5th 1999. Even before George W. Bush had been elected, France was protesting against American "unilateralism", arguing that other countries needed to resist the "hyperpower" and preserve multilateralism.

2 *Occupational Licensing: A Framework for Policymakers*, The White House, July 2015. The report was compiled jointly by officials from the Treasury Department, the Council of Economic Advisers and the Department of Labor.

3 Eberstadt, Nicholas, *Men Without Work: America's Invisible Crisis*, Templeton Press, 2016. US law distinguishes between "felonies", or serious crimes punishable by death or imprisonment in excess of one year, and "misdemeanours" by reference to the maximum sentence possible for the crime under law, not the sentence actually imposed.

4 *The Economist* has been campaigning for drug legalisation ever since the late 1980s. See, notably, a special report by Frances Cairncross, *Stumbling in the Dark*, July 26th 2001.

5 Data taken from a report by the chief economist of General Electric, Marco Annunziata, in September 2016: https://medium.com/@marcoannunziata/how-to-pave-the-way-for-stronger-u-s-growth-d1c1e305dbbe#.rwx22fuxi

6 Kluth, Andreas, "Democracy in California: The People's Will", *The Economist*, April 20th 2011.

7 Gardels, Nathan, "The Third Turn of American Democracy", unpublished chapter for his forthcoming book, provisionally titled *The Great Transformation: Governing in the Age of Turmoil*.

References

Ellwood, David, *The Shock of America: Europe and the Challenge of the Century*, Oxford University Press, 2012.

Elwell, Craig K., *Inflation and the Real Minimum Wage: A Fact Sheet*, Congressional Research Service, January 8th 2014.

Hamel, Gary and Zanini, Michele, "Excess Management is Costing the U.S. $3 trillion Per Year", *Harvard Business Review*, September 5th 2016.

Kleiner, Morris M., "Why License a Florist", *New York Times*, May 28th 2014.

5 Britain, their Britain

Notes

1 *See you soon, Pet*, "pet" being a common term of endearment in north-east England.

2   Born as a public body, the National Endowment for Science, Technology and the Arts in 1998, Nesta was thus renamed in 2012 and became an independent charity providing research and grants to foster innovation.

3   The turnout was 72%, which is higher than in any general election since 1992, but well below the 84.6% turnout in Scotland for its 2014 referendum, which itself topped the highest post-1945 general election turnout of 83.6% in 1950.

4   Most notorious among these was a claim painted on Leave's "battle bus" that the UK was sending £350 million a week to Brussels as its budgetary contribution, a figure which the UK Statistics Authority repeatedly pointed out was false since it failed to take account of the £100 million a week discount that had originally been negotiated by Margaret Thatcher in the 1980s.

5   First presented at a Nuffield Society seminar at Europe House, London, on June 30th 2016, chaired by me and broadcast on July 2nd by the BBC Parliamentary Channel, available on BBC iPlayer. Another speaker at the event, Vernon Bogdanor, a professor at Kings College, London, stressed the point about the special constitutional case for a referendum on the EU.

6   Under the Gini coefficient, a perfectly equal distribution would score 1. So higher scores indicate greater levels of inequality.

7   To understand "at last" see "Guy Fawkes was right", *The Economist*, November 5th 1977, which made the same analysis as this chapter of how the winner-takes-all system was producing unrepresentative government, with the combined Tory and Labour shares of support declining sharply – 40 years ago.

References

Barr, Damian, *Maggie & Me*, Bloomsbury, 2013.

British Social Attitudes Report 33, *Britain Divided? Public attitudes after seven years of austerity*, NatCen Social Research, 2016.

Lanchester, John, "Brexit Blues", *London Review of Books*, July 28th 2016.

Mateos-Garcia, Juan and Bakhshi, Hasan, *The Geography of Creativity in the UK*, Nesta, July 2016.

The Migration Observatory, *Migrants in the UK: An Overview*, University of Oxford, January 28th 2016.

Nathan, Max, Kemeny, Tom, Pratt, Andy and Spencer, Greg, *Creative Economy Employment in the US, Canada and the UK: A Comparative Analysis*, Nesta, March 2016.

Nathan, Max, Pratt, Andy and Rincon-Aznar, Ana, *Creative Economy Employment in the EU and the UK: A Comparative Analysis*, Nesta, December 2015.

Olson, Mancur, *The Rise and Decline of Nations: Economic Growth, Stagflation and Social Rigidities*, Yale University Press, 1982.

6 European paralysis

Notes

1 Greece made it 12 members in 2001, Slovenia, Cyprus, Malta and Slovakia had all joined before the euro-zone crisis commenced in 2010–11, and they were followed by Estonia, Latvia and Lithuania in 2011–14.
2 The IMF also provided emergency funding for three non euro-zone EU countries: Hungary (2008), Latvia (2008) and Romania (2009). It did not however have to provide lending for Spain, whose 2012 bank-recapitalisation plan was funded by the euro-zone's own European Stability Mechanism.
3 Austria, Denmark, Germany, France, Poland, Sweden and Norway.
4 Assigning Nobel prizes by country is tricky, given that intellectuals move around between institutions. The figures in the text sort the prizes (including economics but excluding peace) according to winners' institutional affiliations, and if a prize is shared between more than one person counts that as one prize each. Allocated by the birthplace of the winner, Europe's share would be higher and the decline sharper, at 43% in the 1980s and 31% in both the 1990s and 2000–16, but many Europeans have won their prizes for work done at US (or other) universities, and even take US nationality, so counting by affiliation is more meaningful. Franco Modigliani, for example, who won the economics prize in 1985, was born in Italy but became a US citizen in 1948.
5 Peel, Quentin, "Merkel warns on cost of welfare", *Financial Times*, December 16th 2012.
6 The definition of "longer-serving" was 45 years or more, which therefore meant people who had started work at age 18, and so were likely to have been manual workers of some sort: "Germany attacked over plan to cut retirement age", *Financial Times*, April 21st 2014.
7 Co-authored with director and producer Annalisa Piras and made by Springshot Productions, the film was broadcast by the BBC and by Sky Italia.
8 2011 figures, from *Society at a Glance*, OECD report, 2014.
9 As of December 2015, the euro-zone countries with public debts exceeding 100% of GDP were Belgium (106%), Cyprus (108.9%), Portugal (129%), Italy (132.7%) and Greece (176.9%).

References

Draghi, Mario, "Italy and the World Economy, 1861–2011", Bank of Italy conference, October 12th 2011.
Eurostat, *The EU in the world*, 2015 edition.
Gill, Indermit S. and Raiser, Martin, *Golden Growth: Restoring the Lustre of the European Economic Model*, World Bank Report No. 68168, 2012.

Peet, John, "So much to do, so little time", *The Economist* Special Report on France, November 17th 2012.

World Bank Group, *Doing Business 2016: Measuring Regulatory Quality and Efficiency*.

7 The Japanese puzzle

Notes

1 The term was used as a warning in his farewell address by President Dwight D. Eisenhower on January 17th 1961.

2 This "Nixon shock", as it became known, consisted of President Nixon's decision in August 1971 unilaterally to withdraw the dollar from the system of fixed exchange rates and convertibility to gold that had existed since 1945. This forced all other currencies to find their value by floating freely on foreign-exchange markets.

3 The Plaza accord, named after the Plaza Hotel in New York City where the meeting took place, was an agreement between the US, the UK, France, Japan and West Germany to intervene in currency markets so as to make the dollar depreciate in value. The Louvre accord two years later, agreed at a meeting of the same countries at the Louvre museum in Paris, aimed to halt or at least slow the resulting decline of the dollar so as to restore stability.

4 In his book *Capitalism, Socialism and Democracy* (1942), Schumpeter argued that it was the innovative entry of new entrepreneurs and ideas to replace (that is destroy) old ones that made capitalism work far better than socialism as an economic system. But, like Karl Marx, he feared that creative destruction might end up destroying capitalism itself.

5 Dentsu was initially founded by Hoshiro Mitsunaga as two separate businesses, one in news and the other in advertising, but the two were merged in 1906. They remained combined until 1936, when the news agency was sold to Japan's Imperial news agency, Domei.

6 Shujitsu University "Glocal Forum" on "Globalisation and Corporate Management", Okayama, April 16th 2016. Professor Onzo's presentation was entitled "Globalisation and University Management".

7 Although initially one whistleblower passed information for *FACTA's* first article, subsequently other sources passed further information for *FACTA's* later articles. The whistleblowers' identities have never been revealed, and they are still believed to be working for Olympus.

8 "Immigration to Japan: A narrow passage", *The Economist*, August 20th 2016.

References

Drucker, Peter F., *The Concept of the Corporation*, John Day, 1946.

Emmott, Bill, *The Sun Also Sets: Why Japan will not be Number One*, Simon & Schuster UK 1989; Times Books USA, 1989; Soshisha Japan, 1990.

Kingston, Jeff, *Japan's Quiet Transformation: Social Change and Civil Society in 21st Century Japan*, Routledge, 2004.

Mikitani, Hiroshi and Mikitani, Ryoichi, *The Power to Compete: An Economist and an Entrepreneur on Revitalizing Japan in the Global Economy*, Wiley, 2014.

Van Wolferen, Karel, *The Enigma of Japanese Power: People and Politics in a Stateless Nation*, Alfred Knopf, 1989.

8 Swedish and Swiss Houdinis

Notes

1 After the sharp rise in oil prices in 1973, several, mainly Arab, oil-producing countries leapt to the world's top ranks in terms of GDP per head, as they suddenly had valuable GDPs but fairly few heads. That is why from that date onwards it is more relevant when evaluating Western countries to look at GDP-per-head rankings among the OECD members rather than the world as a whole.

2 A helpful chronology of reforms can be found in an appendix to IFN Working Paper No. 873, 2011, from the Research Institute of Industrial Economics, "The Rise, Fall and Revival of the Swedish Welfare State: What are the Policy Lessons from Sweden", by Andreas Bergh.

3 PISA is short for Programme for International Student Assessment, under which the OECD studies 15-year-old students' scholastic abilities in science, mathematics and reading.

4 In 1970, manufacturing accounted for 23% of Swiss GDP, 24% of US GDP and 27% of UK GDP. So at that time, relative to the UK, Switzerland was more noted for services – the "gnomes of Zurich" as the UK's prime minister, Harold Wilson, had called Swiss financiers – than industry. The reverse is now true. In 2013 comparable figures to Switzerland's 19% were 12% for the US, 11% for France, 10% for the UK, 15% for Italy, but 19% for Japan and 22% for Germany, according to the UN Conference on Trade and Development (UNCTAD), cited in House of Commons Library Briefing Paper 05809, *Manufacturing: International* Comparisons, June 18th 2015.

5 24% is the official Swiss figure for the share of the resident population made up of foreigners. The OECD's figure for the share that is "foreign born" is 28%.

6 The UK figure was 13.1% in 2014, up from 7% in 1993, according to the Migration Observatory at Oxford University. The German figure was 12.9% in 2012, according to the OECD.

References

Booth, Michael, *The Almost Nearly Perfect People: The Truth about the Nordic Miracle*, Jonathan Cape, 2014.

Gill, Indermit S. and Raiser, Martin, *Golden Growth: Restoring the Lustre of the European Economic Model*, World Bank Report No. 68168, 2012.

9 Silver hair and smart drones

Notes

1   See Eurostat, *People in the EU – statistics on demographic changes*, June 2015; and UN Department of Economic and Social Affairs, *World Population Prospects: 2015 revision*.
2   Japan's 2015 total of 60,000 centenarians is almost as high as the US's 73,000 despite a population just one-third the size. The UK's total is 14,500.
3   More accurately, electricity was discovered rather than invented. So by this is meant the period of rapid development of electrical engineering by inventors such as Thomas Edison in the late 19th century.
4   www.livescience.com/49711-japanese-robot-hotel.html
5   "Welcome to the Drone Age", *The Economist*, September 26th 2015.
6   Professor Li's background is a typical Stanford and Silicon Valley story, confirming the continued appeal of the US for the best and brightest: born in China, she studied at Princeton and California Institute of Technology before joining Stanford.
7   The OECD's definition of the average effective age of retirement looks at the age when workers withdraw from the labour market. Statistics are for 1970–2014 from the OECD's *Live Longer, Work Longer* report on ageing and employment policies.
8   *The Temptation of Early Retirement*, report by Gavekal Dragonomics, Beijing, August 3rd 2016.
9   Data in this paragraph from: Ipsos-Mori, "How Britain voted in 2015", August 26th 2015; United States Elections Project; Japan Association for Promoting Fair Elections.

References

Drucker, Peter, "The Next Society", *The Economist* Special Report, November 1st 2001.
Ford, Martin, *The Rise of the Robots: Technology and the Threat of Mass Unemployment*, Basic Books, 2015.
Kurzweil, Ray, *The Singularity is Near: When Humans Transcend Biology*, Viking Press, 2005.
Myrdal, Gunnar, *Asian Drama: An Inquiry into the Poverty of Nations*, Allen Lane, 1968.
Sundararajan, Arun, *The Sharing Economy: The End of Employment and the Rise of Crowd-Based Capitalism*, MIT Press, 2016.

10 Barbarians at the gate

Notes

1 See Pinker, Steven, *The Better Angels of our Nature: Why Violence has Declined*, Viking, 2011.

2 Most notably Charles Krauthammer's September 1990 article in *Foreign Affairs*, "The Unipolar Moment": (www.foreignaffairs.com/articles/1991-02-01/unipolar-moment). A decade later Joseph Nye, a professor at Harvard's Kennedy School of Government, wrote an essay in *The Economist* entitled "The new Rome meets the new barbarians", on March 21st 2002, reflecting on the impact of the September 11th 2001 attacks in the US and arguing that while the US was dominant on many measures, it could not expect to achieve its international goals without allies and a broad consensus (www.economist.com/node/1045181).

3 The phrase was popularised by Paul Kennedy, a British historian at Yale University, in his book *The Rise and Fall of the Great Powers: Economic Change and Military Conflict from 1500 to 2000*, Random House, 1987.

4 Soft power is the concept, pioneered by Nye, that states can get others to do what they want them to do through the power of ideas, information, media, values and other "soft" means, all as an adjunct to "hard" military power and to economic or financial leverage.

5 As editor of *The Economist*, I supported the invasion of Iraq through that publication's pages, based on a belief in the presence of weapons of mass destruction and that the status quo was too dangerous to leave unaltered. I subsequently wrote in a valedictory editorial in 2006 that I still felt we had taken the right decision on the basis of the (evidently bad) information that we had, but that we could and should have been more sceptical about the US's ability and willingness to stabilise and rebuild Iraq after the war.

6 The saying is generally attributed to William McChesney Martin, chairman of the Federal Reserve from 1951 to 1970.

7 I was a trustee of the International Institute for Strategic Studies in 2009–15 and rejoined the board of trustees in November 2016.

8 Transnistria is a strip of land on Moldova's border with Ukraine which has been an "autonomous province", but de facto independent, since a short war in 1992. It is not recognised by the UN.

9 No one with a foreign spouse – her late husband, Michael Aris, was a British academic at Oxford University – or children is allowed to be president. But following Aung San Suu Kyi's party's landslide victory in the 2015 elections she was allowed to nominate the president, Htin Kyaw, and has been given a new title as state counsellor.

10 See Ostrovsky, Arkady, *The Invention of Russia: The Journey from Gorbachev's Freedom to Putin's War*, Atlantic Books, 2015. Ostrovsky, a Russian citizen, is Russia and eastern Europe editor at the *The Economist*.

References

Acheson, Dean, *Present at the Creation: My Years in the State Department*, W. W. Norton and Company, 1969.

Bilmes, Linda and Stiglitz, Joseph, *The Three Trillion Dollar War: The True Cost of the Iraq War*, W. W. Norton and Company, 2008.

Marx, Karl, "The Eighteenth Brumaire of Louis Bonaparte", essay published in 1852.

Permanent Court of Arbitration, press release, July 12th 2016: https://pca-cpa.org/wp-content/uploads/sites/175/2016/07/PH-CN-20160712-Press-Release-No-11-English.pdf

Stiglitz, Joseph, 2015 interview at www.democracynow.org/2015/10/27/nobel_laureate_joseph_stiglitz_on_rewriting_the

11 The fate of the West

Notes

1 Used and popularised by Karl Marx in his *Critique of the Gotha Programme*, 1875, though apparently he borrowed the slogan from earlier socialists.

2 As the 5th Viscount Ridley, he has since 2013 been a Conservative peer in the UK's House of Lords.

3 The film was released in 1962.

References

Fukuyama, Francis, "The End of History", *The National Interest*, summer 1989; followed by his book, *The End of History and the Last Man*, The Free Press and Allen Lane, 1992.

Olson, Mancur, *The Rise and Decline of Nations: Economic Growth, Stagflation and Social Rigidities*, Yale University Press, 1982.

Ridley, Matt, *The Rational Optimist: How Prosperity Evolves*, Harper 2010.

Zakaria, Fareed, *The Post-American World and the Rise of the Rest*, W. W. Norton & Co, 2008.

Acknowledgements

This book has been written while events were swirling all around it, most recently the Brexit referendum, the election of Donald Trump, terrorist attacks in European cities and the resignation of Matteo Renzi as Italy's prime minister after voters' rejection of his constitutional reforms. So it has required publishers to hold their nerve as the book kept on mutating and then to accommodate quite late amendments. I have been extremely fortunate to have had the backing of the strong-nerved Andrew Franklin and Stephen Brough at Profile Books and Clive Priddle at Public Affairs in New York. All have been enthusiastic, supportive and tolerant, while still providing the necessary discipline of the production schedule.

Stephen Brough, as lead editor, made numerous helpful suggestions and criticisms while working his way through successive drafts; Clive Priddle ensured that readers on both sides of the Atlantic were kept firmly in the author's mind; and my longstanding Japanese agent, Manami Tamaoki, made it possible for the future of the West to be considered also in the land of the rising sun by recruiting Nikkei Books to publish in Japan. I am also grateful to my successor-but-one in the editor's chair at *The Economist*, Zanny Minton-Beddoes, for allowing the book to appear under The Economist Books imprint, and to Daniel Franklin, executive editor, for providing a very constructive critique of a late draft. I am honoured and delighted to be back under *The Economist*'s logo.

As for previous books, Christopher Wilson dug up the data for the graphs as well as fact-checking the final text under considerable time pressure. Paul Forty at Profile shepherded the book through the editing and production process with skill and precision, while Penny Williams copy-edited the text in several versions with great care and efficiency. All errors and omissions remain however entirely my responsibility.

I think of *The Fate of the West* as a personal project of research, analysis and advocacy that stands alongside the educational charity, The Wake Up Foundation, which I have set up with my friend and film-making collaborator Annalisa Piras. The foundation, which is dedicated to public education about the trends of decline and division in western societies described here, has published in January 2017 a new statistical indicator, The Wake Up 2050 Index, of how well western countries are shaping up in the face of long-term trends such as demography, globalisation and technological innovation, which can also serve as useful supplementary data for this book. The foundation has, moreover, sought to "Wake Up Europe" to the paralysis outlined in Chapter 6 by generating public events around screenings of Annalisa's documentary, *The Great European Disaster Movie*. We will now organise new events and debates around the themes of this book, online, on social media and live. The battle to save the world's most successful political idea is well and truly under way, and we intend to carry on the fight.

Index

Page numbers in *italics* refer specifically to figures.